SAY WE ARE NATIONS

SAY WE ARE
NATIONS

Documents of Politics and Protest
in Indigenous America since 1887

EDITED BY

Daniel M. Cobb

The University of North Carolina Press CHAPEL HILL

This book was published with the assistance of the H. Eugene and Lillian Youngs Lehman Fund of the University of North Carolina Press. A complete list of books published in the Lehman Series appears at the end of the book.

Designed by Alyssa D'Avanzo
Set in Calluna by codeMantra, Inc.
Manufactured in the United States of America

The paper in this book meets the guidelines for permanence and durability of the Committee on Production Guidelines for Book Longevity of the Council on Library Resources.

The University of North Carolina Press has been a member of the Green Press Initiative since 2003.

Cover illustration: Ariana Chavis, *Recognition, Part 1*. Used with permission.

Library of Congress Cataloging-in-Publication Data
Cobb, Daniel M., compiler.

Say we are nations : documents of politics and protest in indigenous America since 1887 / Daniel M. Cobb.

pages cm. — (H. Eugene and Lillian Youngs Lehman series)

Includes bibliographical references and index.

ISBN 978-1-4696-2480-8 (pbk : alk. paper) — ISBN 978-1-4696-2481-5 (ebook)

1. Indigenous peoples—United States—Social conditions—Sources. 2. Indigenous peoples—Legal status, laws, etc.—United States—Sources. 3. Indigenous peoples—United States—Government relations—Sources. 4. Indigenous peoples—Civil rights—United States—Sources. 5. Indigenous peoples—United States—Politics and government—Sources. I. Title. II. Series: H. Eugene and Lillian Youngs Lehman series.

E93.C66 2015

323.1197′073—dc23

2015010506

To Kevin Swope and Jason Stiffler,
friends and heroes

Contents

Map and Figures

Acknowledgments

I traveled a long road in completing this book and accumulated many debts along the way. A Lester J. Cappon Fellowship in Documentary Editing in the summer of 2009 afforded an opportunity to draft the proposal and identify documents in the rich collections of Chicago's Newberry Library. Presentations at Helsinki University's Maple Leaf and Eagle Conference in North American Studies, Stockholm University, and Dartmouth College in 2010 provided settings for me to work through my initial thoughts on the topic. An invitation to contribute a chapter to the edited volume *Native Diasporas* pushed me to clarify my thinking in regard to the assertion of a global indigenous identity in the context of Native activism before and after the Cold War.[1] For these opportunities, I thank Allan Winkler, Markku Henriksson, Clara Sue Kidwell, Bo Persson, Gunlög Fur, Ben Madley, Colin Calloway, Gregory Smithers, and Brooke Newman. The History Department at Miami University and the Department of American Studies and Center for Global Initiatives at the University of North Carolina generously supported my international travels.

In my first year at the University of North Carolina, I developed an upper-division, research-intensive course on Native politics and activism since 1887 inspired by and founded on the material I had identified for this volume. Students selected primary documents and spent the better part of the semester transcribing and conducting the research necessary to contextualize them. I believe there is no better way for teachers to encourage student engagement than to involve them directly in what we are most passionate about—to invite them to be co-creators of new knowledge. That's exactly what my students have become each time I've taught the course. They have challenged me to think about Native activism in a different light, and their unique interests caused me to pursue themes and avenues of investigation that I would not have otherwise. So, to the approximately seventy-five scholars who have gone "Beyond Red Power" with me since 2010, I say thank you for being outstanding students *and* teachers. A special note of gratitude is due to Ariana Chavis for graciously allowing me to use her original work, *Recognition, Part 1*, as the cover art.

I was also fortunate in being able to call upon colleagues for assistance in tracking down documents I had encountered in reading their brilliant work. My gratitude goes to John Troutman, Christian McMillen, Tisa Wenger, Katherine M. B. Osburn, Keith Richotte, J. Kēhaulani Kauanui, Jean Dennison, and Jacqueline Solis in this regard (even though some of the documents didn't make it into the volume). Thanks, too, to Cindy Kelly, president of the Atomic Heritage Foundation, Barbara Leigh Smith of Evergreen State College, Chickasaw legal scholar Alex Pearl, and Diné poet, musician, and activist Lyla June Johnston for granting permission to include excerpts from the Russell Jim interview, Osage constitution case study, "3/256," and "Call Me Human," respectively. Dave Posthumus provided invaluable service by transcribing and translating the Lakota language used by Armando Iron Elk and Faith Spotted Eagle in chapter 5. I thank Bill Wingell and Jason Kaplan, too, for allowing me to include their photographs of the Alcatraz occupation and Yakama elder Russell Jim. Maureen Booth, Jennifer Klang, Shyamalika Ghoshal, and George Franchois of the U.S. Department of the Interior Library delivered critical assistance at a rather late hour, as well.

In researching and writing about the 1960s, my life has been made much richer by virtue of getting to know many of the people who made that history. More meaningful still have been the ongoing relationships, some of which are now more than a decade old. I am particularly thankful for Jeri (Cross) Redcorn's and Sandra (Johnson) Osawa's willingness to let me include the words they wrote as college students attending the Workshop on American Indian Affairs. Angela Russell graciously permitted me to include her reflections on participating in the Selma-to-Montgomery March originally published in *Americans before Columbus*. Della Warrior has always been generous, sharing her life experiences and personal papers with me. In addition to leading to the inclusion of Clyde Warrior's words in this volume, my relationship with her set the next destination of my intellectual journey, a biography of her late husband.

Mark Simpson-Vos, editorial director of the University of North Carolina Press, has been a stalwart supporter of this project from its inception all the way through to its completion. I am so very thankful for his patient encouragement and keen insights over the years. The readers of this volume's prospectus and earlier iterations provided critical feedback and were instrumental in streamlining its organization, sharpening its focus, and correcting at least one bad date. Any errors that remain are my responsibility alone.

And last, I would like to close with the words of Ponca activist Clyde Warrior. "The foundation of any individual . . . is his family," he wrote in 1965. "In today's society when the 'chips are down' and an individual needs help . . . he can only turn to his family. . . . This is a painful lesson everyone learns as they grow older."[2] The five years it took to write *Say We Are Nations* taught me the truth of this insight. I thank my wife, N. Nicole Cobb, and my daughters, Anna and Molly, for once again understanding the demands of my solitary craft. As they have always done, my parents read and offered critical feedback on every word of every page. And my dad, a skilled anthropologist whose interest in Native America inspired my own, is the "someone" referred to in the introduction who read all of these documents aloud the second time so I could check the transcriptions for accuracy.

SAY WE ARE NATIONS

Introduction

A Reflexive Historiography

Over the past several decades, reflexivity has transformed the field of anthropology. It began as a critique of the ethnographic method, but I consider the concerns it raises applicable to any scholarly enterprise. Essentially, reflexivity refers to the process of consciously locating ourselves in the work we create. Reflecting on our positionality allows us to think critically about the intersubjectivity of the stories we tell—to recognize that there is an awful lot about "us" in what we write about "them" (no matter who the "us" or "them" happen to be). The importance of reflexivity to scholarship about the past has not been lost on historians. In fact, even Frederick Jackson Turner, propounder of the infamous "frontier thesis" in 1893, recognized that there's a lot about "now" in what gets written about "then." "When . . . we consider that each man is conditioned by the age in which he lives and must perforce write with limitations and prepossessions," he observed in 1891, "I think we shall all agree that no historian can say the ultimate word." One would like to think that this self-awareness would have injected Turner with a dose of humility. It didn't.[1]

Indigenous people and scholars of American Indian and indigenous studies are well aware of the power of history—and of the need to understand the consequences of its being "conditioned by the age" of its authors. For too long a time, non-Indians like Turner wrote as though American Indian history began in 1492—set in motion, of course, by the "discovery" of the "New World." From that point forward, at least according to these texts, indigenous peoples became supporting actors in the story of "America"—bit players in a "master narrative" that celebrated the founding and expansion of the United States. At worst, Indians were cast as treacherous villains and bloodthirsty savages; at best, as co-conspirators in their own undoing or "tragic heroes" who valiantly resisted before accepting the inevitability of their demise. "For Native people," Paul Chaat Smith (Comanche) and Ann McMullen of the National Museum of the American Indian noted, "history itself became another battleground, another weapon of conquest."[2]

Since the 1960s, revisionist scholarship has reimagined the historical and contemporary experiences of Native peoples by adopting a decidedly less "westward facing" point of view. At the heart of the new narrative rests a story of indigenous survival, which Chaat Smith aptly described as "one of the most extraordinary stories in human history."[3] The creation of this new narrative, however, developed unevenly. Most of the revisionist work focused on the early colonial period and carried through to the end of the nineteenth century. Stopping there unwittingly reinforced the very argument—epitomized by Turner's frontier thesis—that the "New Indian History" had set out to complicate. Even during the years around the Quincentennary in 1992, a moment indigenous people seized upon to celebrate five hundred years of surviving colonialism, few scholars had much to say about how that story unfolded after 1900.[4] The ethnohistorical research methodologies, analytical interpretations, and narrative constructions that so fundamentally recast our understanding of the sixteenth, seventeenth, eighteenth, and nineteenth centuries just did not seem to reach very far into the twentieth.[5]

IT'S HERE THAT I would like to shift into a reflexive mode of historiography. I started my graduate work in 1996, right in the midst of this exciting, creative, and dynamic moment. As someone interested in the Native 1960s, I found myself puzzling over why historians framed twentieth-century American Indian history so differently from earlier times. The more I thought about it, the less sense it made to compartmentalize the years following 1887 into neat policy periods that corresponded with the actions the federal government took against Indians rather than its complicated relationships with or the actions of Native people. It didn't make sense to settle for allotment, assimilation, reorganization, termination, and self-determination, when we could be thinking in terms of middle grounds, borderlands, diplomats, negotiators, playoff systems, and alliances. I found politics more compelling than policies. And I began to frame the preceding century of American Indian history as a continuation of the encounters that James Axtell had defined as mutual and reciprocal, temporally and spatially fluid, and generally capacious in his essay "Colonial Encounters: Beyond 1992."[6]

My first attempt to imagine politics as continuing encounters focused on a case study of the 1960's War on Poverty in Oklahoma. Looking at the people engaged in the politics of the Community Action Program, in turn, convinced me of a real need to think more broadly about activism during this era, which tended to be overshadowed by what came after it—the American Indian Movement (AIM) and its brand of Red Power. Influenced by the work of Loretta Fowler, James C. Scott, and Jean and John Comaroff, I conceived of activism as politically purposeful acts rather than just militancy. A few years after finishing my Ph.D. in 2003, I had the good fortune of coediting a volume with Fowler that took these ideas and applied them to the period from the late nineteenth century to the present. The contributors to *Beyond Red Power* effectively transformed policies into shifting contexts for rather than determinants of political action and decentered the militancy of the 1970s by situating it in the context of more than a century of activism.[7]

In looking at the generation of intellectuals, reformers, and radicals that preceded the American Indian Movement, I wanted to understand the Native 1960s on its own terms. For instance, as important as Paul Chaat Smith's and Robert Warrior's *Like a Hurricane: The Indian Movement from Alcatraz to Wounded Knee* was (and continues to be), I recognized a need to push back on the idea that the sixties "showed up in the Red Nation a few years late and mostly took place in the seventies."[8] Standing Rock Sioux scholar Vine Deloria Jr. critiqued this tendency to engage in history creep in an interview I conducted with him in 2001. "What you're talking about really," he said, "is moving everything that happened in the Seventies into the Sixties and pretending that it happened then."[9]

In crafting an alternative narrative of Native activism during the 1960s, I wanted to demonstrate that it was part of a much larger story—and that, in fact, our understanding of the 1960s (and of "United States history") was incomplete if American Indian stories remained on the periphery. In the end, I concluded that the people, ideas, events, and issues I wrote about in *Native Activism in Cold War America* were influenced by and shapers of the larger domestic and international histories of which they were a part— from the struggle for black equality and the War on Poverty to the youth movement and decolonization. In so doing, I contributed to the crafting of what historians Fred Hoxie, Peter Mancall, and James Merrell described as "an intellectual framework for understanding the distinctiveness—and the interconnectedness—of Indian and non-Indian history." The contributors to *Why You Can't Teach United States History without American Indians* have moved this important project forward.[10]

In a way perhaps only he could (and probably without even knowing it), Vine Deloria played a particularly important role in clarifying the intellectual intersections I had been investigating. It happened after I asked him about his role as executive director of the National Congress of American Indians (NCAI) during the 1960s. "At NCAI," he told me, "I was looking for some kind of intellectual format of how you would justify overturning termination and at the same time escape this big push for integration that civil rights was doing." In 1966 he had the opportunity to make that distinction when the NCAI garnered media attention during an emergency meeting in Santa Fe, New Mexico, to protest against the Interior Department's unwillingness to consult Indians on new legislation. "Well, what are we gonna say?" Deloria remembered a fellow NCAI member asking him. "I said, 'Look, self-determination was a big cry after World War I. . . . If we're gonna say we're nations, and we got sovereignty, and our treaties are as valid as other treaties, then we gotta talk the language of the larger world—not just the Indian of it.'"[11] In my mind, these words epitomized the approach Native activists took during the struggle for sovereignty between the mid-1950s and late 1960s.

Informed once again by the innovative work of historian Fred Hoxie—and bolstered by Paul Rosier's *Serving Their Country* and David Martinez's *The American Indian Intellectual Tradition*—I began exploring whether the approach described by Deloria might be considered part of a political and intellectual *tradition*. And that, in turn, led me back into the archives, to the voices of Native activists before and after the period I had focused on in my book, and to this collection of primary documents.[12]

Say We Are Nations showcases letters, congressional testimonies, interviews, excerpts from autobiographies, essays, formal lectures, and student writings to illustrate how, from the late nineteenth century to the opening decades of the twenty-first, American Indians asserted sovereignty by rhetorically and literally connecting issues they cared passionately about to larger domestic and international concerns, events, ideas, and movements. Talking the language of the larger world meant relating perennial concerns over treaty rights, land, and sovereignty to Reconstruction and the Paris Peace Conference, Christianity and civilization, civil rights and international law, nuclear waste and climate change. It also meant invoking "American" ideas of citizenship, consent of the governed, representation, rights, democracy, liberty, justice, and freedom—but investing them with indigenized meanings.

As delicate an ideational dance as this proved to be, it became still more complicated. If civil rights were a part of the larger world's language, for instance, so was race. The same could be said of blood. These ideas may have originated outside of Native America, but they have also been internalized and made real by Native people. They continue to figure significantly in contemporary assertions of sovereignty and constructions of nationhood. And what of the issue of understanding? It is one thing to talk the language of the larger world; it is something completely different to have your audience make the correct translation. If ever there were continuity across centuries of political encounters between Natives and newcomers, it can be found in the disparity between what was said and what was heard (or, at least, written down).

COVERING MORE THAN one hundred years of political activism and protest in a space as diverse as Native America is no small feat. With that in mind, I would like to offer a few words about what this book is and what it is not. *Say We Are Nations* is a collection of fifty-five documents organized into five chapters that move chronologically from the late nineteenth century to the early twenty-first century. I have intentionally chosen documents that provide geographic, topical, temporal, and interpretive breadth. Many of them have either never been published or focus on individuals, communities, time periods, and ideas that are not discussed in depth in textbooks and other document volumes, including Native Hawaii, Alaska Natives, the 1960s, southern Indians, gender and sexuality, and hemispheric and global indigenous rights.[13]

Because of this, readers familiar with twentieth-century American Indian history may note the absence of some of the "usual suspects" in terms of personalities and documents. This was intentional. The book is not meant to be exhaustive or canonical. In fact, while I have chosen some documents that may be familiar, even those I have presented in ways that, I hope, make them seem unfamiliar. I want the documents to cast history in a different light—one that reveals new people, places, events, and ideas and alternative ways of thinking *about* these people, places, events, and ideas. I have also carefully selected illustrations that I hope will be read as documents in their own right. Perhaps there will be found in these documents new avenues for teaching and research.

While I do not intend for you to approach the pages that follow as comprising *the* great documents in American politics and protest since 1887, they do contain great documents. The ideas, issues, and insights they hold make them so. But it will be your job to do the work of intellectual excavation. In the spirit of reflexivity and intersubjectivity, I have explained how I came to this project, and why I framed it the way that I did. I have also provided enough contextual information at the beginning of each chapter

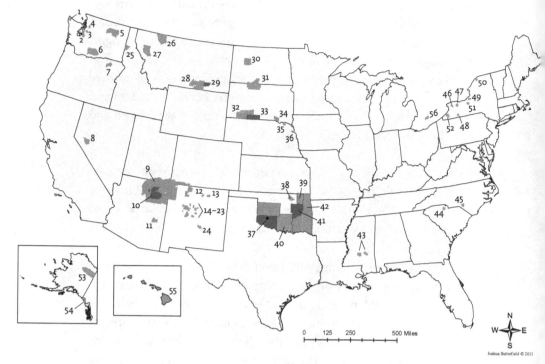

1. Makah	16. Santa Clara	31. Standing Rock	45. Lumbee
2. Nisqually	17. San Ildefonso	32. Pine Ridge	46. Tuscarora
3. Puyallup	18. Nambé	33. Rosebud	47. Tonawanda
4. Tulalip	19. Tesuque	34. Yankton	48. Allegheny
5. Colville	20. Cochiti	35. Santee Sioux	49. Oneida
6. Yakama	21. Santa Ana	36. Ho-Chunk	50. St. Regis
7. Umatilla	22. Santo Domingo	37. Caddo	51. Onondaga
8. Walker River	23. Sandia	38. Ponca	52. Cattaraugus
9. Diné	24. Isleta	39. Osage	53. Gwich'in
10. Hopi	25. Coeur d'Alene	40. Chickasaw	54. Tlingit
11. Fort McDowell	26. Blackfeet	41. Muscogee	55. Kanaka Maoli
12. Taos	27. Flathead	42. Cherokee	56. Six Nations Reserve
13. Picunis	28. Crow	43. Mississippi Band of Choctaw Indians	
14. San Juan	29. N. Cheyenne		
15. Zia	30. Fort Berthold	44. Catawba (in S.C.)	

Indigenous America, 2015. Indigenous nations are rising. During the 2010 census, 5.2 million people identified themselves as American Indian and Alaska Native. Another 1.2 million individuals identified as Native Hawaiian and Other Pacific Islander. The United States recognized 566 tribes and administered 325 reservations.

and in individual introductions for you to begin making sense of the documents. I did not, however, want to fall into the trap of doing the interpretive work for you. Instead, I offer themes, implications, comparisons, and potential connections. The questions and considerations are meant to encourage you to engage with some of the things that I consider most important to think about. But I also know that the authors may have more to say to you—and that it depends on what you bring to the table.

A final note: the most significant decision I made in writing about the Native 1960s was to seek out, talk to, and learn from the people who made the history. The interviews I conducted literally changed everything. The individuals I spoke with allowed me to make sense of the documentary record in ways that would otherwise have been impossible—and they told me stories the archives could never have told. But it wasn't just what people told me; it was how—the meaning was in their voices and in the inflections in their voices as much as the words. It was revelatory.

In preparing this volume, I used dictation software to do the first round of transcriptions. To check for accuracy, I then followed the resulting text as someone read the original documents in their entirety a second time. Suffice it to say that I did not go into the project thinking I would hear every word of every document read aloud not once but twice. But I am glad I did. As with the oral interviews I conducted, hearing the words afforded new insight. So, I would encourage you to try it. I think you will find, as I did, that literally hearing these men and women say they are nations will allow you to comprehend their words in a completely different and, I think, profoundly meaningful way.

PART I

CONTESTING CITIZENSHIP, 1887–1924

At the end of the nineteenth century and for the first three-and-a-half decades of the twentieth, American Indians contended with a federal government and majority society wedded to the policies of allotment and assimilation. Inaugurated in 1887, the General Allotment (Dawes) Act proposed to convert the 138 million acres of tribally owned reservation lands remaining in Native America into individually owned plots of from 40 to 320 acres. Meanwhile, the larger assimilation project of which it was a part aspired to effect the complete replacement of one identity (Indian) with another (white). These two mutually reinforcing aspects of what President Theodore Roosevelt called a "mighty pulverizing engine to break up the tribal mass" had to do with more than land or cultural practice. They addressed a question that vexed the minds of missionaries, federal bureaucrats, members of Congress, and reformers alike—the question of belonging.[1]

The cant of citizenship emerged as the dominant rhetorical vehicle to talk about what it meant to belong in the United States of America. Inclusion and incorporation offered convenient, even optimistic, desiderata. A settler state, whose existence was made possible only through the ruin of indigenous nations, now offered the survivors of that destructive process a place in the new body politic. But it would come at a cost, and a great one at that. Even the "Friends of the Indian" possessed a narrow, singular conception of citizenship. This citizenship of sameness had little room for cultural pluralism and did not countenance the perpetual continuation of separate political identities.[2]

The process of incorporating indigenous peoples into the United States extended beyond reservation communities and became integral to the American imperial project abroad. It took a variety of forms from Latin America and the Caribbean to the Philippines but proved most complete in the Hawaiian Islands, where the overthrow of the Hawaiian monarchy in 1893 paved the way for annexation in 1898 and statehood in 1959. As they had in the contiguous United States, assimilative pressures accelerated the extension of territorial, economic, and governmental control. As the common refrain of "benevolent assimilation" conveyed, the imperative to be the same—even in the absence of U.S. citizenship—guided the nation's engagement with indigenous peoples.[3]

When the United States entered World War I (1914–18) in 1917, the question of belonging took on new meanings. The war served as a transformative force in the lives of American Indians, as many of them left their homes in search of work in war industries or volunteered to fight overseas. And yet, while approximately sixteen thousand Native people served in the military, not all of them had volunteered. Conscription happened unevenly, and it presented a problem. How could a country that did not acknowledge someone's legal personhood draft that person to fight in its war? As the documents in this chapter attest, some Native communities solved that problem by arguing that their citizens belonged to their own nations and, by extension, went into the military as allies. Some Lakotas, Dakotas, Ojibwes, Goshutes, and Creeks, among others, drew a harder line, reasoning that a settler state they considered illegitimate could not compel them to serve. And still others contended that, in the wake of war, Congress should honor the fact that so many Native people volunteered by bestowing U.S. citizenship.[4]

The General Allotment Act always had built within it a pathway to U.S. citizenship—one inextricably bound to private land ownership and conflated with competence. The war shortened the distance Native people had to travel—and ultimately left them without a choice of whether they even wanted to go down that road. Between 1919 and 1924, Congress enacted legislation extending U.S. citizenship to veterans and then to all American Indians. As we will see, some welcomed the "gift," some refused it, and some sought creative ways of making it compatible with tribal sovereignty. The last of these became particularly important as the assimilationist juggernaut continued through the 1920s and manifested itself in such things as bans on ceremonial practices, allotment, inequitable leases, reduced spending on health and education, and passage of legislation that sought to settle disputed land claims in favor of non-Indians.[5]

Another critical dimension of Native activism during this period grew out of President Woodrow Wilson's rationale for U.S. intervention and his vision for the postwar world. In April 1917, he told a reluctant public that the "world must be made safe for democracy." Eight months later, in a special address to Congress, Wilson enunciated the Fourteen Points to give meaning and purpose to the Great War. Among the principles were the right of national self-determination, the adjustment of colonial claims, and the formation of an international body, a League of Nations, "for the purpose of affording mutual guarantees of political independence and territorial integrity to great and small states alike." While Congress refused to join the League of Nations, its import was not lost on Indian rights advocates. Native people well understood the need for the right of self-determination.[6]

The following documents demonstrate some of the ways in which Native people offered their own answers to the question of belonging during the late nineteenth and early twentieth centuries. They constructed blockades to stop the pulverizing engine of progress and built new track to direct it away from their communities. But contests over allotment, assimilation, citizenship, incorporation, and inclusion did not simply place "Native peoples" in opposition to "whites." Rather, these were multivocal affairs that emerged from and served as an impetus for unexpected conversations within and between Native and non-Native communities. Some of the authors in the following documents attempted to delineate nonindigenous and indigenous worlds; others articulated a nebulous space between them—a third space of sovereignty. Talking back to civilization and saying we are nations, then, did not result in a dialogue but an intricate fugue.[7]

1

"My Own Nation" (1899)[8]

Queen Liliʻuokalani

In 1887, the same year the U.S. Congress passed the General Allotment Act, American missionaries and businessmen forced Hawaiʻi's King Kalakaua to sign the infamous "Bayonet Constitution," a document that ceded monarchical power to a settler-dominated cabinet opposed to indigenous sovereignty. Though denounced by the Kanaka Maoli (Native Hawaiians), the Bayonet Constitution marked a turning point in the push for annexation. The support it gained on the mainland conveyed to the world that the United States meant to act on its ambition for an empire beyond its continental borders—to make Indians out of Native Hawaiians. After Kalakaua's untimely death in 1891, it fell to his sister, Liliʻuokalani (1838–1917), to prevent the U.S. Congress from ratifying an annexation treaty and to advocate for a new constitution that enfranchised the Kanaka Maoli. Although she did not succeed on either count, Liliʻuokalani galvanized an ongoing resistance movement. Consider how and why she deployed concepts such as citizenship, civilization, indigeneity, self-determination, sovereignty, constitutionalism, representation, patriotism, international law, and Christianity in defense of Hawaiian nationhood.[9]

It has been suggested to me that the American general reader is not well informed regarding the social and political conditions which have come about in the Sandwich Islands, and that it would be well here to give some expression to my own observation of them.[10] Space will only permit, however, a mere outline.

It has been said that the Hawaiian people under the rule of the chiefs were most degraded, that under the monarchy their condition greatly improved, but that the native government in any form had at last become intolerable to the more enlightened part of the community. . . . It is more to the point that Kalakaua's reign was, in a material sense, the golden age of Hawaiian history. The wealth and importance of the Islands enormously increased, and always as a direct consequence of the king's acts. It has been currently supposed that the policy and foresight of the "missionary party" is to be credited with all that he accomplished, since they succeeded in abrogating so many of his prerogatives, and absorbing the lion's share of the benefits derived from it. It should, however, be only necessary to remember that the measures which brought about our accession of wealth were not at all in line with the policy of annexation to the United States, which was the very essence of the dominant "missionary" idea. In fact, his progressive foreign policy was well calculated to discourage it.

And for this reason, probably, they could not be satisfied even with the splendid results which our continued nationality offered them. They were not grateful for a prosperity which must sooner or later, while enriching them, also elevate the masses of the Hawaiian people into a self-governing class, and depose them from that primacy in our political affairs which they chiefly valued. They became fiercely jealous of every measure which promised to benefit the native people, or to stimulate their national pride. Every possible embarrassment and humiliation were heaped upon my brother. And because I was suspected of having the welfare of the whole people also at heart (and what sovereign with a grain of wisdom could be otherwise minded?), I must be made to feel yet more severely that my kingdom was but the assured prey of these "conquistadores."

. . . [In 1893] I proposed to promulgate a new constitution. I have already shown that two-thirds of my people declared their dissatisfaction with the old one; as well they might, for it was a document originally designed for a republic, hastily altered when the conspirators found that they had not the courage to assassinate the king. It is alleged that my proposed constitution was to make such changes as to give to the sovereign more power, and to the cabinet or legislature less, and that only subjects, in distinction from temporary residents, could exercise suffrage. In other words, that I was to restore some of the ancient rights of my people. I had listened to whatever had been advised, had examined whatever drafts of constitutions others had brought me, and promised but little.

But, supposing I had thought it wise to limit the exercise of suffrage to those who owed allegiance to no other country; is that different from the usage in all other civilized nations on earth? Is there another country where a man would be allowed to vote, to seek for office, to hold the most

Queen Liliʻuokalani's activism took many forms. In addition to engaging in formal diplomacy, she wrote poetry, songs, and chants to give her people strength. A quilt she made during her imprisonment at Iolani Palace stands as testimony of the love she felt for her nation. National Portrait Gallery, Smithsonian Institution, Washington, D.C.; gift of the Bernice Pauahi Bishop Museum/Art Resource, NY.

responsible of positions, without becoming naturalized, and reserving to himself the privilege of protection under the guns of a foreign man-of-war at any moment when he should quarrel with the government under which he lived? Yet this is exactly what the quasi Americans, who call themselves Hawaiians now and Americans when it suits them, claim the right to do at Honolulu.

The right to grant a constitution to the nation has been, since the very first one was granted, a prerogative of the Hawaiian sovereigns. . . .

While in Boston [in December 1896 and January 1897] I was constantly asked if there was any political significance in my visit to America, and if I expected to see the President. It seemed wise to say nothing about my purpose at that time, but frankness would now indicate an opposite course. By the first vessel that arrived from Honolulu after I had reached San Francisco, documents were sent to me by the patriotic leagues of the native Hawaiian people, those associations of which I have already spoken in full; and these representative bodies of my own nation prayed me to undertake certain measures for the general good of Hawai'i. Further messages of similar purport reached me while I was visiting my Boston friends.[11]

All the communications received, whether personally or in form, from individuals or from the above-mentioned organizations, were in advocacy of one desired end. This was to ask President [Grover] Cleveland that the former form of government unjustly taken from us by the persons who in 1892 and 1893 represented the United States should be restored, and that this restoration should undo the wrong which had been done to the Hawaiian people, and returned to them the queen, to whom constitutionally, and also by their own choice, they had a perfect right.

This was further in the line of the only instructions which to this day have ever been given by the United States to the so-called Republic of Hawai'i, and those were that the President acknowledges *the right of the Hawaiian people to choose their own form of government.* Were that one sentence literally carried out in fact today, and the Hawaiians sustained in the carrying out of the same, it would be all that either my people or myself could ask.

The second package of documents received by me in Boston was addressed to President [William] McKinley, and was similar to the others I already had. . . .[12] Accompanying these papers were other documents, showing that full power was accorded to me, not only as their queen, but individually, to represent the real people of Hawai'i, and in so doing to act in any way my judgment should dictate for the good of the Hawaiians, to whom the Creator gave those beautiful islands in the Pacific. Commissions were also issued to Mr. Joseph Heleluhe, empowering him to act with me; he having been chosen by the Hawaiians as the special envoy of those deprived by the Provisional Government, not only of the franchise, but also of any representation at the capital of that American nation to which they have never ceased to look for the redress of national wrongs, brought upon them by the hasty action of United States officers.[13]

When I speak at this time of the Hawaiian people, I refer to the children of the soil—the native inhabitants of the Hawaiian Islands and their descendants. Two delegations claiming to represent Hawai'i have visited Washington at intervals during the past four years in the cause of annexation, besides which other individuals have been sent on to assist in this attempt to defraud an aboriginal people of their birthrights—rights dear to the patriotic hearts of even the weakest nation. Lately these aliens have called themselves Hawaiians.

They are not and never were Hawaiians. Although some have had positions under the monarchy which they solemnly swore by oath of office to uphold and sustain, they retained their American birthright. When they overthrew my government, and placed themselves under the protectorate established by John L. Stevens—as he so states in writing,—they designated themselves as Americans; as such they called on him to raise their flag on the building of the Hawaiian Government.[14] When it pleased the Provisional Government to give their control another name, they called it the Republic of Hawai'i. To gain the sympathy of the American people, they made the national day of the Independence of the United States their own, and made speeches claiming to be American citizens. Such has been their custom at Honolulu, although in Washington they represent themselves as Hawaiians. . . .

Perhaps there is a kind of right, depending upon the precedents of all ages, and known as the "Right of Conquest," under which robbers and marauders may establish themselves in possession of whatsoever they are strong enough to ravish from their fellows. I will not pretend to decide how far civilization and Christian enlightenment have outlawed it. But we have known for many years that our Island monarchy has relied upon the protection always extended to us by the policy and the assured friendship of the great American republic. . . .

The conspirators, having actually gained possession of the machinery of government, and the recognition of foreign ministers, refused to surrender their conquest. So it happens that, overawed by the power of the United States to the extent that they can neither themselves throw off the usurpers, nor obtain assistance from other friendly states, the people of the Islands have no voice in determining their future, but are virtually relegated to the condition of the aborigines of the American continent.

It is not for me to consider this matter from the American point of view; although the pending question of annexation involves nothing less than a departure from the established policy of that country, and an ominous change in its foreign relations. . . . Is the American Republic of States to degenerate, and become a colonizer and a land-grabber?

And is this prospect satisfactory to a people who rely upon self-government for their liberties, and whose guaranty of liberty and autonomy to the whole western hemisphere, the grand Monroe Doctrine, appealing to the respect and the sense of justice of the masses of every nation on earth, has made any attack upon it practically impossible to the statesmen and rulers of armed empires?[15] There is little question but that the United States could become a successful rival of the European nations in the race for conquest, and could create a vast military and naval power, if such is its ambition. But is such an ambition laudable? Is such a departure from its established principles patriotic or politic?

Here, at least for the present, I rest my pen. During my stay in the capital, I suppose I must have met, by name and by card, at least five thousand callers. From most of these, by word, by grasp of hand, or at least by expression of countenance, I have received a sympathy and encouragement of which I cannot write fully. Let it be understood that I have not failed to notice it, and to be not only flattered by its universality, but further very grateful that I have had the opportunity to know the real American people, quite distinct from those who have assumed this honored name when it suited their selfish ends.

But for the Hawaiian people, for the forty thousand of my own race and blood, descendants of those who welcomed the devoted and pious missionaries of seventy years ago—for them has this mission of mine accomplished anything?

Oh, honest Americans, as Christians hear me for my downtrodden people! Their form of government is as dear to them as yours is precious to you. Quite as warmly as you love your country, so they love theirs. With all your goodly possessions, covering a territory so immense that there yet remain parts unexplored, possessing islands that, although near at hand, had to be neutral ground in time of war, do not covet the little vineyard of Naboth's, so far from your shores, lest the punishment of Ahab fall upon you, if not in your day, in that of your children, for "be not deceived, God is not mocked."[16] The people to whom your fathers told of the living God, and taught to call "father," and whom the sons now seek to despoil and destroy are crying aloud to Him in their time of trouble; and He will keep His promise, and will listen to the voices of His Hawaiian children lamenting for their homes.

It is for them that I would give the last drop of my blood; it is for them that I would spend, nay, am spending, everything belonging to me. Will it be in vain? It is for the American people and their representatives in Congress to answer these questions. As they deal with me and my people, kindly, generously, and justly, so may the Great Ruler of all nations deal with the grand and glorious nation of the United States of America.

2

"Keep Our Treaties" (1906)[17]

Chitto Harjo

As Lili'uokalani's opposition to annexation faltered, Native nations within the continental United States defended their homelands from a different form of incorporation. Allotment intended to integrate reservations into the United States by allocating parcels of tribally owned property to individual Indians and opening the remaining "surplus land" to homesteaders. It proceeded unevenly. In Oklahoma Territory and Indian Territory pressure intensified, and resistance took many forms. Lone Wolf, a Kiowa leader, sued the United States to prevent the dismantling of the Kiowa, Comanche, and Apache Reservation, only to be defeated in *Lone Wolf v. Hitchcock* (1903). Plenary power, the Supreme Court affirmed, enabled Congress to abrogate treaties arbitrarily. After separate legislation extended the Dawes Act to Indian Territory, dissenters refused to sign tribal rolls or accept allotments. The Creeks splintered, and as Oklahoma moved toward statehood in 1906, Chitto Harjo (1846–1911) took the Creek opposition's case before a Senate investigating committee in Tulsa. Consider the connection he made between land ownership and nationhood, his strategic deployment of history, memory, and race, and the central place treaty making, consent, and justice held in his defense of Creek sovereignty.[18]

I will begin with a recital of the relations of the Creeks with the Government of the United States. . . . And I will explain it so you will understand it. . . . My ancestors and my people were the inhabitants of this great country from 1492. I mean by that from the time the white man first came to this country until now. It was my home and the home of my people from time immemorial, and is today, I think, the home of my people.

Away back in that time—in 1492—there was man by the name of Columbus came from across the great ocean, and he discovered this country for the white man—this country which was at that time the home of my people. What did he find when he first arrived here? Did he find a white man standing on this continent then, or did he find a black man standing here? Did he find either a black man or a white man standing on this continent then?

... I stood here first and Columbus first discovered me. I want to know what did he say to the red man at that time? He was on one of the great four roads that led to light. At that time Columbus received the information that was given to him by my people. My ancestor informed him that he was ready to accept this light he proposed to give him and walk these four roads of light and have his children under his direction. He told him it is all right. He told him, "The land is all yours; the law is all yours." He said it was right. He told him, "I will always take care of you. If your people meet with any troubles I will take these troubles away. I will stand before you and behind you and on each side of you and your people, and if any people come into your country I will take them away and you shall live in peace under me." "My arms," he said, "are very long." He told him to come within his protecting arms and he said, "If anything comes against you for your ruin I will stand by you and preserve you and defend you and protect you." ...

He told me that as long as the sun shone and the sky is up yonder these agreements shall be kept. That was the first agreement that we had with the white man. He said as long as the sun rises it shall last; as long as the waters run it shall last; as long as grass grows it shall last. That was what it was to be and we agreed on those terms. That was what the agreement was, and we signed our names to that agreement and to those terms. ... That is what he said, and we believed it. I think there is nothing that has been done by the people should abrogate them. We have kept every term of that agreement. The grass is growing, the waters run, the sun shines, the light is with us, and the agreement is with us yet, for the God that is above us all witnessed that agreement.

... Now, coming down to 1832 and referring to the agreements between the Creek people and the Government of the United States: What has occurred since 1832 until today?[19] It seems that some people forget what has occurred. After all, we are all of one blood; we have the one God and we live in the same land. I have always lived back yonder in what is now the State of Alabama. We had our homes back there; my people had their homes back there. We had our troubles back there and we had no one to defend us. At that time when I had these troubles it was to take my country away from me. I had no other troubles. The troubles were always about taking my country away from me. I could live in peace with all else, but they wanted my country and I was in trouble defending it.

It was no use. They were bound to take my country away from me. It may have been that my country had to be taken away from me, but it was not justice. I have always been asking for justice. I never asked for anything else but justice. I never had justice. First, it was this and then it was something else that was taken away from me and my people, so we couldn't stay there any more. It was not because a man had to stand on the outside of what was right that brought the troubles. What was to be done was all set out yonder in the light and all men knew what the law and the agreement was. It was a treaty—a solemn treaty—but what difference did that make? I want to say this to you to-day, because I don't want these ancient agreements between the Indian and the white man violated. . . .

Then it was the overtures of the Government to my people to leave their land, the home of their fathers, the land that they loved. . . . He said, "Go away out there to this land toward the setting sun, and take your people with you and locate them there, and I will give you that land forever, and I will protect you and your children in it forever." That was the agreement and the treaty, and I and my people came out here and we settled on this land, and I carried out these agreements and treaties in all points and violated none. I came over and located here.

What took place in 1861? I had made my home here with my people, and I was living well out here with my people. We were all prospering. We had a great deal of property here, all over this country. We had come here and taken possession of it under our treaty. We had laws that were living laws, and I was living here under the laws. You are my fathers, and I tell you that in 1861, I was living here in peace and plenty with my people, and we were happy; and then my white fathers rose in arms against each other to fight each other. They did fight each other. At that day Abraham Lincoln was President of the United States and our Great Father. He was in Washington and I was away off down here. My white brothers divided into factions and went to war.

When the white people raised in arms and tried to destroy one another, it was not for the purpose of destroying my people at all. It was not for the purpose of destroying treaties with the Indians. They did not think of that and the Indian was not the cause of that great war at all. The cause of that war was because there was a people that were black in skin and color, who had always been in slavery. In my old home in Alabama and all through the south part of the nation and out in this country, these black people were held in slavery and up in the North there were no slaves. The people of that part of the United States determined to set the black people free, and the people in the South determined that they should not, and they went to war about it. In that war the Indians had not any part. It was not their war at all.

The purpose of the war was to set these black people at liberty, and I had nothing to do with it. He told me to come out here and have my laws back, and I came out here with my people and had my own laws, and was living under them. On account of some of your own sons—the ancient brothers of mine—they came over here and caused me to enroll along with my people on your side.[20] I left my home and my country and everything I had in the world and went rolling on toward the Federal Army. I left my laws and my government, I left my people and my country and my home, I left everything and went with the Federal Army for my father in Washington. I left them all in order to stand by my treaties. I left everything and I arrived in Kansas—I mean it was at Leavenworth where I arrived. It was a town away up in Kansas on the Missouri River. I arrived at Fort Leavenworth to do what I could for my father's country and stand by my treaties. . . .

Things should not have been that way but that is the way they were. The father at Washington was not able to keep his treaty with me and I had to leave my country, as I have stated, and go into the Federal Army. Then I got a weapon in my hands, for I raised my hand and went into the Army to help to defend my treaties and my country and the Federal Army. I went in as a Union soldier. When I took the oath I raised my hand and called God to witness that I was ready to die in the cause that was right and to help my father defend his treaties. All this time the fire was going on and the war and the battles were going on, and today I have conquered all and regained these treaties that I have with the Government. I believe that everything wholly and fully came back to me on account of the position I took in that war. I think that. I thought then, and I think today, that is the way to do—to stand up and be a man that keeps his word all the time and under all circumstances. That is what I did, and I know that in doing so I regained again all my old treaties, for the father at Washington conquered in that war, and he promised me that if I was faithful to my treaties I should have them all back again. I was faithful to my treaties and I got them all back again, and today I am living under them and with them. I never agreed to the exchanging of lands and I never agreed to the allotting of my lands. . . . Your Government . . . said that if anyone trespassed on my rights or questioned them to let him know and he would take care of them and protect them.[21]

I always thought that this would be done. I believe yet it will be done. I don't know what the trouble is now. I don't know anything about it. I think that my lands are all cut up. I have never asked that be done, but I understand it has been done. I don't know why it was done. My treaty said that it never would be done unless I wanted it done. That anything I did not want to be done contrary to that treaty would not be done. . . . I never had made these requests. I went through death for this cause, and I now hold the release this Government gave me. I served the father faithfully; and as a reward I regained my country back again and I and my children will remain on it, and live upon it as we did in the old time. I believe it. I know it is right. I know it is justice.

I hear that the Government is cutting up my land and is giving it away to black people. I want to know if this is so. It can't be so, for it is not the treaty. These black people, who are they? They are negroes that came in here as slaves. They have no right to this land. It never was given to them. It was given to me and my people and we paid for it with our land back in Alabama. The black people have no right to it. Then can it be that the Government is giving it—my land—to the negro?[22] I hear it is, and they are selling it. This can't be so. It wouldn't be justice. I am informed and believe it to be true that some citizens of the United States have titles to land that was given to my fathers and my people by the Government. If it was given to me, what right has the United States to take it from me without first asking my consent? That I would like to know. . . .

I believe the officers of the United States ought to take care of the rights of me and my people first and then afterwards look out for their own interests. I have reason to believe and I do believe that they are more concerned in their own welfare than the welfare or rights of the Indian—lots of them are. I believe some of them are honest men, but not many. A man ought first to dispossess himself of all thought or wish to do me or my country wrong. He should never think of doing wrong to this country or to the rights of my people. After he has done that, then maybe he can do something for himself in that regard; but first he must protect the Indians and their rights in this country. He is the servant of the Government and he is sent here to do that and he should not be permitted to do anything else.

All that I am begging of you, honorable Senators, is that these ancient agreements and treaties wherein you promised to take care of me and my people be fulfilled, and that you will remove all the difficulties that have been raised in reference to my people and their country, and I ask you to see that these promises are faithfully kept. . . .

3

"We Can Establish Our Rights" (1913)[23]

Cherokee Freedmen

Many indigenous peoples practiced captive taking and slavery prior to contact with Europe. By the nineteenth century, some southeastern Indians developed chattel slavery. In a pernicious paradox, treating other human beings as property became a way for Native nations to demonstrate their civilization. The Civil War and Reconstruction transformed the politics of race and nation in Indian Territory. In 1866, the U.S. government forced the Cherokees, among others, to enfranchise their emancipated slaves, referred to as "Freedmen." The creation of tribal rolls, allotment, and the distribution of monetary awards from claims cases brought the meaning of citizenship back to the fore during the late nineteenth and early twentieth centuries. Were Cherokee Freedmen, in the absence of kin relations, entitled to the same rights and entitlements as Cherokees who were citizens "by blood?" And who possessed the power to decide? In this memorial submitted to Congress in 1913, the Cherokee Freedmen provided their response to those questions. Consider whether their reckoning of citizenship delineated race from nation.[24]

To the Congress of the United States:

We, the undersigned, representing the Cherokee freedmen who have been wrongfully excluded from the final rolls of the Cherokee Nation of Oklahoma, do hereby memorialize Congress to enact legislation which will protect us in the rights guaranteed us under treaties between the United States and said nation, under the laws of Congress, and the rules and regulations of the Interior Department, and the decisions of the courts.

By the act of Congress of June 10, 1896 (the Indian appropriation bill), the rolls of citizenship of the several tribes, as they then existed, were confirmed, yet a number of our people whose names appear upon the various rolls have been denied their rights.[25]

Under the act of June 28, 1898, the Commission to the Five Tribes was directed as follows: "It shall make a roll of Cherokee freedmen in strict compliance with the decree of the Court of Claims rendered the 3d day of February, 1896."

The direction was plain and simple, yet it was not obeyed.

The court in this opinion clearly set out the rights of the Cherokee freedmen, and we call your attention the following extract: "Said commissioners, in ascertaining the identity of the freedmen entitled to share under this decree, *shall accept* what is known as the authenticated Cherokee roll, the same being on file in the office of the Secretary of the Interior, having been furnished to him, and purporting to have been taken by the Cherokee Nation in 1880, for the purpose of showing the number of freedmen entitled at that time to citizenship in said nation ***and their descendants."

The Secretary of Interior in his letter of instructions told the commission what it should do, and had the commission followed the law and his instructions there would have been no trouble, but the commission did neither. He informed them that "The roll of 1880 made by the Cherokee Nation is to be accepted by you as conclusive of the rights of all persons whose names are found thereon and of their descendants to be enrolled by you, ***no evidence was to be accepted tending to disprove the citizenship of any person whose name was upon the roll of 1880."[26]

Notwithstanding the decree of the court and the strong language of the Secretary, the commission did fail and neglect to properly place upon the final roll the names of a number of freedmen who were on the 1880 roll. Many of the freedmen whose names were on that roll and their descendants have been and still are wrongfully denied membership in said nation, and they will lose their valuable rights unless some action is taken by Congress. There can be no reasonable excuse offered for the neglect of the Commission to the Five Tribes, for it was fully instructed what to do in regard to the Cherokee freedmen. . . .

Many of the people have lived in the Cherokee Nation all their lives, some of them have occupied and cultivated the same tract of land for from 30 to 40 years, and some were permitted to make tentative selections. They have raised stock and crops, built houses and barns, have developed the agricultural wealth of the Cherokee country. They have voted, held office, and exercised all the rights of citizenship. They applied for enrollment within the time fixed by law. All of them have been enrolled once as citizens and many of them twice by the Government, and these rolls have been approved by the Secretary of the Interior, and many of them at various payments, were paid as members of the Cherokee Nation of Indians.

The act of Congress provided for the removal of intruders; none of these freedmen were disturbed.

Under the act of June 28, 1898, authority was given to the chief or to any member of the tribe to bring suits against any person holding wrongful possession of lands in the Cherokee country, yet no action was brought against any of your petitioners. Under the act of 1902 the Secretary was to cause allottees to be placed in possession, but the Secretary did not remove the freedmen claimants. This shows how they were regarded before the final rolls were made up and before they were wrongfully left off of the final rolls, which will deprive them of their interest in the tribal property, and they will be driven from the homes they have occupied for years, and others will be deprived from making their rightful selections.

By reason of valuable oil and gas deposits in the lands, which by rights belong to your petitioners, the same—worth many millions of dollars—we will lose, also be deprived of other property, and our homes if Congress does not give us relief.

We are satisfied that the records of the Interior Department cover all the facts, and that the questions involved could be settled fairly and justly within a very short time.

We therefore pray Congress to give us a chance to present our cases to a committee of Congress, to any court, or to the Secretary of the Interior. We know that we can establish our rights, and we are only asking for just and fair treatment.

4

"That the Smaller Peoples May Be Safe" (1918)[27]

Arthur C. Parker

Founded in 1911, the Society of American Indians (SAI) represented an indigenous version of what African American intellectual W. E. B. Du Bois referred to as the "Talented Tenth." Its membership included Native people from many walks of life, but its leadership largely consisted of professionals. Seneca archaeologist, folklorist, and museum curator Arthur C. Parker (1881–1955) served as a central figure and editor of SAI's journal. Like many of his peers, Parker put his training to unexpected uses. Rather than advocating for the obliteration of tribal identities, Parker approached Seneca stories as living texts, challenged binaries that cast "Indian" in opposition (and as inferior) to "white," attacked pseudoscientific theories purporting Native racial inferiority, and castigated the pretentious underpinnings of Western education and Indian policy. Consider how Parker used concepts such as materialism, civilization, democracy, citizenship, and experience to connect his critique of federal-Indian relations and his defense of Native rights to issues and ideas that rested at the heart of progressivism and U.S. involvement in World War I? What do you make of his proposed solution?[28]

Complaint against the existing order is not always indicative of anarchism; it may be on the other hand a healthy call to greater progress and wider application of world justice. Complaints against the Indian Office have been continual since its creation but at irregular intervals these complaints become more acute and again die down to a low, almost inaudible rumble.[29] It would be an interesting study to trace the curve of complaint against this branch of the Government's activities and to determine the various causes that directed it.

Complaint against the Indian Bureau is not lodged without cause, but whatever the specific cause, the complaint is indicative of one or more evils that affect the living condition, the vital requirements of the Indians. The Bureau may be blamable. Congress may be at fault, or the errors and imperfections of modern "civilized society" may be the factors that react to the injury of the complaining people. Perhaps all these factors are responsible for the conditions bringing forth the complaint. We ought to inquire, and soberly, just what the basic trouble is and then with courage correct what we can. What we cannot correct we must seek in other ways to overcome, or, we must determine that the Indians become properly adjusted, that they may live notwithstanding the environment that militates against them.

Before we venture too far we ought to find out definitely whether or not society is not itself blameworthy for some of the defects we credit to governmental agencies. Certainly it appears to be, for the thousand frauds could never have been perpetrated on Indians, despoiling them of lands, money, resources and even life, itself, had not human society, our so-called "civilization" permitted it—which forces us to inquire whether or not a true civilization could or would permit such encroachments upon the lives and liberties of other men as have been made upon the red race in America. If we say that real civilization could not and would not permit such injustice and lack of consideration, then we must admit now, what the future will attribute to us in abundant measures, a lack of real civilization. In a large measure we are still barbarians restrained mostly by the prohibitions and penalties imposed by statutes, and not by the overwhelming force of our moral convictions. But, in material attainment we may lay some claim to civilization. This attainment has been possible largely by the subordination of human society to the direction of economic agencies. In other words, our relations one to another, our measures of expediency and our government are largely directed and controlled by the rules, customs and the laws of trade and barter. We hedge these things about by protective laws and in every way seek to conserve and encourage commerce, even though human lives are impaired, lost or dwarfed. Our aim as expressed by our attainments has been *material acquisition* and has not been spiritual expansion and *spiritual freedom*.

It is because we have been playing the game of "*Get*" that we have robbed the Indian. He did not know what he was playing, did not know the rules of the game, did not know that he had his lands and allotments stacked like chips; he only knew that every time the white man said, "Come on, let's deal with one another," that *he* lost something. The game was too complex for the red man, and not because he did not himself barter, but because he did not have the means of making an elaborate set of rules and have the power to enforce them. The result has been that the man who knew the rules got the possessions of the men who did not. It was an unequal game. How was the red man to know that when he signed something that he thought was a promise to deliver a hundred beaver skins that one year later he must lose all his land because what he thought and what he was told differed from what reality proved the paper he signed to be. How were the Indians to know that the treaties they signed were documents that contained verbiage that could be construed differently from what they understood. The Indians *lost* and the laws of the land and the courts sanctioned the winnings of the man or men who knew the rules of the game. Does not the law say that when you sign your name to a document you are bound to perform what the document says? That's the rule of the game; society sanctions it. How the history of the Indian's experience with the white man rings with complaint against the rules of this commercial game played by predatory society. Do the Indians' complaints indicate nothing but pique or do they point out an evil that infects and affects all civilization built up on the "economic theory"?

Yet, how shall we of today change the order of society and rebuild civilization? Only as awakened conscience and intelligence causes us all to do so. But until we do change our way we shall continue to approve and even encourage the exploitation of all weaker peoples—peoples who are less acquainted with the rules of this game.

So much for our indictment of civilization. We have robbed the Indian because we are civilized and because it is a part of civilization to do so. Yet our higher ideals of a true relation of men one with the other disapprove of our entrenched, legalized buccaneering. . . .

The complaints of the Indians and their friends when reduced to analysis are found to consist of protests against certain actions that are admitted by all to be inconsistent with our democratic ideals. The Indians are not, and have not, been treated in a democratic way. We govern them, but not with their cooperation or consent; conversely, we *impose* our will upon them. In making laws for them and for their government we seldom or never consult their wishes. In our administration of Indian affairs we do not seek to make the Indians affected well acquainted with our aims. Except in a perfunctory legal way we do not publish those laws for their benefit. Very seldom have they knowledge of any contemplated action by the Indian Department. They are but silent, passive spectators of their own fate and so far as the laws and administrative policy goes have no part in it. They move as they are moved. . . .

The remedy would be the inauguration of a consistent policy philo-sophically constructed upon democratic principles. You never can do this by any sort of process that leaves the Indian Bureau in existence as an autocratic institution with the power to arbitrarily impose government. Though an autocratic bureau may have a perfect machine for doing what it desires with Indians; though its card indexes and loose leaf ledgers may be the latest, it will still fail in accomplishing a democratic end. This will be simply because in handling Indian money and property it also handles as commodities and chattels the souls and the liberties of men, and by its short-sighted paternalism prevents that most necessary of all things in a changing environment,—*experience*. Experience is a biological requisite for survival.

Therefore, if we are consistent in our aim to bring democracy to all the peoples of the earth let us deal with the Indians in a democratic way. It would be democratic for Congress to assert now, and without further delay, that all Indians within the United States of America are citizens or candidate citizens of the land. If their lands and trust funds are held under special tenure this would not then injure the status of the people as citizens. . . .

The Government through its Congress and the Department of Indian Affairs should never forget that the making of citizens who are intelligent men and women and who shall be responsive to all the requirements of a democracy is the chief function of all special dealings with the Indian on the part of the Government. Until the Government recognizes the primary right of the Indians to have full knowledge of their affairs, of acts affecting their personal rights and property, it will be making "democracy unsafe" for Indians. Indeed, a persistence of the present policy will work hardship that will be cumulative in its effects, for the natural impulses is to evade or break laws that one has had no part in framing.

The Data of Solution

Just how a speedy settlement of the details that make up the "Indian problem" may be brought about has been frequently set forth. To summarize these details of adjustment we shall but name them. 1st, a definite aim logically projected; 2d, a defined statute; 3d, admission of Indian claims to the Court of Claims for adjudication; 4th, the breaking up of tribal funds into individual apportionments; 5th, the cessation of annuities; 6th, definite and genuine participation in affairs that concern their personal and landed interests; 7th, knowledge beforehand of contemplated action; 8th, opportunity to acquire experience and to feel the weight of responsibility; 9th, real citizenship and genuine protection where special interests are involved.

If anything else is to be added to this category it might be an insistence on the part of the Government that frauds committed upon Indians will not be tolerated, notwithstanding the fact that to highly civilized businessmen who have power and a knowledge of the law's quirks, may defraud in a "perfectly legitimate way." Moral principle should rule in such transactions and the Government should insist that the moral principle have precedence over legal loopholes.

We are making war against autocracy in order, as we have stated our aims, "to make the world safe for democracy." This paper, criticizing, as it does an existing order, may be called too highly theoretical, yet we are engaged in a gigantic world war over a theory—the theory of the right of the smaller peoples to determine how they shall live and be governed, and we are warring that the smaller peoples may be safe. We are making war that on earth democracy, government by the consent of the governed, may triumph as the working theory of human society. Perhaps, then, it will be well for us to reconstruct our theory of Indian administration, and in our practical affairs follow the theory of making democracy safe for the Indian.

But we shall never get anywhere until we break the grip of the Indian Department in its repressing hold upon the lives and the development of the Indians. So long as the Indian Office is constituted as it is, it will insist upon thinking for the Indians and denying them the experience they should naturally have. If we can do nothing else let us say that the Bureau shall be limited to be a Department of Indian Disbursements charged with paying out that which treaties, contracts and Congress order. Then if we still desire to send men who are to superintend the social hygiene, the civilization, of the Indians, let us insist that they be men with training, human insight and the love of God and their fellow men in their hearts. This point cannot be over-emphasized, for the converse is true—Indians cannot be civilized and made men of acumen by ex-slave-drivers or by uncouth brutes without sympathy.

Our American Indians are today in France on the battle line, fighting that liberty, fraternity and equality of opportunity may prevail throughout the world. Are they to return and find that they alone of all humankind are denied these blood-bought privileges? We who remain here to labor, to think and to conserve true democracy are responsible for the answer!

5

"Another Kaiser in America" (1918)[30]

Carlos Montezuma

What does it mean to be civilized, and how can a nation call itself that and then proceed to exploit and oppress another people? Many indigenous protestors raised these questions during the late nineteenth and early twentieth centuries. Few did it more vociferously than Carlos Montezuma (1866–1923). A Yavapai physician taken captive as a child, sold to and adopted by a non-Indian, and educated at the University of Illinois and Chicago Medical College, Montezuma argued that exploitation and oppression extended from the denial of citizenship. Without it, American Indians existed outside the law and, from his point of view, had no rights. Montezuma took an uncompromising stance on the solution—grant U.S. citizenship and abolish the Indian Service. As conservative as Montezuma may sound to twenty-first-century ears, one might also hear the voice of a race radical. Consider his views on reservations, wardship, consent, civilization, morality, democracy, and, above all, freedom. How did he situate these ideas in the context of World War I and national self-determination? Do you think he saw a future for tribal sovereignty?[31]

Never in the history of America had there been such demonstration of rejoicing as when the wire waving over the country proclaimed that the war had ended.[32] "Now, free the Indians," comes to WASSAJA.[33] There is no use of talking, THIS MUST BE DONE. The people throughout America think the Indians are free and citizens. Again, we say, it is not so. The Indians are not free and citizens. Reservation life is not freedom. It is bondage. The Indian Bureau of the Interior Department of the United States is un-American. It holds down the Indians worse than slaves. Who have a better right to be free and citizens of America than the Indians? And yet, they are wards and counted outside of laws that govern other races in the United States. How can the liberty-loving country withhold any longer from the Indians their just rights? Now, we have gained freedom for other races or nations, it is up to Congress to pass a bill to free the Indians. For fifty years we Indians have been imprisoned on reservations. No nation has been so patient for their rights as the Indian race.

Just imagine between six and seven thousand volunteers in the army and navy, fighting for freedom (which they do not enjoy themselves,) and they have made good by the report of the press. At a crisis, does not that show that they are equal to it? Let us hope their services may not be overlooked. They fought for freedom and equal rights. Would it be right to keep them in slavery on reservations and under the heel of the Indian Bureau? Good common sense would say, "Not on your life." What would you do with them? As they have nobly carried themselves as men, when the country needed them, so should they be encouraged to be free and give them their citizenship to go where they please, in order to make their living. Most of them were judged upon as incompetent. Now what has the slave-holding Indian Bureau have to say?

What keeps the Indians from becoming free and citizens? We are not wrong, when we say, IT IS THE INDIAN BUREAU. In order to free the Indians and have them citizens, the right way is to abolish the Indian Bureau, because it is another Kaiser in America, relative to the Indian race. We have done away with one, let the people of the United States do the same with the Indian Bureau. Some people will say it is too radical. These same people have been saying that for these many years, and have not done anything to make the Indian man free or done anything in any way to see that they are citizens. In order to do what is right for a man, you must give him his rights. That is what we are seeking for the Indian race. THE RIGHTS THAT BELONG TO THE INDIANS.

We believe and know the Indians are in position to be freed and that they are ready to be given their citizenship. We assert that the only obstacle in the way for the Indians to gain their freedom and citizenship is the Indian Bureau.

The Indian Bureau

An institution that thinks more of itself than for the object for which it was instituted, that institution is no longer useful. When an organized body becomes useless, it turns into a poison. That is its way with the Indian Bureau. It has forgotten its object, now it is only a routine of making reports, receiving reports and filing reports. Outside of that, it has no more idea of the Indian's interest than a cat. In Washington they are ashamed to see and be seen with an Indian on the street. They send the Indian back to the reservation as soon as possible.

The Indian Bureau does not take the Indian by the hand and lead him out into the world. They would be the last ones to do such a thing. But they will set every obstacle in the way that leads to FREEDOM and CITIZENSHIP for the Indians. They will poison the minds of the public about the Indians and will insist they are a necessity, and without them the Indians would starve and die. They who differ with them are branded as frauds and self-exploiters. They will bring forth backers such as the Government of the United States, Civil Service, Indian Rights Association, Mohonk Conference, churches, and men and women of prominence, such as philanthropists, statesman, authors, artists and others from every walk of life.

Pity does not help. The above mentioned backers of the Indian Bureau are backers because they pity the poor Indians. How human it is to shift one's personal responsibility onto an organization or a bureau. When an organization or bureau goes so far as to KEEP ONE FROM HIS RIGHTS, MAKES ONE WORTHLESS AND DEPENDENT, then it is about time to CALL A HALT.

The Indian Bureau has been in existence for half a century. Time enough has been given to it to bear fruit, and it has born fruit out of the Indians. Out of a splendid race the Indian Bureau has demoralized it in every way to a state that words cannot express. The mind of the Indian is not free. He has been dependent on the Washington Father too much. He has been taught to depend upon the Indian Agent, and employees of the Indian Service. HE WAS A FREE MAN ONCE, but since the Indian Bureau's birth, he has been kept as a prisoner within the confines of the reservation system, which no ADOPTED AMERICAN WOULD TOLERATE. He moves and has his being in an atmosphere that is not an American. For fifty years he has been living in a world by himself. Such is the fate of the Indians at the hands of the Indian Bureau. Friends and America, can such autocracy be tolerated after battling and winning for FREEDOM, EQUAL RIGHTS, DEMOCRACY AND JUSTICE for the whole world?

National Peace Conference

If there will be a Peace Conference of all the nations after the war, the Society of American Indians should delegate a representative from the Indian race.[34] Why? Because we Indians are a nation. We Indians have never received justice from the hands of the United States. We have been

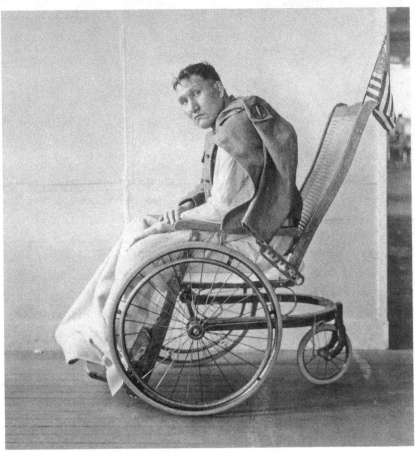

Fred Fast Horse (Rosebud Sioux) was partially paralyzed by wounds suffered during World War I. This image invites multiple readings of being, belonging, and the meaning of citizenship. He died in 1919. Accession Number 1962-08-6323. Wanamaker Collection, Mathers Museum of World Cultures, Indiana University, Bloomington.

relegated to the outside realm of humanity. There is no picture as black as the history of our race. You may speak about abuses and mistreatment received by the Belgians, Bohemians, Poles, Serbians and other nations of the old country, their griefs and wild kings are no comparison to the treatment of the Indians at the hands of the American Government. Five hundred years have rolled by and the Indians are not free yet. Five hundred years since the invasion of the pale faced race on the domain of the Indians and they do not enjoy the rights of human beings. This righteous war is a mockery to the Indian race, if we are not allowed at the Peace Conference.

6

"Our Hearts Are Almost Broken" (1919)[35]

No Heart et al.

Native people responded to the remaking of the spaces in which they lived—and of their very selves—in innumerable ways. Some embraced assimilation and left their birthplaces never to return. Others overtly resisted allotment through legal action or opted for subversion via accommodation, turning externally imposed institutions to their own purposes and driving hard bargains with federal agents interested in opening tribal lands. Those of a younger generation attended boarding schools and used what they learned to redefine the meaning of being Indian, reconfigure the boundaries of community, and defend the rights of their people. Everyday life served as another arena for taking politically purposeful action. This included everything from the language spoken in the home and childrearing to foodways, ceremonial practice, and artistic expression. This letter, written by Standing Rock Sioux leaders to Commissioner of Indian Affairs Cato Sells in 1919, shows that Native people also enacted agency through dance. Consider how the authors deployed the language of citizenship, morality, sacrifice, and patriotism to protect Lakota values and ways of being and belonging.[36]

Dear Sir:

We, the undersigned members of the Standing Rock Indian Reservation of North Dakota, hereby write and explain to you the difficulties we are having regarding our Indian dances on this Reservation.

Our Superintendent, Mr. James B. Kitch has recently announced that Indian dances are absolutely prohibited by the Indian Office on account of complaints made to you from this Reservation. We are advised that the complaints as stated to you are as follows:

That our Indian dances have caused many family separations; that divorces are getting common on account of the Indian dances; that the Indians are giving their property away at these dances and that these dances are getting worse every year on this Reservation.

We regret to hear of this false statement which has been made to you. It seems to us as though our Superintendent must be blindfolded if the Indians of this Reservation are doing as stated to you.

Regarding divorces on this Reservation we beg to say we feel that it is not our fault, nor do we advise them to do so. We are absolutely innocent, but do blame the lawyers more than anybody else.

The North Dakota Legislature passed a law in 1915 giving an Indian the same right as the white man to apply for a divorce. We understand that this law was passed with the consent of the Indian Office, so it would seem as though the Superintendent has no power to prevent the Indians from getting divorces. There are [men?] who never participate in the Indian dances who have got divorces and there are others who have been given patent in fee for their lands, bought Automobiles and spent all their money and on account of spending all their money in a foolish way have broken up their family. These persons have never participated in our dances, so you see this matter has been stated to you falsely.

We have ever since 1868 been obedient to the United States Government.[37] We have done our very best to comply with the regulations on this Reservation. We have sent our children to school to be educated to learn to manage their future life affairs. We have given our boys to a great World War. Many of our boys have been killed and some are wounded, account of this our hearts are almost broken but again we are glad that we have done our part in this great war.

We feel, however, that we did not gain the confidence of this great government since we hear of the restriction placed upon us.

It seems that all other Reservations throughout the United States are having their Indian dances frequently. There are some dances which are against the law which we understand are carried on at the Fort Peck Reservation in Montana. These dances are known as Sun dances.

On this Reservation, as we know, the returned students are allowed to dance, but it seems that the Reservations of this State are the only Reservations upon which dancing is strictly forbidden.

In the year 1882 our friend the White Haired Inspector Col. McLaughlin made an agreement with us that we could continue all dances as long as we lived.[38] We were to learn the white mans ways; learn to farm and on Saturdays we were to dance. There are now very few of us left, we are getting old and cannot enjoy ourselves in dancing the white man's dances. We have a dance known as the Grass dance but that is almost out of existence.[39] We are now dancing what is known as the side step or one step.

We do not paint up like we used to, but dance with our citizen clothes on. We dance with the boys that come back from the great war. We have no other way to enjoy ourselves when our soldier boys return but by dancing. There is no evil created in our doings. What is the difference in Indians dancing and white men dancing? There is no more temptation in the Indians dance than there is in the white mans. We do not give things away in our dancing like we used to do. The only time that we do give anything at dances is when there are donations to be made to the Red Cross, War Work Fund and Liberty Loans and we feel that it is our duty to do so. Our Superintendent knows what we have done toward the above.

Those who complain that we have given away our property at our dances, as we believe are all Missionary. If we had gave them all the money that we have donated toward the great world war we believe that they would not say anything against our dancing. We believe that they are German sympathizers or otherwise they would not make such false statements to you.

What else can we do for the United States Government that we may be recognized as obedient people to this great country? We have gave little to the churches. We hope that this restriction will be removed and that we may have the pleasure of meeting you personally at the coming Fourth of July celebration to be held at the Headquarters of the Standing Rock Agency.

We are your obedient Indians of the Standing Rock Agency, North Dakota.

7

"I Want to Be Free" (1920)[40]

Porfirio Mirabel

Incorporation through U.S. citizenship occurred unevenly during the late nineteenth and early twentieth centuries. Between 1919 and 1924, however, Congress enacted legislation to extend it to veterans of World War I and then to all American Indians born in the United States. While those with mindsets similar to Parker, Montezuma, and the Society of American Indians rejoiced, not everyone shared their enthusiasm. This should have come as no surprise to federal legislators, given the positions taken by many Native people during hearings conducted by a House committee in 1920. The Pueblos of San Juan, Taos, Picuris, Santa Clara, San Ildefonso, Nambe, and Tesuque, for instance, petitioned to be excluded from any citizenship legislation and demanded that the federal government continue its trust relationship with them. In this document, Porfirio Mirabel of Taos explains his views on the most significant issues confronting his community. Consider how he viewed the citizenship issue through the lens of land ownership and connected both to an indigenous definition of freedom. Does the exchange suggest that Mirabel and the committee were speaking the same language?[41]

Mr. MIRABEL (interpreted by Mr. Lorenzo Martinez).[42] Gentlemen of the committee, I am here today representing my pueblo of Taos. I am a man of this age, and I have the opportunity to meet you, the committee from Washington, at this stage. I am not an old man, but age is about 65 to 70 years old. I am glad to have the chance to talk to you and put before you what is needed at my pueblo. . . . I will tell you what I know of the conditions of my pueblo of Taos. It seems to me that when we were under the control of the Spanish Government, land was given us of which we are in charge, and are now taking care of it. It seems to me that at that time I never knew that we have ever sold any part of our land that was turned over by the Spanish Government to us.[43] Since that time, as I said, this land was turned over to our hands from the center of the survey, called for from the center of the cemetery by the old treaty, 3 miles that way [indicating] east, west, north, south—3 miles. . . . This land lately, not very many years ago, the Government survey came up to Taos. They surveyed the grant, but the surveyor, after it was done, we recognized that it was reduced about a mile or half a mile or a mile of what we knew as the area as it was turned over to us. . . .

The CHAIRMAN.[44] The Government took that away themselves first by this survey?

Mr. MIRABEL. Yes.

The CHAIRMAN. Then, for a great many years they never had had them?

Mr. MIRABEL. No, sir. But a great many years is not away back. As I said, since then the league recognized the whole according to what the Spanish Government gave us. Then at one time there came a revolution of Americans and Mexicans, and the head men of the Pueblo of Taos were arrested and taken under authority at that time—taken to town to be prosecuted under that act of their deed. Father Martinez at that time was a priest there. He went to the pueblo and told the Indians that if he has the ability of doing so that he would take so much land if the Indians would allow it to him, and he will protect the lives of those 12 Indians who were to be hanged at that time. The Indians believed what the priest said, so they decided that they would give it, for fear of having those 12 chiefs or governors hanged. But the reverse of that was done, according to the promise to the chief. As I said, there is a certain place like a trench made. From that trench on down to a certain boundary, the entire tract, they gave to the priest.

The CHAIRMAN. Did the priest keep faith with them? Did he save those men?

Mr. MIRABEL. No, sir.

The CHAIRMAN. He let them be hanged?

Mr. MIRABEL. They were hanged.

The CHAIRMAN. And he took the property?

Mr. MIRABEL. Yes: he took the property. . . .

The CHAIRMAN. How long ago was that? . . .

Mr. MARTINEZ. It was in 1847.

The CHAIRMAN. Is that your knowledge of it?

Mr. MARTINEZ. As to the days of the month they have no knowledge. As I recognize and know it, it is in 1847.

The CHAIRMAN. If your story is true, of course, that land was never fairly taken away and there ought to be some way to turn it back to them.[45]

Mr. MARTINEZ. I have been acting as interpreter mostly since I came back from school. I am pretty well up in the knowledge of this account or story that I am telling.

The CHAIRMAN. You are a graduate of Carlisle?[46]

Mr. MARTINEZ. Not graduated, but partly. I started in according to my ability.

The CHAIRMAN. When you finished that school what grade were you in?

Mr. MARTINEZ. The fifth grade, I think it was. . . .

The CHAIRMAN. Go ahead.

Mr. MIRABEL. This is the only tract of land my ancestors have ever agreed to let it out of their hands under the provisions of the deed they had with Father Martinez. We understand it today that the said Martinez has made his deed according to his own desire and own wish. . . . The heirs of the priest hold the land now. . . .

Mr. HAYDEN.[47] At Taos they are not asking the Government to buy them more land?

Mr. MARTINEZ. We wait to ask the Government about this disposed land of Martinez. It encroaches on us right inside of the grant, and that cuts off the grazing of our cattle, our horses, our animals, on the west side of the village.

Mr. HAYDEN. Then, all that the tribe would like to have is that it would like to recover from the priest, Martinez?

Mr. MIRABEL. Yes: if that could be done. It is only disposed of by the field. We would like to have that back, if possible. . . .

Mr. HERNANDEZ.[48] Is it not a fact that this land question, in connection with the lands you speak of that have been in possession of other people in Taos Valley, has been thrashed out in the United States Court, and even went as far as the Supreme Court of the United States about 40 years ago?[49]

Mr. MIRABEL. No, sir. . . .

Mr. HERNANDEZ. So in regard to the land lying south of the pueblo, and where the town of Taos now stands, you remember that your people had a lawsuit in regard to that land, and it went to the Supreme Court of the United States, and the Supreme Court held that you had a right to sell that land and that it went out of your possession by your own free will and accord. Do you remember that?

Mr. MARTINEZ. No, sir: I do not know anything about it.

The CHAIRMAN. Is that the fact?

Mr. HERNANDEZ. Yes. In regard to this Martinez tract, I have always thought this Martinez tract had been settled by the decision of the Supreme Court of the United States. I do not know about it, but that is my impression. . . .

Mr. HERNANDEZ. Is it not a fact that your people occupy now, as you claim, considerably more than 3 miles east of the pueblo?

Mr. MARTINEZ. Under our ancestors' traditions we did. Since we came to live in the Taos it embraces all the mountains southwest to Maxwell, and down to the center of the Taos Lake. We have two lakes.

Mr. HERNANDEZ. That is about 15 miles?

Mr. MARTINEZ. . . . It seems that the reservation was made under the United States Government and it became forest land. It seems to me then, as I remember, that I was working for my people as an interpreter. Then the first surveyor came there, and he went over there and he talked to me and told me about conditions of the land and of the watershed. Then we petitioned the Government to let us have what we claimed under our traditions, under our ancestors. . . .

Mr. HERNANDEZ. As a matter of fact, you have plenty of land to cultivate, and you do cultivate enough to raise crops enough to keep yourselves, to maintain yourselves in carry on?

Mr. MARTINEZ. I will ask Mirabel to say.

Mr. MIRABEL. I know, since I have been in Taos in all my life, we are laborers and farmers and we work for the protection and maintaining of our families with our work. But in those old days we have not enough ability or intelligence to cultivate our lands and break our lands. We don't do it that way or plan it in our climate.

Mr. HERNANDEZ. As a matter of fact, you lease considerable of the tillable land to the people who live around there, don't you?

Mr. MARTINEZ. Yes. This leasing I have referred to many of the inspectors, or men from Washington who claim that they are from Washington. I have been always opposed to leasing the cultivated land of my people.

Mr. HERNANDEZ. But you do lease it?

Mr. MARTINEZ. Yes. There is a class of Indians when they cannot find feed for their family they do it.

Mr. HERNANDEZ. Is it a fact also, Lorenzo, that you have toward the west and north, about, I should say, 1000 acres of good vega pasture land?

Mr. MARTINEZ. Yes; right near the pueblo.

Mr. HERNANDEZ. Showing, as a matter of fact, that you know the Indians of the pueblo of Taos have considerable land now that is not under cultivation which can be cultivated if they had the means to do it with?

Mr. MARTINEZ. We had at one time land which was lying idle.

The CHAIRMAN. Just one more question. Has the witness anything further on his mind that he has not told us and that he wants to tell in one final question?

Mr. MIRABEL. Only one thing: yes. One thing I fear very much is about citizenship. There is a bill pending on that in the House or Senate.

The CHAIRMAN. What do you want done with that?

Mr. MIRABEL. All that I ask the Government of the United States is that we want to be left alone and not to be made citizens, to be as always we have been from the old time of our ancestors' time, not molesting us any as to the citizenship. We do not want to be citizens.

Mr. CARTER.[50] Is it your understanding that when you are made citizens of the United States under the bill you are speaking about that you will have to pay taxes?

Mr. MIRABEL. That is what I want to know. I am here before you gentlemen from Washington to tell you what I am not willing. I am before you, as I said, and I want to ask that we do not want to pay taxes. We do not want to be taxed.

Mr. CARTER. Did anybody tell you that this bill required you to pay taxes?

Mr. MIRABEL. I did not hear anything.

Mr. CARTER. This bill does not require you to pay taxes. The only thing the bill does is that it gives you, if you desire, the right to vote and the right to sit on a jury when the case is of your own people or tribe.

Mr. MIRABEL. I am not educated and can not very much explain about this, whether we were to pay taxes or what this bill is. I am not educated. I cannot answer directly.

Mr. CARTER. Tell him that I wrote that bill myself and I am an Indian, and I wrote it for the benefit of the Indians. . . . And that I wrote it with a view not imposing anything upon the Indians, but with a view to giving him some of the rights and liberties which he does not now have.

Mr. MARTINEZ. He said to ask you about that man. What person is this that passed this bill? Who is that man that passed this bill? Where is he from?

Mr. CARTER. I am the man that drafted the bill. I belong to the Choctaw and Chickasaw Tribe of Indians. . . . And I was undertaking to do the same thing for all the Indians which has been done for the Choctaws and Chickasaws, and I want to repeat again that this bill does not tax your land. It does not place any burden on you at all. The only thing it does is that it gives you the right to vote, if you want to. You do not, under the bill, have to vote, and you do not have to take any part in the white man's government if you do not wish, except that when one of your men is arrested and tried for anything it gives you the right to serve on the jury and say whether he is guilty or not. That is all.

The CHAIRMAN. Knowing these facts that Mr. Carter has told you, do you still feel that you do not want the help of this bill?

Mr. MIRABEL. I do not want to be wiped out. I want to be free, as I have always been. We do not want to be citizens.

Mr. CHAIRMAN. You and your people want to be left alone, just as you are now?

Mr. MARTINEZ. What was the question?

Mr. CHAIRMAN. Do he and his people want to be left alone as they are now?

Mr. MIRABEL. No, sir: we do not want to be left alone by the United States. We want its protection always.

The CHAIRMAN. That is what you have now. You and your people do not want any change in your present condition except that would like to get little more land.

Mr. MIRABEL. Yes.

8

"I Am Going to Geneva" (1923)[51]

Deskaheh

Like the Pueblos, the Six Nations of the Iroquois Confederacy rejected the imposition of U.S. citizenship in 1924. Moreover, the Senecas, Cayugas, Onondagas, Oneidas, Mohawks, and Tuscaroras looked upon the national border established between the United States and Canada, which cut through ancestral Iroquois lands, as artificial. That did not stop the Canadian government from conscripting Iroquois, arbitrarily extending Canadian citizenship, and attempting to dismantle the Six Nations Reserve on the Grand River, land set aside for the Iroquois by King George III in 1784. Incensed by these actions, the Confederacy Council of the Six Nations directed Cayuga hereditary chief Deskaheh (Levi General, 1873–1925), speaker of the Confederacy Council, to take their case before the newly formed League of Nations in Geneva in 1923. In August of that year, he issued the following statement in London. Consider Deskaheh's use of history and memory and the position he took on citizenship. How did he relate them to sovereignty, the place of the Iroquois among the family of nations, treaty making, and international law?[52]

I am on my way to the League of Nations, and stopped off to tell why, to you who care to know. I go because your Imperial Government refused my plea, for protection of my people as of right against subjugation by Canada. The Canadian "Indian Office" took that refusal to mean that it could do as it wished with us. The officials wished to treat us as children and use the rod. This trouble has been going from bad to worse because we are not children. It became serious three years ago, when the object, to break us up in the end as tribesmen, became too plain for any doubt. Then I came to London to complain under the pledge of the Crown.

These were our grievances. When our men returned home from fighting for you, and three hundred went, leaving forty asleep under the sod, the Indian Office undertook a new scheme to enforce Canadian citizenship upon us, one at a time, but regardless of whether we consented to the conditions. They call it over there "enfranchising" us, although we have our own franchises, men, and women, too, and are quite satisfied on that score. We would not have consented to take Canada's franchises if she had asked us politely to do so. We are Red Indians, but what is more, we are Iroquois: the People of the Six Nations; the Mohawk, the Onondaga, the Oneida, the Cayuga, the Seneca, the Tuscarora.

We are willing to remain allies of the British as against days of danger, as we have been for two hundred and fifty years, and faithful allies, too; but we wish no one-sided alliance, nor will we ever be subjects of another people, even of the British, if we can help it. Any of our people may freely renounce allegiance to the Six Nations, but we object to the Dominion Government rewarding those becoming British subjects by turning over to them portions of our National Funds happening to be in Dominion hands, and such is the practice of the Indian Office.[53] We are burdened with scores of apostates quitting us for Canadian enfranchisement, who have returned to us as British paupers after squandering their ill-gotten monies.

So the move of the Indian Office, the department of "The Savages," as that office calls itself in Canada, to "enfranchise" more of us and weaken our ranks, did not work. Then the Indian Office undertook to lend our returned soldiers money to buy farms, a generous measure you may think. But all who knew how to farm really had all the land they needed. Those who did not know how would fail. There were a few only who, tempted at the site of the money, gave mortgages to the Indian Office as security for the loans. That Office took those mortgages readily, for, if not paid, the fact would afford a reason, partially good, for pushing political dominion within our borders by use of the domestic Courts of Canada. Courts are established to deal out justice, but not to seize power. We were not blind. Our Council—the very same in which Captain Joseph Brant used to sit—knew that no domestic Courts have a right to apply the law of one people over another.

Our Counsel knew, too, that if the Indian Office could by hook or by crook buy and sell our lands piece by piece, when our own Government had not consented, the Six Nations would slowly but surely be scattered to the winds and soon be gone forever as a separate people, swallowed up in the alien population surrounding us, not of our blood. So our Council resisted and stood its ground. I then became a marked man and would be in a Canadian prison now on some trumped-up charge if the Mounted Police had caught me—and they tried. They have recently caught and jailed many of my people for being loyal to their own Six Nations, for that is looked on now over our border in the Dominion as a crime or a contempt of court on our part subject to punishment by Canada. Wishing to send me upon this mission, my people insisted that I seek asylum south of the Great Lakes, while they were raising the necessary funds to send me. I went and they worked and saved and raised the money.

The Indian Office is now practicing what it calls law enforcement. It is experimenting on our people with the penal laws of Canada in reference to what may be eaten and drunk, and as to what may be done on certain days. We know nothing of those laws, but we learn that certain of them are quite old and some quite new. We had nothing to do with the making of them. Under colour of those laws, nevertheless, the Dominion Government has lately violated the Six Nation domain, and has wrongfully seized many of my people and cast them into Canadian prisons. That is where it has recently put several of our loyal members who, refusing to ask leave of the Indian Office Autocrats under the Indian Act, used fuel from their own woodlands to preserve their own lives in winter season. To keep warm Canadian farmers do not have to ask leave of anyone. This impressment of a domestic judiciary into service for subjugation of tribal Red Men is in imitation of a policy devised by the government of the United States. Not satisfied with those autocratic measures of a civil sort, the Dominion Government has at last committed an act of war upon us, without just cause, by making an hostile invasion of our domain in December last with a Canadian armed force, remaining since in our midst, with the result of serious trouble for our Council in its efforts to carry on our own duly constituted Government.

Along with these aggressions the Indian Office has denied us the use of our own public funds. Those funds arose from cessions of parts of our domain on the Grand River to the British Crown, made mostly over 100 years ago, with the agreement that the sale monies should be retained by the British Crown, but in express trust, for the use of the Six Nations and under Royal promise to pay to us the interest monies annually earned thereon. The Crown, for convenience, turned over to the Dominion Government, soon after the establishment of the Dominion, those funds for administration according to the terms of that trust and promise, and they are now held at Ottawa, except the large sums which have been wasted and misappropriated, and for which no accounting has been rendered, although the Six Nations have long tried to get one. The principal and the earnings are now being used by the Indian Office for such objects as it sees fit. For many years the earnings of those funds have been depleted by payments made through the Indian Office to men, alien to us, in reward for political services of no concern to the Six Nations. And now that Office is using those funds to incite rebellion among our own people, with the purpose to set up in place of our duly constituted Council a Six Nation Government devised by Canadians, to rest in fact upon Canadian authority supported by mounted police. No revenue from those funds has been available for use by the Six Nation Council or as income for my people for upwards of two years last past, with the result that our officials are for the first time serving without pay. Moneys for meeting the necessary expenses of any peaceful resistance to these aggressions practiced upon us we have had to raise through loans and contributions. When we issued our own public bonds to secure our own people and friends who made those advances, the Indian Office undertook to defame our credit and financial honour, using Canadian newspapers for that purpose. But we got the money—good friends over here have helped us.

During the last year we have offered to submit to impartial arbitration the justice of our cause but our offer was rejected by the Dominion Government. We in turn rejected its proposal that our differences be submitted for judgment to a Canadian Government tribunal to be set up for that special purpose. We would accept no tribunal not free to be impartial between us.

The Indian Office decided since that time to conduct an investigation into our morality. No doubt you will soon be hearing that we are a wicked people. That step is intended by the Indian Office to divert attention from its own wrong-doings. We will submit our morality to no other people for judgment, least of all to officials of a Government whose double standard is matter of record in its own so-called laws to which they say we must submit. No one before ever said Must to the Six Nations, or dictated terms of surrender to them. That law the "Indian Act" so-called, provides that in the case of Red people, a widowed mother or wife may not inherit from her deceased husband except as she established before officials of that Indian Office that she is a woman of good moral character. The Canadians have no such law applying to their own women. You said that the three hundred men we sent over here were good. They were sons and husbands of our women.

I am going to Geneva, and I suppose many stones have been placed in my path. But I must go there because your Imperial Government refused to keep good the British Crown's promise of protection, pledged not only by Royal document delivered to Captain Brant, which we hold, but under the old covenant chain of friendship that Sir William Johnson and Captain Brant kept bright so long. Our document reads that the Six Nations, as the King's faithful allies, may settle upon the Grand River lands as a safe retreat under his protection for them and their posterity forever. Your Colonial Secretary, who spoke for you, thought that our covenant chain was no longer good. He cast us off two years ago. He held that the British Crown was no longer responsible to us.[54]

We deny that such responsibility could be transferred to the Dominion of Canada without our consent, and we never consented. Our memory is not short. It is as true today, I am sorry to say, as it was two hundred years ago, that the nearest neighbors of the Six Nations, if they are of European stock, cannot be trusted to be just to us. That was the reason Sir William Johnson received his appointment from London to deal for you with us and not from the local governments of the British colonies which adjoined our domains. We have neighbors now hungry for lands we still own. They long for a very valuable tract of ours adjoining the City of Brantford, which even the Canadian Courts say is ours, yet the Indian Office will not permit us to use that land, to have any income from it, or to make a sale of it for ourselves.

If we have no special claim on British justice on the score of faithful and very useful services of our fathers in British need of long ago, as we believed we had, we who live to-day have a special right at Geneva. We helped to make possible the League of Nations, and did our full share by your side in the Great War. Now we mean to look to the League of Nations for the protection we so much need, to prevent complete destruction of our Government and the obliteration of the Iroquois race which would soon follow.

9

"It Is Our Way of Life" (1924)[55]

All-Pueblo Council

The continued assault on tribal lands and traditional practices did not come as a surprise to the Pueblos. By the 1920s, these politically distinct and linguistically diverse communities concentrated along the Rio Grande Valley in present-day New Mexico had grown accustomed to dealing with the unwanted presence of outsiders. Indeed, the All-Pueblo Council had been in existence since 1598, the year the Spanish colonial project began in earnest. During the late nineteenth and early twentieth centuries, Pueblos fended off invasive salvage anthropologists, challenged assimilationists, and confronted local, state, and federal interests on taking possession of Pueblo land. No sooner had the Pueblos defeated the Bursum Bill, which aimed to dispossess them, than they had to fight for their spiritual lives. This document, signed by seventy-four delegates from fourteen Pueblos, exposes a matrix of subjection that threatened Pueblo notions of being and belonging. But it also reveals a sophisticated strategy of using the values, principles, and institutions of an oppressive system against itself. Consider, in particular, their use of a rights-based discourse that would have been familiar to non-Indians.[56]

The Council of All the New Mexico Pueblos, assembled at Santo Domingo Pueblo this Fifth day of May, 1924, issues the following declaration, addressed to the Pueblo Indians, to all Indian, and to the people of the United States.

We have met because our most fundamental right of religious liberty is threatened and is actually at this time being nullified. And we make as our first declaration the statement that our religion to us is sacred and is more important to us than anything else in our life. The religious beliefs and ceremonies and forms of prayer of each of our Pueblos are as old as the world and they are holy. Our happiness, our moral behaviors, our unity as a people and the peace and joyfulness of our homes, are all a part of our religion and are dependent on its continuation.

To pass this religion, with its hidden sacred knowledge and its many forms of prayer, on to our children, is our supreme duty to our ancestors and to our many hearts and to the God whom we know. Our religion is a true religion and it is our way of life.

We must tell how our religious freedom is threatened and is denied to us. We specify first the order issued by the Commissioner of Indian Affairs to Indian Superintendents, dated April 26th, 1921. In that lengthy order, the Commissioner gives a list of "Indian Offenses for which corrective penalties are provided." He places upon local Superintendents the duty of determining whether Indian religious observances "cause the reckless giving away of property"; are "excessive"; promote "Idleness, danger of health and shiftless indifference to family welfare." "In all such instances the regulations should be enforced." And one of our present Superintendents of the Pueblos thus states his attitude in a printed Government report: "Until the old customs and Indian practices are broken up among this people we cannot hope for a great amount of progress. The secret dance is perhaps one of the greatest evils. What goes on I will not attempt to say but I firmly believe that it is little less than a ribald system of debauchery."

We denounce as untrue, shamefully untrue and without any basis of fact or appearance, and contrary to the abundant testimony of White scholars who have recorded our religious customs, this statement, and we point out that the Commissioner's orders, quoted here, to be interpreted and enforced by the Superintendents, is an instrument of religious persecution.

We next refer to the circular addressed "To all Indians," signed by the Commissioner of Indian Affairs and dated February 24, 1923. He states, "I could issue an order against these useless and harmful performances, but I would much rather have you give them up of your own free will and, therefore, I ask you now in this letter to do so. If at the end of one year the reports which I receive show that you are doing as requested, I shall be very glad, but if the reports show that you reject this plea, then some other course will have to be taken." And on February 14th, 1923, the Commissioner addressed all Superintendents commending to their attention the proposals of certain Christian missionaries, stating that "the suggestions agreed in the main with his attitude." Among these suggestions were the following:

"2. That the Indian dances be limited to one each month in the daylight hours of one day in the mid-week and at one center in each district; the months of March, April, June, July and August being excepted (no dances these months).

"3. That none take part in these dances or be present who are under 50 years of age.

"4. That a careful propaganda be undertaken to educate public opinion against the (Indian) dance."

We Pueblo Indians of course have not consented to abandon our religion. And now the Commissioner of Indian Affairs has just visited the Pueblos, and he went to Taos Pueblo and there he gave an order which will destroy the ancient good Indian religion of Taos if the order is enforced. He ordered that from this time on the boys could no longer be withdrawn temporarily from the Government school to be given their religious instruction. These boys would stay longer in school to make up for the time lost, and there is no issue about the Indians not wanting their children to be educated in the Government schools. But if the right to withdraw the children for religious instruction be withdrawn, then the Indian religion will die. The two or three boys taken out of school each year are the boys who will learn all the religious system of the tribe, and they in turn will pass on this knowledge to the generation to come.

When issuing this order to the Taos Pueblos, the Commissioner denounced the old customs and religions and he used harsh words about us who are faithful to the religious life of the race. He called us "half-animal."

And now we will call attention to the fact that when our children go to school, as they all must do and we want them to do, they are compelled to receive the teachings of the Christian religion no matter what the parents or the clans may desire. And the parents, the clans and the tribes are not even given the privilege of saying which branch of denomination of the Christian religion their children shall be taught. Thus a division is made between the parents and the children. And now if we are to be, according to the Commissioner's new order, forbidden to instruct our own children in the religion of their fathers, the Indian religion will quickly die and we shall be robbed of that which is most sacred and dear in our life.

We address the Indians and the people of the United States, and we ask them to read the guarantees of religious liberty which we have received. We came into the United States through the Treaty of Guadalupe Hidalgo, and that treaty guaranteed to all the Inhabitants of the Southwest, that until such time as they were made citizens of the United States "they should be maintained in the free enjoyment of their liberty and property, and secured in the free exercise of their religion without restriction." And we call attention to the covenant, which was a treaty, made between the

United States and the People of New Mexico, whose words are embodied in the enabling act making New Mexico a State in the Constitution of New Mexico.

"And said convention shall provide by an ordinance irrevocably and without the consent of the United States and the people of said State:
"First: Perfect toleration of religious sentiment shall be secured, and no *inhabitant* of this state shall ever be molested in person or property on account of his or her mode of religious worship."

We conclude this statement by asking the citizens of the United States: Shall the Commissioner of Indian Affairs be permitted to revoke these guarantees which the Congress of the United States itself could not revoke under the Constitution? We are but a few people in the Pueblos. We have inherited and kept pure from many ages a religion which, we are told, is full of beauty even to the White Persons. To ourselves at least, our religion is more precious than even our lives. The fair-play and generosity of the American people came to the rescue of the Pueblos when it was proposed to take away their lands. Will the American people not come to our rescue now, when it is proposed to take away our very souls?

We request and authorize the various organizations friendly to the Indians' cause to act with and for us in this crisis. This appeal has been written with the help of representatives of these organizations though what it says is our own thought and our own plea.

Most of all we say to all the Pueblos who we represent—to all the ten thousand Pueblo Indians, and likewise to the Hopi and Navajo Indians: This is the time of the great question. Shall we peacefully but strongly and deathlessly hold to the religion of our fathers, to our own religion, which binds us together and makes us the brothers and children of God? There is no future for the race of the Indians if its religion is killed. We must be faithful to each other now.

PART II

RECLAIMING A FUTURE, 1934–1954

Native communities continued to struggle for their right to exist as distinct peoples through the late 1920s and early 1930s. The number of new allotments declined, but supplementary legislation and all manner of dubious dealings at the grassroots level ensured that the divesting of the tribal estate persisted.[1] By 1934, less than fifty years after passage of the General Allotment Act, the federal government had liquidated nearly 100 million acres of tribal lands. Compressed into one solid mass, the remaining 48 million acres scattered across Native America would have fit within the boundaries of the state of South Dakota with room to spare. Meanwhile, missionaries were still at play in the fields of the lord, and the Office of Indian Affairs issued circulars outlawing dances, giveaways, and other ceremonial practices. In classic colonial fashion, externally imposed institutions within tribal communities, such as Indian police forces and Courts of Indian Offenses, empowered some Indian people to control and punish others.[2]

Controversies over land claims, treaty rights, and ceremonial practices, along with worsening conditions on reservations and gross administrative mismanagement, entered the public sphere in the 1920s. Heightened awareness of this dire situation translated into a reevaluation of federal-Indian relations in the form of the Committee of 100 on Indian Affairs in 1923, staffed by several Society of American Indians members, and the Meriam Report, an exhaustive survey of all aspects of the federal government's administration of Indian affairs published in 1928. While neither of these investigations advocated for the abandonment of allotment or assimilation, they did intersect with ongoing grassroots rights movements throughout Indian Country. In so doing, they contributed to major reforms during the 1930s.[3]

Catalyzed by the onset of the Great Depression and President Franklin D. Roosevelt's eclectic response to it, the Office of Indian Affairs redefined federal-Indian relations. The Indian Reorganization Act of 1934, championed by Indian Commissioner John Collier, an eccentric reformer and Indian rights advocate who cut his political teeth in controversies surrounding the Pueblos during the 1920s, ended allotment and the attacks on American Indian ceremonial practices. In the place of old draconian policies, the legislation instituted mechanisms for increased tribal self-government, land reconsolidation, and economic development. Collier's administration also articulated the inherent rights of tribal governments, supported land claims litigation, and embraced cultural pluralism through its support of arts and crafts.[4]

World War II, however, brought important changes. For one, it immediately derailed the Indian New Deal along with the rest of the Roosevelt administration's domestic reform agenda.[5] But the war and its aftermath also presented new opportunities and contributed to revitalization efforts. Approximately twenty-five thousand American Indian men and women served in the U.S. Army, Navy, Marines, Air Force, and auxiliary corps, while another forty thousand sought opportunities in war industries outside reservation communities. American Indians reinvigorated old warrior societies and created new ones; they conducted ceremonies to send loved ones off to war and to welcome them home; they wrote songs and created dances to celebrate military valor and mourn loss. Increased mobility during and after the war bolstered communities in places such as Los Angeles, Seattle, Phoenix, Denver, Oklahoma City, and Chicago and expanded regional networks between reservations and cities.[6]

Whether or not they served in the military, many Native people looked at the postwar world with grand expectations just as other Americans did. Returned soldiers expected their efforts to lead to a Double Victory over fascism abroad and racism at home. Meanwhile, tribal governments anticipated the return of or adequate compensation for reservation lands seized by the United States in the name of winning the war. Others, such as the hundreds of Aleuts living in isolated villages near Unimak Island, sought restitution for the loss of their homes and livelihood due to displacement and internment.[7] The war and its aftermath also conjured old threats in new guises. Massive dam-building projects in the Northeast and across the West threatened tribal lands, as well as treaty-guaranteed hunting, fishing, and water rights. And the question of belonging returned with a vengeance as a new generation of assimilationists touting the citizenship of sameness renewed their efforts of incorporation in the form of a federal policy known as termination.[8]

From the mid-1930s to the early 1950s, as the documents in this chapter show, American Indians continued to articulate visions for their communities that reclaimed a future from a majority society bent on consigning

Ho-Chunk educator Henry Roe Cloud, standing to the left of President Calvin Coolidge, attended an off-reservation school, an elite preparatory school, and Yale. Active in the Society of American Indians, he served on the secretary of the interior's Committee of One Hundred (pictured here) in December 1923, a pivotal moment of transition in federal-Indian relations. National Photo Company Collection, Library of Congress, Washington, D.C.

Native peoples to the past. For much of this period, acting on the right of self-determination included refusing to assimilate, defending traditional practices, protesting violations of treaty rights, protecting tribal lands, and demanding restitution. But asserting the right of self-determination also manifested itself in unexpected ways as Native people scrutinized and critiqued their would-be friends' plans to promote tribal self-government. In each instance, Native people engaged in a sophisticated process of indigenizing words, concepts, and issues familiar to the society that surrounded them. In so doing, they articulated a vision of a future on terms of their own making.

10

"As One Indian to Another" (1934)[9]

Henry Roe Cloud

The Indian New Deal has a mixed legacy. Insofar as it ended allotment, its significance would be difficult to overstate. And yet it did not realize all that it set out to achieve. The blame did not rest, as John Collier believed, solely with his opponents in Congress and Indian Country. Instead, trouble also extended from his romantic ideas about indigenous peoples, his inability to take criticism, and flaws in the Indian Reorganization Act (IRA). In this document, however, Ho-Chunk reformer and Indian Service employee Henry Roe Cloud (1884–1950) focused on the IRA's strengths. A Yale graduate, educator, Society of American Indians founder, and Meriam Report contributor, Roe Cloud served as Collier's point person in a series of congresses held in Indian Country to generate support for the legislation, including this one in Anadarko, Oklahoma, in March 1934. Consider what he believed to be the IRA's virtues—and, given his past experiences, why he invested such confidence in Collier's reforms. Does his construction of Indian economic thought and "racial character" ring true?[10]

I would like to give my personal opinion on this whole bill and it might be interesting to some of you. . . . I am not speaking officially for the United States government in any sense of the word. I am just talking as one Indian to another. Now I happen to be in favor of this bill for the following reasons:

. . . In the first place for the organization of these chartered communities that we have been hearing about, there will be allowed five hundred thousand dollars for the purpose of purchasing additional lands for the Indian people. There will be an annual sum of two million dollars to enlarge the territory of these chartered communities and that sum of two million dollars a year will be an annual affair so far as I understand it now. There are one hundred thousand Indians who have land leased and some Indians have felt that it was rather an injustice to those who are still holding onto their lands to give these Indians who have squandered their inheritance and their lands, and turn around and give them some more land. But the Commissioner feels very strongly this way about it.

The issuing of the patent in fees at the time they did when Secretary Lane and Commissioner Cato Sells sent competency commissioners all over the United States declaring a great number of Indians as competent to become fee patent Indians, that was one of the gravest and most serious errors that the United States government ever committed against the Indians. The Indians' lack of the sense of the value of his holdings and lands, as all of you know, is notorious. Suppose that we as Indians require three or four more generations of training and experience before we shall come to a proper realization of the value of lands such as the white man has today by thousands of years of experience and in the handling of these kinds of values, the white people have been struggling for the possession of their small acres across the seas for centuries and they developed a strong sense of ownership in land when they first landed on these shores. Because the Indian had so many acres of this whole community to roam over, he did not value the land that he had.

If I had a million dollars in my pocket, it isn't worth anything to me to hand you one dollar of it. I wouldn't miss that one dollar because I have a million dollars, less one, in my other pocket. If I have millions of acres what do I care for one single acre. Not until the Indian had lost all his lands did he begin to realize the value of his own lands.

Now in the meantime, the white people have used every artifice and means and even trickery, to get a hold of these lands that the Indians owned, and these figures that the Commissioner gave today are appalling, indeed, very, very appalling to me that from something like one hundred thirty-eight million of acres, we have dropped down to forty-seven million of acres in the hands of Indians with ninety-one million acres lost. Just think of the terrible loss that is to the Indians of America. Now the loss of lands causes certain following things: It makes a people poor, without resources, and consequently, they cannot build houses and comfortable places in which to live and bye and bye they do not have enough to eat and the consequences of unsanitary housing conditions and lack of proper food bring on all kinds of diseases. And that is why the Commissioner today stated that the death rate among the Indians is twice as that among the whites. Now where there are white people living and Indian people living alongside of them, every time a white man dies, two Indians die and it would not be so very long before the Indian race would perish from the earth. If that condition of affairs continues, it all harks back to the loss of our lands. We don't have any estate to give us the production and the income to provide us with a wherewithal to live.

In the first place, the Indian, when the white man came to this country, lost his buffalo; and in the second place, he lost the elk and deer; and in the third place, he finds himself hard-pressed for a place to hunt even small game; and in the fourth place, he has lost this vast territory of land involving his health and bringing about a high death rate and therefore a future that is mighty gloomy, indeed.

Now if the present allotment law of 1887 is going to continue, it will mean that those dark consequences that the Indian is suffering today will continue and the future of our race, no one can guess but in the most gloomy terms, I for one, would like to see all Indian tribes brought back into such a condition where they begin to increase and increase.... In one of the great gatherings of Indian Congresses, Commissioner Collier stood up and told them that everything in this country is organized except the Indian people. He told them that in organization there is strength and that as long as the Indian remains an undivided unit, pure and simple, and not willing to organize with his fellow tribesmen and put in an intertribal organization for the putting through of things that require national attention or even state attention, so long as that situation exists he is going to be pushed to the wall and the white man is going to get the best of him every time....

The reason that we as Indian people, do not progress and forge ahead very fast is because we are looking to Washington and the Secretary of the Interior and Superintendents on each reservation to do the things for us that are necessary. What will happen if we take those powers and functions into ourselves and begin to exercise them on our own behalf? The reaction that that sort of a program will be such tremendous development among the Indians as that we will begin to see the most wonderful and wonderful Indian leaders among both men and women and that is the secret of the meaning of self-government which this bill is seeking to bring back to the Indian people everywhere.

Now some tribes may not feel they are ready to begin that thing because the responsibilities are tremendous and great. When you consider that the budget estimates and the expenditures of those moneys is left to the initial judgment of the American Indian people themselves and to be considered by the Budget Bureau and Congress, and finally adopted according to the well considered planning and thinking of the Indian people, you can realize that is a great responsibility. How else can you develop the sense of finance and business among the Indians, two of the weakest parts of our racial character, because we have never had experience along those lines. How else can you develop those two things in the line of character unless you give the Indians a chance to do those things?

... The feature about tribal claims where if an amendment is provided and no set off is made to these claims by the United States government, that alone means millions and millions in savings to the Indian people if they should listen to the voice of this bill and I want to say emphatically, if such a bill were brought to any group of white people from across the seas, these Bohemians, the Czechoslovakians, Romanians, and Russian communities in the United States, if any man came out of Washington and offered them a bill of this kind, they wouldn't hesitate two seconds and they would grab it. Never such a wonderful thing came out of Washington to the Indian people such as we have been offered in this day. Now I want to emphasize one thing that is this: This thing would go over big in Congress if the Indian people got behind it themselves and that is what the President is expecting to see. That is what Congress is expecting to see and that is what the Secretary of the Interior is hoping for and that is what Mr. Collier, Commissioner of Indian Affairs, has come out to ask you to give. Now in view of all those benefits, of all those wonderful provisions about the gift of lands and the gift of moneys, of organization proposal and self-government in order to put a rainbow in the Sky for us Indian people instead of a stormy, black future, I think that every tribe ought to think very seriously, indeed, before they cast this thing to the ground. ...

And the last word I want to say is on the educational feature. I happen to be a man dealing in education of young, Indian people. All my life I have been interested in education. Fifty thousand dollars is the initial sum offered for the education of the bright, young Indians of every tribe. Now there is no reason why the Commissioner of Indian Affairs could not increase that amount to two hundred thousand dollars a year if the Indian people showed him that that amount was necessary to take care of the higher education and professional education of the Indians. But you must begin somewhere, so he puts it down to fifty thousand dollars. He has to be diplomatical and tactful and he has to be wise in the presence of this bill and put it in a way that will appeal and finally get passage. It is far easier to ask for more money by presenting the increased need in that respect, of Congress than if he asked fifteen thousand dollars, in addition, that he would like to use in picking out a Comanche, Cheyenne, Arapahoe, a

Kiowa, Wichita or Apache Indian who shows a special promise. Here is $15,000 for that purpose. . . .

You don't even sign a formal contract and whenever you are unemployed, the government is not going to ask you to pay it back. I wish I had had that opportunity when I was a young lad and had to work my way. I sold cigars, cigarettes and chewing tobacco and Navajo rugs, and crawled on my hands and knees planting flowers for rich people back East in order to earn my way through school. No government, nor friend ever rose up and said: "I will lend you this money. You don't need to pay one-half of it back. You can pay a small amount of interest on the other half and I won't ask you to go into a contract and whenever you go into a job and pay it back." I wish somebody would have offered me that opportunity. But you have it now. Your children, your sons and daughters, have it now provided in this bill. This whole thing means the rehabilitation of our family life and new self-respect.

We may have in our hearts the fires that have been low for centuries will be burning again and become bright and brighter because of the scheme of this bill. It means that your agriculture, the things you have built up for over a thousand years as a race of people, will be re-evaluated and re-established and you can look upon your people and my people as again a proud race of people instead of having this thing Mr. Collier, the Commissioner, calls an inferiority complex. Everybody up high but the Indian down here. He tries to restore the Indian race so that the Indian may be on a par in his mind and heart. That is the great objective that he is striving for and the Indian race, if it really understood the spirit and the contents and the accomplishment that this bill is aiming at, would become very friendly, indeed, toward the whole proposition.

We make mistakes all along our lives. The white people make mistakes. Every Commissioner comes in here and has a new policy and experiments with us, and now this Commissioner comes in here and says "Experiment with yourselves and see where you get," and in an experimentation of that kind I know of no better cause; no race of people has ever been known on the face of the earth to progress and go forward unless they experimented on themselves, by themselves, and for themselves.

11

"Fooled So Many Times" (1934)[11]

George White Bull and Oliver Prue

As Collier, Roe Cloud, and other members of the Indian Office moved from one congress to the next during the spring of 1934, Native representatives scrutinized the particulars of the Indian Reorganization Act (IRA). Some questioned whether the emphasis on retribalizing land fractionated by allotment would lead to segregation; others hinted that it smacked of communism. The critical stances, Standing Rock Sioux scholar Vine Deloria Jr., observed, revealed "that most Indians had adjusted to the allotment act, and the selfishness that Senator Henry Dawes believed an essential part of civilized life had taken hold in many tribes so that they were reluctant to pool their resources and lands and try to revive the old tribal ways." Consider how Deloria's assertion stands in relation to Roe Cloud's evaluation of Indian economic thought. Do the concerns raised by George White Bull and Oliver Prue, Lakota delegates from Standing Rock and Rosebud in North and South Dakota, confirm or complicate their analyses? How do their understandings of past relations with the federal government shape their attitudes toward the IRA?[12]

George White Bull from Standing Rock: Mr. Chairman. We have such a good interpreter that I am going to say a few words. I wish to extend my appreciation to the Officials for all the good things that they have done for us. But, in the middle there, there are some things that is detrimental to us and we fear them. Under the allotment system they have been after us for quite a number of years, using every means, employing fraud and deceit and eventually made us accept and go into the allotment system, under which we are now being governed. We believed in the allotment system as presented and we are now kind of getting accustomed to that way of being governed. All the officials are interested in the passage of the now proposed Bill or the new Bill, which contains some very good provisions in that Bill.[13]

Now, if, as a precaution and safeguard, if they will make a law guarding that Bill with a penalty of so many years' imprisonment and a fine of so many dollars attached to anyone who violates or breaks up this Bill, annuls or voids this Bill, I believe that nobody shall attempt to break up this Bill. What I have reference to is the regulations governing the allotment system of which are now past. I believe that something is not very clear in our minds and that is this, that the passage of the new Bill would in turn jeopardize our interests in some of the allotment and treaties that are known by the year '68, '78, and '89. Treaties that are known by the years would be jeopardized and that part of those will be relinquished if we accept the new proposed Bill.

I also believe that immediate action concerning this Bill is unnecessary as I just mentioned that some of the contents of the Bill are not clearly understood by all of us and there are a large number waiting at home and I feel that the delegations should take the matter home on their respective jurisdictions and there acquaint themselves, study the Bill, analyze it to the fullest extent. It may seem simple to you English speaking people, in whose language the Bill is constructed, but on the other hand the Indians that are involved, by the gift of God, they have an entirely different dialect, or language, of their own and some of them do not speak the English language so I think that the matter should be referred back to the people at home and there digested fully and then acted upon according to the wishes of the entire people after they have thoroughly acquainted themselves with the provisions.

One more thing I wish to say. Something that is to be readily observed by the delegates present here is that among the delegates are some who are landless that are very anxious for the passage and the acceptance of the Bill, and the reason for this anxiety, I believe, is that in the provisions of the Bill a credit system or the loan of money was mentioned. As I said awhile ago, we are getting, some of us are getting accustomed to the allotment system; that is, live on our allotments, utilize that land for their livelihood, utilize the water, the wood, timber and grass and maybe a garden spot and, more, a majority of these people that are utilizing their allotments are full bloods and can not speak English and they are reluctant about hasty acceptance of the Bill, fearing that some authority would come and take away what they now hold and claim as their own. That is all I wish to say.

I have some claims and suits against the U.S. Government.[14] We are looking forward to the day when a judgment shall be reached in connection with our claims that we may realize some compensation on behalf of the claims. How does it happen there are no monies to settle our claims and reach judgment on our claims or pay the amount of those claims, but when a time comes for the transfer of our allotments into another system then we are told that a large amount of money—millions—would be appropriated for this purpose? I believe that it would be an easy matter for us to reach an early decision in this matter had the Government been anxious to settle our claims and pay up our claims in full than if a new proposition were presented. I believe we would have been just as anxious to answer just as readily and go into it wholeheartedly. Also, because by the settlement of our just claims we know our rights and we would have no fear towards any other matter that they may present. I believe that if they go into an immediate decision on this matter and take final action on it here it would be just the same as taking bread and butter out of the mouths of the younger generation and taking it from the old and indigent Indians. . . .

Mr. Collier: Now I do want to say a word about the matter of claims against the Government. . . . There is one very real connection between this proposed Bill that we are discussing and your claim. One real connection, and it has to do with what will happen to your judgment after it is paid to you. Maybe you think, "We Sioux are going to get $100,000,000 net," and that is a lot of money. But, I have told you today how the Government, without the consent of the Indian, has misappropriated more than that much Indian trust money since 1900. If you just take one tribe of Indians alone: the Osage Tribe in Oklahoma. Since 1915, $245,000,000 has been paid into the Tribal fund of the Osage Tribe: $245,000,000. And do you know how much of that is gone already, thrown away, eaten up, wasted? $220,000,000 of that is gone. If you want to find out how it went, get the issue of *Collier's Weekly* that is on the stands right now and you will read all about how the Osage tribal fund has been misappropriated, or ask Mr. Henry Roe Cloud; he will tell you about it.

Now, if this Bill becomes law, this Bill we are discussing at this Congress, and then if you Sioux Indians go ahead under the Bill and take your charters and then, if you get your judgment from the Court of Claims, then not a dollar of that money can be spent by the Government except with your consent. You can protect your fund from misappropriation. Under existing law you would be powerless to protect your tribal fund from misappropriation. That is the only connection that this Bill would have with your claim. . . .

Mr. Oliver Prue [from Rosebud]: There is a thing that I want to question in regard to this petition, but before I make any statement I want to make a general statement on it. From times gone by, the Secretary of the Interior has been empowered with authority to act and to do as he pleases in all matters relating to Indians. We are selected as delegates to come to this Congress and listen on both sides of the question and thresh out the matters and try to understand it thoroughly and then without taking any action on our part, to take the case home, back to the people whom we represent. Therefore, it is believed, those being the conditions under which we came, if it is just a little matter of local concern right at this meeting that the whole Congress is requested to act on, our delegation is not at liberty to take part even in that case.

Last night, our Attorney, Major Case, gave us a nice talk and he complimented Mr. Collier, the Commissioner, on the character of the man and his sincerity in everything and his earnest desire to do something worthwhile for our people, and we also, our Rosebud Delegation, believe with Mr. Case.[15] From past experience in years gone by, we have come to learn to distrust all Government officials that come out here to negotiate with our people and we really have been fooled so many times, time and again, that we just simply distrust every Government official that came out here, however true they may be. (Applause.)We have listened to Mr. Collier for two days now and he has presented some very good material for us to listen to, but we have had so much experience in the past and even right now, maybe one matter brought up sounds good, looks good, and pleasant to hear about, etc., and yet we hear another thing again and then another thing. The matter has been passed along like a basketball. Thrown from one player to another until we don't know what it is.

12

"Let Us Try a New Deal" (1934)[16]

Christine Galler

In Chemawa, Oregon, delegates from the Klamath, Spokane, Yakama, Warm Springs, Colville, Taholah, Nez Perce, and Flathead reservations—speakers of approximately twenty different languages—expressed their views to Collier's team. Among them was Christine Galler (1884–1936), an Okanogan woman from the Omak Colville District Association, who served as both an interpreter and delegate. Better known today as Christal Quin-tasket, she published the acclaimed novel *Cogewea* under her Okanogan name Hu-mi-shu-ma or Mourning Dove in 1927.[17] On the first day of the conference, she cautioned federal officials to reconsider whose language presented a challenge: "You have many words that even an interpreter needs an interpreter for."[18] On what ground does Galler, who experienced allotment, spent part of her adult life as a migrant laborer, and became the first woman elected to the Colville tribal council in 1935, rest her case in favor of the Indian Reorganization Act.

I have spoken many times before the white people; and I am sure I am going to speak to you. . . . Ladies and gentlemen: My education did not come to me on a silver spoon. I am one of seven children. We children were very, extremely poor. My mother and father were prejudiced against education. What I have learned was through the hard ways. I learned of my own free will and I am proud today to say that I learned the education of the white man's language and tongue. What little education I have I worked hard for it. And it was through the Indian school as a stepping stone. It was here that I first accomplished my education. I fought for 25 years for the cause of the Indian people. The reason I have fought for my people is this: I owe it to them, old men and the old women of the Colville Indians. It is for their benefit that I speak for them today. I am a woman and you might think it funny that the Colvilles elect a woman for a delegate but the capacity of an Indian woman's head has the same amount as a man or a white man. Any woman can do what a man or a white man can do in any instance.

It is all up to you whether we will go back to the blanket. To those people who are not in favor of the bill, there is always a place for them. If they want to keep their allotments and their land they can ask the government for them. John Collier could take every foot of land, if they wish to, with the stroke of the pen according to law and we would lose every bit of ground we have. He has given us this privilege to find what kind of people we are. That is why he sent this Congress before you.

Someone said a while back that if it wasn't for the government we would be retarded back to an environment where our children would not have an opportunity like the white people. Due to them, all over the Indian reservations there are schools that your children could attend, like Chemawa.[19] There are schools for your children to go to. There is always a place for you if you don't want to be self-governing and to pay your obligations of taxes and being a citizen of the United States, to direct in any way what you want done.

We have been driven. We have been led by the white people for 122 years since the white people came into this country. We have never been given the choice of our leaders. We have no voice in anything. And now you are opposed to this bill of Collier's. He has worked for 15 years for the Indians cause. You want to be driven to it because you are not accustomed to lead your people. Your people as a people, industrious and self-governing, can do just what you want if you have the Federal Court to back you in your cause.

Ladies and gentlemen: I hope you are not going to think I am radical. I hope that you don't think that I am like Emma Goldman or any other woman, but as an Indian, my heart is with the Indians.[20] Let us hope that with this new form of government will not be imposing on our old people, that you younger men and women will have a voice in the government of the U.S. Let us try a new deal. It cannot be any worse than what it has been. You can say the government has stolen your land away from you. For the wagon, the implements, the government has given us direct compensation. That word "education" in exchange for the bow and arrow. That you can be thankful for. I thank you ladies and gentlemen.

13

"If We Have the Land, We Have Everything" (1934)[21]

Albert Sandoval, Fred Nelson, Frank Cadman, and Jim Shirley

The Navajos or Diné delivered Collier a blow when they voted not to endorse the Indian Reorganization Act in 1935. During a congress held in Fort Defiance, Arizona, in March 1934, Diné delegates articulated some of the concerns that led them to this decision. Of paramount importance was a stock reduction program implemented by the federal government that led to the destruction of hundreds of thousands of sheep and goats—all of it done in the name of erosion control, soil conservation, and range management. Diné men and women could no longer provide for their families and struggled to find wage work. But stock reduction worked even greater hardships by attacking Diné identity. Consider the alternative solutions to stock reduction advanced by the delegates, the deep connections to livestock and land they attempted to get Collier to understand, and whether you find the Indian commissioner's response to be adequate. In 1920 Porfirio Mirabel saw the issue of citizenship as inseparable from (and subordinate to) Pueblo concerns over the land. Would it be fair to say that a similar dynamic was at work in Dinétah?[22]

Albert Sandoval, Delegate from Southern Navajo: The speakers ahead of me have given little stories when they started their talks. When I was in school I read a little story. When the white people first came across the ocean and first came in contact with us, the Indians, they began to push the Indian back. Finally, a general and an Indian Chief had a meeting. They sat on a log together. The Chief kept telling the General to move over and give him more room. He kept pushing him over and pushing him over. Well, finally, the General said, "There is no more space left for me to move on." He was on the end of the log. Then the Chief said, "That is just the way you people are doing us. You are pushing us back and pushing us back, until we are on the end of the log."

That is the situation now with us, the Navajos. The white man gave us a little space, of grants. We found out right away that wasn't big enough and we asked for extensions. The white man was beginning to say "No more room for me to move back." But we know there is plenty of room, plenty of land back there. The only way I see to get enough land is to adopt the resolution that has been prepared here. That is the only thing, I think, that will help us out, because we have been fighting for this for years. I am much in sympathy with that resolution, although it is going to bring on a lot of harsh talk and scolding back home, but I do not see any other way out, except to take it the way the resolution reads.[23]

Fred Nelson, Delegate from Hopi Jurisdiction: Friends, Commissioner, and Staff from Washington: There have been a lot of things brought out in this Council, and before going on and adopting this new resolution that is afoot, we would like to refute a proposal that we made at the Tuba City Council, the resolution at the Council to reduce our sheep a hundred thousand. I think we should refute that resolution before we go ahead with this new proposal. At the time, when we passed that resolution that we were to reduce our sheep 100,000 head, most of you here, if not all, were present at that meeting.

Now, at that time, we tried to propose that this reduction of sheep be left until our next meeting. Our argument at that time was, that we would like to consult our people back home before going on with the proposal to reduce our sheep. In spite of the fact that we tried to carry over this proposal plan at the time, we were asked to make our resolution to reduce our sheep.

Now, the government, at that time gave us an outline of a program that we were to be compensated for, in this proposal. That we were to be given employment, and things in that line. It seems the program, as it was outlined at that time, is not fully carried out, and for our part, we have carried it out. We think it not fair to do our part and the government does not meet us half-way. I think we have done our part, and now the proposal that is afoot, that we were to be taxed at dipping time 10¢ per head for all the sheep and goats that we were to dip this summer, or that we were to be taxed 10% of the wages we were to earn from this E.C.W. work.[24]

Now, that is something complicated to us. It seems to us the wages are not sufficient for us, as wage earners, and it seems we should not be taxed, at that. We are only getting $42.00 a month on the E.C.W., at most. Out of this amount, $4.20 is to be taxed, out of the sum of money we are to earn in a month. If we were to get a loan from the Federal government in order to purchase these surplus goats, instead of using that money for purchasing our stock, is there any way that we could use that money for leasing land outside of the reservation. Would that save our goats? Is it possible that we could get a loan and lease some ranges in order to transfer what surplus stock we have, to control our range here on the reservation.

For the white people, the good old dollar is where they get their sustenance of life and the Navajos get their sustenance of life from the goats and the sheep, so it would not be fair to the Navajo to give up their goats and not the white people part of their dollars. We depend upon the goats and sheep for our life, our income, everything, the same as you depend upon your American dollar for your sustenance of life. That is what is puzzling us. We are wondering, having gone twice as far, and you have gone halfway back, which doesn't seem to appeal to the Navajo. . . .[25]

Commissioner [John Collier]: I want to say something else, which is a confession, and which puts me in agreement with our friend, who has just been speaking about something that he feels. He feels it hurts him and it hurts you, this idea of giving up sheep and goats. It just *hurts*. Two years ago, at the beginning of the great storm that descended upon the Navajo reservation, I was going through the Navajo reservation and saw the terrible things it was doing to your stock.

I saw the cattle standing with icicles hanging clear to the ground, of their frozen breath and I saw sheep dead, frozen in the cold. And it hurt me just like it hurt you and I hurried back to Washington. I was not then the Commissioner, I was the Secretary of the Indian Defense Organization, and I started a very intense campaign back in Washington. A campaign to get money to save your goats and sheep and we got from Congress, as I recall, $150,000 to help get feed to your stock. And it was not enough and so I kept on fighting, I was so anxious to save the sheep and the goats, and the cattle. And there were people back in Washington who said: "You are making a mistake because there are too many sheep and goats. The range is overgrazed and the blizzard is sent by God to cut down the sheep and goats and save the range from overgrazing." And that made me very mad when they said that. I wrote statements and the papers published them and members of Congress put them in the record and there was a very great to-do about it.

Well, later on, I have found that I was mistaken. That there were too many stock. That I was not really doing the right thing. But I tell you, I felt it just as strongly as any of you do about your sheep and goats. I had to learn that bitter fact which you all know now, that the range is overgrazed and has been very greatly damaged, and is going down fast so that if we go on the present way, there will be no food there for the goats or the sheep or the people in a few years. That is a hard fact and I have had to learn it and have had to admit my error of two years ago. And then having learned that, which is the truth, I went to work along with all of your other friends, to see if there was a way to save your soil and build it up again and restore your prosperity, and, therefore, all these millions of dollars are being spent because we know it is possible to save your range and restore your range, and to add enormously to your well being, but it does require a temporary reduction of stock.

The other question is, could not the money be used to rent land outside the reservation and move that many stock off and get them off the reservation in that way. We have gone into that rather carefully and the answer we get is that on the whole it cannot be done. Some help can be had from renting land off the reservation, but not enough. . . .

Frank Cadman, Delegate from Southern Navajo: . . . When we get very sick, when we need a physician, we go and look for the best physician and the best medicine we can find and when we find that medicine, we are satisfied. Now, in regard to our land—our land seems to be very sick. And the plan that is put out so that it can be brought back to normal state, I favor. That is the land erosion control. And the proposed plan to re-establish our reservation or bring back the soil that is in a state of deterioration, is the erosion control plan. That is the only thing that would solve it and bring back the soil. I favor it, and we should be willing to accept it.

We have been hearing about this plan for a long time, until they have actually come out here and actually brought with them an exhibition of what the erosion control really is and they have an experimental station at Mexican Springs now, so we may look at what is meant by erosion control. And another reason why I favor the erosion control plan, in that I would not fall out or be offended if these people did not succeed after they have put forth every effort to bring back the soil and bring back the range, if I neglected the seed, and let the seed fail; when I look at the soil, that is all patched, that if we lose it by putting forth every effort, then I would not feel bad. But when there is a solution that will solve the problem, we ought to be able to take it. The erosion plan is the remedy and solution for that thing. . . .

Jim Shirley, Alternate from Southern Navajo: There are two sources of life, of living, I wish to convey to you. The two forces are the land and livestock. One force is the land, from which we get mineral, from which we raise crops, from which we get our sustenances of life, and the other source is the livestock, and for the livestock, we cannot get by, we cannot profit by having livestock when our range is deteriorated. Therefore, we need to develop our soil that we may be able to take care of our livestock, and, therefore, we cannot put the livestock before land. We have to have the range before we can have livestock and for that reason, people may criticize and they may have the opinion that we are more or less deciding to handicap them in having reduction, in cutting off that source of living that we get from livestock, but the bigger question is the land question. If we have the land, we have everything.

14

"We Have Heard Your Talk" (1934)[26]

Joe Chitto

In the South, where Indians struggled to carve out a place for themselves in a space defined largely in terms of black and white, many Indians seized upon the opportunity to organize. But Collier's initiatives proved to be more complicated and contradictory than first imagined. In North Carolina, the Indian Reorganization Act's blood quantum requirements undermined the Lumbees, and Collier proved unable or unwilling to accept Lumbee conceptions of community. The Mississippi Band of Choctaws also met with frustration when they attempted to organize a government outside the purview of the local Office of Indian Affairs. Among its leaders was Joe Chitto, secretary of the Mississippi Choctaw Indian Federation. Consider why he chose to quote at length from ninety-year-old correspondence to express his dissatisfaction with the Collier administration and its failure to follow through on the promise of self-government in this letter drafted in August 1934.[27]

Sir:

In 1842 the Government sent a board of Commissioners to Mississippi to investigate the wrong perpetrated on the Choctaw Indians under the 14 article of the Dancing Rabbit Creek Treaty.

The United States Emigrating Agent, John J. McRae, convened the Indians at Hopaka, in Leake County, and urged them in [torrid] terms, to enroll for removal to the west, and renewed in the name of the Government, the lavish promises the [that] had been made. Col. Cobb, the Choctaw chief, and one of the shrewdest men the nation ever produced replied to Mr. McRae's speech. For your information we copy this speech as given by Claiborne's Mississippi History page 513.

"Brother: We have heard your talk as from the lips of our father, the Great White Chief at Washington, and my people have called on me to speak to you. The Red man has no books, and when he wishes to make known his views, like his fathers before him, he speaks it from his mouth. He is afraid of writing. When he speaks, he knows what he says; The Great Spirit hears him. Writing is the invention of the pale faces; it gives birth to error and feuds. The Great Spirit talks. We hear him in the thunder, in the rushing winds, and the mighty waters. But he never writes.

Brother: When you were young we were strong; we fought by your side; but our arms are broken now. You have grown large. My people have become small.

Brother: My voice is weak; you can scarcely hear me; it is not the shout of a warrior, but the wail of an infant. I have lost it in the mourning over the misfortunes of my people. These are their graves, and in those aged pines you hear the ghosts of the departed. Their ashes are here, and we have been left to protect them. Our warriors are nearly all gone to the far country west; but here are our dead. Shall we go, too, and give their bones to the wolves?

Brother: Two sleeps have passed since we heard your talk. We have thought upon it. You ask us to leave our country, and tell us it is our Father's wish. We would not desire to displease our Father. We respect him, and you his child. But the Choctaws always thinks. We want time to answer.

Brother: Our hearts are full. Twelve winters ago our chief sold our country. Every warrior that you see here was opposed to the treaty. If the dead could have been counted, it would never have been made; but alas! Though they stood around, they could not be seen nor heard. Their tears came in the rain-drops and their voices in the wailing wind, but the pale faces knew it not, and our land was taken away.

Brother: We do not now complain. The Choctaw suffers, but he never weeps. You have the strong arm and we cannot resist. But the pale-face worships the Great Spirit. So does the Red man. The Great Spirit loves truth. When you took our country, you promised us land. There is your promise in the book. Twelve times have the trees dropped their leaves, and yet we have received no land. Our houses have been taken from us. The white man's plow turns up the bones of our Fathers. We dare not kindle our fires; but yet you said we might remain and you would give us land.

Brother: Is this truth? But we believe now that our Great Father knows our condition—he will listen to us. We are as mourning orphans in our country; but our Father will take us by the hand. When he fulfills his promises, we will answer his talk. He means well. We know it. But we cannot think now. Grief has made children of us. When our business is settled we shall be men again, and talk to our Great Father about what he has proposed.

Brother: You stand in the moccasins of a Great Chief; you speak the words of a mighty nation, and your talk was long. My people are small; their shadow scarcely reaches to your knee; they are scattered and gone; when I shout I hear my voice in the depths of the woods, but no answering shout comes back. My words, therefore are few. I have nothing more to say, but to tell what I have said to the tall Chief of the pale faces, whose brother stands by your side."

You see how the Government treated our fathers, and now after more than one hundred years, the remnant of the once powerful Choctaws took Mr. Collier at his word, met, elected Chief, Sec., and Council. Adopted constitution and by-laws, and submitted them to you and asked for recognition; to be told by you that you would not recognize our Federation. It makes us Choctaws wonder if the Government ever makes its promise good to the Indians.

15

"Eliminate This Discrimination" (1941)[28]

Elizabeth and Roy Peratrovich

When the Japanese attacked Pearl Harbor on December 7, 1941, the American people readied for war. Alaska Natives felt the need for a Double Victory against fascism abroad and racism at home as much as any community in the United States. Acquired from Russia by the United States in 1867, Alaska soon attained territorial status. Native land and citizenship rights, however, were ill-defined and routinely abused. Elizabeth Peratrovich (1911–58) and Roy Peratrovich (1908–89), a Tlingit couple with leadership roles in the Alaska Native Brotherhood and Alaska Native Sisterhood, advocated for citizenship rights and fought against segregation.[29] With support from Governor Earnest Gruening, a grassroots movement ultimately led the territorial legislature to adopt an Anti-Discrimination Act in February 1945. Though a long battle for sovereignty lay ahead, Alaska Natives had found their Martin Luther King Jr. Consider how the couple deployed concepts of patriotism, democracy, and citizenship in this letter protesting the discrimination they and others experienced after the attack on Pearl Harbor.[30]

December 30, 1941

Dear Mr. Gruening,

My attention has been called to a business establishment in Douglas, namely, "Douglas Inn," which has a sign on the door which reads, "No Natives Allowed."

In view of the present emergency, when unity is being stressed, don't you think that it is very Un-American? We have always contended that we are entitled to every benefit that is accorded our so-called White Brothers. We pay the required taxes, taxes in some instances that we feel are unjust, such as the School tax. Our Native people pay the School tax each year to educate the White children, yet they try to exclude our children from these schools.

In the present emergency our Native boys are being called upon to defend our beloved country, just as the White boys. There is no distinction being made there, but yet when we try to patronize some business establishments we are told in most cases that Natives are not allowed.

The proprietor of "Douglas Inn" does not seem to realize that our Native boys are just as willing as the White boys to lay down their lives to protect the freedom that he enjoys. Instead he shows his appreciation by having a "No Natives Allowed" [sign] on his door.

We were shocked when the Jews were discriminated against in Germany. Stories were told of public places having signs, "No Jews Allowed." All freedom-loving people in our country were horrified at these reports, yet it is being practiced in our country.

We, as Indians, consider this an outrage because we are the real Natives of Alaska by reason of our ancestors who have guarded these shores and woods for years past. We will still be here to guard our beloved country while hordes of uninterested whites will be fleeing South.

When a Norwegian, Swedish, or an Irishman makes a fool of himself in any of these business establishments, he is asked to leave and that is not held against all of the Norwegians, Swedes, or what have you. We ask that we be accorded the same considerations. If our people misbehave, send the parties concerned out, but let those that conduct themselves respectfully be free to come and go.

We know that you have the interest of the Native people at heart and we are asking that you use your influence to eliminate this discrimination, not only in Juneau or Douglas, but in the whole Territory.

16

"I Am Here to Keep the Land" (1945)[31]

Martin Cross

During the 1930s and 1940s, the federal government constructed dams across the South and West to provide flood control, irrigation, and rural electrification. Severe flooding along the Missouri River in 1943 prompted a massive project known as the Pick-Sloan Plan that extended from Montana to South Dakota. Tribal communities stood to lose the most and gain the least from the undertaking, but this did not stop the federal government from setting it in motion, using "eminent domain" as justification. Leaders of the Three Affiliated Tribes of the Fort Berthold Reservation argued that Pick-Sloan violated their rights under the 1851 Treaty of Fort Laramie.[32] In this testimony, Martin Cross (1906–64), the Gros Ventre chairman of the Three Affiliated Tribes, attempted to convey the devastating impact it would have. Consider what this former commander of the Department of North Dakota's All-Indian American Legion Post must have thought of the contradiction between what the United States fought for overseas and what his community was experiencing at home—and what gave the land its value.[33]

I am delegated here with three other men to voice the adverse disapproval of the construction of the proposed Garrison Dam. We wish to present evidence, testimony, and data in support, and substantiate our claim. Most of our reservation, the best irrigable land, and about 370 well-improved Indian homes will be in the flooded area. An unestimated amount of coal, timber, and wildlife will be destroyed. The United States Army Engineer Corps, with the assistance of the State Water Commission, seem to think that Garrison Dam is the logical point for the construction of a water reservoir.

Lieutenant Colonel Goodall, of the Omaha District Office of the United States Army Engineer Corps, seems to think that the Indian land in the flooded area can be acquired by eminent domain if necessary. We question the legality of this process, on the ground that the treaty law between the

United States Government and the Indians is binding and not subject to eminent domain.

Since I have no legal talent, I must rely on other authority to interpret this legal point. I want to raise that question to be considered, but I want to come out openly against the construction of the Garrison Dam, not only from the legal standpoint, but from the destructiveness and the setback of our Indian people. I believe that this group of men composing this honorable body are adamant foes of abuse and, being such, that they will not permit the Army engineers to carry out their program, their plan. And I want to have the Indian Department interpret the legal point of the treaty between the tribes and the Government. . . .

Mr. Chairman.[34] What is the character of the land which would be taken?

Mr. Cross. That would be the best land we have, along the river, the best irrigable land, and our homes are situated along this Valley.

Mr. Chairman. You say that the homes of the Indians are now built upon the land that would be flooded? . . . How many homes are there?

Mr. Cross. Well, there are . . . about 531 homes. Out of these, about 436 would be in the flooded area. . . .

The Chairman. Well, then, what you are saying is that three-fourths of the homes of the Affiliated Tribes would be flooded? . . . And you would have to move off and take up your homes somewhere else?

Mr. Cross. That is right.

The Chairman. These Indians raise agricultural crops? . . . What kind of crops?

Mr. Cross. They raised spring wheat, they raise oats, corn, and a few potatoes, and a little alfalfa. . . .

The Chairman. And of the agricultural land, two-thirds would be taken if the dam were built? . . . Would the Indians be willing to exchange that land for other land, if other land were available?

Mr. Cross. No, sir.

The Chairman. No, you say?

Mr. Cross. No, sir.

The Chairman. Is there any other land available?

Mr. Cross. The War Department has proposed a relocation area north of Killdeer in the Badlands. . . .

The Chairman. You call that the Bad Lands.

Mr. Cross. That is the Badlands. That is right close to the Montana line. I was a member of the delegation that viewed this territory. We do not want it.

Senator Moore.[35] Is it rough and poor land?

Mr. Cross. Rough and poor land. It is mostly breaks, and good country for rattlesnakes and horned toads.

The Chairman. It is not good country for Indians?

Mr. Cross. That is right.

The Chairman. Well, what is the value of this land per acre; have you any idea?

Mr. Cross. In the relocation area?

The Chairman. No, no.

Mr. Cross. Our own?

The Chairman. Yes.

Mr. Cross. I was not permitted to tell that. I would say around $150. That is my personal opinion.

The Chairman. You say you are not permitted to tell it?

Mr. Cross. No, sir. . . . We are not here on the question of selling our land. We want to keep it. . . .

Senator Langer.[36] It is not for sale at all?

Mr. Cross. That is right. I am not here to sell land. I am here to keep the land. . . . And I also would like to report that the Indians will not gain any benefit from this dam. There is no possibility for us other than destructive. There are no benefits to be derived from this dam.[37]

17

"We Are Still a Sovereign Nation" (1949)[38]

Hopi Traditionalist Movement

Despite the miscarriages of justice at home, Native peoples had the highest per capita rate of service during World War II. But support for serving in the war was not universal, and concerns about the kind of world it created abounded. While previous documents illuminated the grand expectation of "Double Victory" and the translation of it into a rights agenda, Native people also turned to the advent of the atomic age and its implications. As Alaska Natives fought for equal rights and the Three Affiliated Tribes called for the honoring of treaties, the Hopis in the village of Shungopavi took the dropping of atomic bombs on Hiroshima and Nagasaki in August 1945 as a sign that they were to begin sharing teachings given to them years before. The movement manifested itself in statements such as this letter sent to President Harry S. Truman on 28 March 1949. Consider how the authors asserted a vision of sovereignty, citizenship, and belonging that was at once distinctively Hopi and inseparable from Cold War geopolitics.[39]

To the President:

We, the hereditary Hopi Chieftains of the Hopi Pueblos of Hotevilla, Shungopovy, and Mushongnovi humbly request a word with you.

Thoroughly acquainted with the wisdom and knowledge of our traditional form of government and our religious principles, sacredly authorized and entrusted to speak, act, and to execute our duties and obligations for all the common people throughout this land of the Hopi Empire, in accordance with the fundamental principles of life, which were laid down for us by our Great Spirit, Masau'u and by our forefathers, we hereby assembled in the Hopi Pueblo of Shungopovy on March 9, 13, 26, and 28 of this year 1949 for the purpose of making known to the government of the United States and others in this land that the Hopi Empire is still in existence, its traditional path unbroken and its religious order intact and practiced, and the capstone Tablets, upon which are written in the boundaries of the Hopi Empire are still in the hands of the Chiefs of Oraibi and Hote-villa Pueblos.

Firmly believing that the time has now come for us the highest leaders of our respective pueblos to speak and to re-examine ourselves, our sacred duties, our past and present deeds, to look to the future and to study carefully all the important and pressing policies that are coming to us from Indian Bureau at the present time, we met here.

What we say is from our hearts. We speak truths that are based upon our own tradition and religion. We speak as the first people in this land you call America. And we speak to you, a white man, the last people who came to our shores seeking freedom of worship, speech, assembly and a right to life, liberty and the pursuit of happiness. And we are speaking to all the American Indian people.

Today we, Hopi and white man, come face to face at the crossroad of our respective life. At last our paths have crossed and it was foretold it would be at the most critical time in the history of mankind. Everywhere people are confused. What we decide now and do hereafter will be the fate of our respective people. Because we Hopi leaders are following our traditional instructions, we must make our position clear to you and we expect you to do the same to us.

Allow us to mention some of the vital issues which have aroused us to action and which we recognized them to be the last desperate move on the part of the leaders in Washington, D.C. They are as follows:

1. From the Land Claims Commission in Washington, D.C. a letter requesting us to file in our claim to land we believed we are entitled to before the five-year limit beginning August 13, 1946 is expired. We were told that after the five-year limit is expired we cannot file any claim.

2. We are being told by the Superintendent at Keams Canyon Agency about leasing of our land to some Oil Companies to drill for oil. We are told to make the decision on whether to lease out our land and control all that goes with it or we may refuse to do so. But, we were told if we refused, them [sic] these Oil Companies might send their smart lawyers to Washington, D.C. for the purpose of inducing some Senators and Congressman to change certain laws that will take away our rights and authority to our land and placing that authority in another department where they will be leasing out our land at will.

3. We've heard that a $90,000,000 is being appropriated for the purpose of carrying out the provisions of the Act No. S. 2363 which read: To promote the rehabilitation of the Navajo and Hopi Tribes of Indians and the

better utilization of the resources of the Navajo and Hopi Reservation, and for other purposes.

4. Recently we were told about the Hoover Commission's proposal to Congress the launching of a program to convert the country's 400,000 Indians into "full, tax-paying citizens" under state jurisdiction.

5. Now we heard about the North Atlantic security treaty which would bind the United States, Canada, and six European nations to an alliance in which an attack against one would be considered an attack against all.[40]

Now these vital issues coming to us from Washington touch the very core of the Hopi life, a peaceful life. By this we know it is time for us to speak and act. It is now time for us as highest leaders of our respective people to come to a definite understanding of our positions before we go forward into the future and before you embark upon your new program. We want the people everywhere to know our stand, the Hopi people. It is of utmost importance that we do this now.

The Hopi form of government was established solely upon the religious and traditional grounds. The divine plan of life in this land was laid out for us by great Spirit, Masau'u. This plan cannot be changed. The Hopi life is all set according to the fundamental principles of life of this divine plan. We can not do otherwise but to follow this plan. There is no other way for us. We also know that the white people and all other races everywhere are following certain traditional and religious principles. What have they done with them?

Now we are all talking about the judgment day. We all are aware of that fact because we are all going to that same point no matter what religion we believed in. In the light of our Hopi prophecy it is going to take place here and will be completed in the Hopi Empire. So for this reason we urge you to give these thoughts your most careful consideration and to reexamine your past deeds and future plans. Again we say let us set our house in order now.

This land is a sacred home of the Hopi people and all the Indian Race in this land. It was given to the Hopi people the task to guard this land not by force of arms, not by killing, not by confiscating of properties of others, but by humble prayers, by obedience to our traditional and religious instructions and by being faithful to our Great Spirit Masau'u. We are still a sovereign nation. Our flag still flies throughout our land (our ancient ruins). We have never abandoned our sovereignty to any foreign power or nation. We've been self governing people long before any white man came to our shores. What Great Spirit made and planned no power on earth can change.

The boundaries of our Empire were established permanently and were written upon Stone Tablets which are still with us. Another was given to his white brother who after emerging of the first people to this new land went east with the understanding that he will return with his Stone Tablet to the Hopis. These Stone Tablets when put together and if they agree will prove to the whole world that this land truly belongs to the Hopi people and that they are true brothers. Then the white brother will restore order and judge all people here who have been unfaithful to their traditional and religious principles and who have mistreated his people.

Now, we ask you Mr. President, the American people and you, our own people, American Indians, to give these words of ours your most serious considerations. Let us all reexamine ourselves and see where we stand today. Great Spirit, Masau'u has granted us the Indians, the first right to this land. This is our sacred soil.

Today we are being asked to file our land claims in the Land Claims Commission in Washington, D.C. We, as hereditary Chieftains of the Hopi Tribe, cannot and will not file any claims according to the Provisions set up by the Land Claims Commission because we have never been consulted in regards to setting up these provisions. Besides we have already laid claim to this whole western hemisphere long before Columbus's great, great grandmother was born. We will not ask a white man, who came to us recently, for a piece of land that is already ours. We think that white people should be thinking about asking for a permit to build their homes upon our land.

Neither will we lease any part of our land for oil development at this time. This land is not for leasing or for sale. This is our sacred soil. Our true brother has not yet arrived. Any prospecting, drilling and leasing on our land that is being done now is without our knowledge and consent. We will not be held responsible for it.

We have been told that there is a $90,000,000 being appropriated by the Indian Bureau for the Hopi and Navajo Indians. We have heard of other large appropriations before but where all that money goes we have never been able to find out. We are still poor, even poorer because of the reduction of our land, stock, farms, and it seems as though the Indian Bureau or whoever is planning new lives for us now is ready to reduce us, the Hopi people, under this new plan. Why, we do not need all that money, and we do not ask for it. We are self-supporting people. We are not starving. People starve only when they neglect their farms or when someone denies them a right to make a decent living or when they become too lazy to work. Maybe the Indian Bureau is starving. Maybe a Navajo is starving. They are asking for it. True, there are the aged, the blind and the crippled need help. So we will not accept any new theories that the Indian Bureau is planning for our lives under this new appropriation. Neither will we abandon our homes.

Now we cannot understand why since its establishment the government of the United States has taken over everything we owned either by force, bribery, trickery, and sometimes by reckless killing, making himself very rich, and after all these years of neglect of the American Indians have the courage today in announcing to the world a plan which will "convert the country's 400,000 Indians into 'full, tax-paying citizens' under state jurisdiction." Are you ever going to be satisfied with all the wealth you have now because of us, the Indians? There is something terribly wrong with your system of government because after all these years, we the Indians are still licking on the bones and crumbs that fall to us from your tables. Have you forgotten the meaning of Thanksgiving Day? Have the American people, white people, forgotten the treaties with the Indians, your duties and obligations as guardians?

Now we have heard about the Atlantic security treaty which we understood will bind the United States, Canada and six other European nations to an alliance in which an attack against one would be considered an attack against all.

We, the traditional leaders want you and the American people to know that we will stand firmly upon our own traditional and religious grounds. And that *we will not bind* ourselves to any foreign nation at this time. Neither will we go with you on a wild and reckless adventure which we know will lead us only to a total ruin. Our Hopi form of government is all set and ready for such eventuality. We have met all other rich and powerful nations who have come to our shores, from the Early Spanish Conquistadors down to the present government of the United States all of whom have used force in trying to wipe out our existence here in our own home. We want to come to our own destiny in our own way. We have no enemy. We will neither show our bows and arrows to anyone at this time. This is our only way to everlasting life and happiness. Our tradition and religious training forbid us to harm, kill and molest anyone. We, therefore, objected to our boys being forced to be trained for war to become murderers and destroyers. It is you who should protect us. What nation who has taken up arms ever brought peace and happiness to his people?

All the laws under the Constitution of the United States were made without our consent, knowledge, and approval, yet we are being forced to do everything that we know are contrary to our religious principles and those principles of the Constitutions of the United States.

Now we ask you, American people, what has become of your religion and your tradition? Where do we stand today? The time has now come for all of us as leaders of our people to re-examine ourselves, our past deeds, and our future plans. The judgment day will soon be upon us. Let us make haste and set our house in order before it is too late.

We believe these to be truths and from our hearts and for these reasons we, Hopi Chieftains, urge you to give these thoughts your most earnest considerations. And after a thorough and careful consideration we want to hear from you at your earliest convenience. This is our sacred duty to our people.

18

"I Had No One to Help Me" (1953)[41]

Jake Herman

During World War I, Lakotas volunteered to serve in the military, raised money for the Red Cross, and leased their lands to support soldiers overseas. The agency superintendent arranging the leases at Pine Ridge, however, aggressively made tribal lands and individual allotments available—to the point that Lakotas could not raise their own livestock. By 1920, tribal leaders demanded his removal and the termination of the leases. Lakotas answered the call again in 1941, nonetheless. And the federal government, just as it had before, sought land on Pine Ridge—but this time eminent domain was used to seize more than 300,000 acres for an aerial gunnery and bombing range. In this 1953 testimony advocating for compensation, Jake Herman (1890–1969), a member of the tribal council recounted the hardships his family and at least 124 other Lakota families experienced. Consider how Herman's account echoes that of Hattie Twiss, another tribal council member who faced eviction. "[The federal official] stated that it is wartime and we did not have any rights," she recalled. "I retorted that I believed that is what we were fighting for."[42]

One day, the first part of August 1942, one of my friends came to me very excited and said we were going to have to move out of our homes in ten days because the Army was going to take over our lands. The Indian people were shocked. Great confusion followed and people were asking what was going to happen to them. Although we knew that some land was to be taken, no one was told which tracts of land. Then after a few days we still had received no information as to what lands were involved, and many of us began to believe that the story was only a rumor. No one seemed to know what was going on. Someone said the Government was going to take a strip of land from the northern part of the Pine Ridge Reservation. A few of us then put up tents to live in and began rolling our barbed wire fences and tearing down our houses, but most of the people did not know what to do or what was going to happen.

A few weeks later, by word-of-mouth, we learned there was to be a meeting of all landowners at Kyle, South Dakota. Not very many of the Indian people managed to attend this meeting at Kyle because they had not been notified; but the meeting was conducted, nevertheless, by Superintendent W. O. Roberts, assisted by a Mrs. Heinemann, Social Worker from Pine Ridge. The Superintendent called the meeting to order and spoke very briefly, "The other day there were two Army Officers who came to Pine Ridge to see me and they want this scope of land, describing it. These Army men said "We are here to tell you, Mr. Roberts, that we need this land for a bombing range, and we need it now, so we will give the people ten days to move out of this area." Superintendent Roberts explained that he asked if the people could not have more time to move, but they replied, "Mr. Roberts, the Army is going to start shooting on this range in ten days." The Superintendent went on to say that if we did not vacate our lands within that time, we would be shocked. He informed us there would be men coming out to appraise our land and that we should stay there until this was done. He also told us not to worry and that we would be rehabilitated in some way for our losses. A few of the people asked questions about their livestock and were told that if they were not out of the area within ten days, or if they strayed back into the area, they would be shot. At this time the Indian people were greatly frightened and bewildered. Some of us went to the Agent's Office at Pine Ridge inquiring what to do. The only help we were offered at that time was a small loan of $50 or $100 to assist in leasing new lands, if we could find something to lease, and we were required to reimburse the tribe out of the money to be gotten from the sale of our original land.

The reservation roads at this time were jammed with wagonloads of household and farm equipment and people were moving hastily what they could salvage. A great number of those who did not live in the bombing range were forced to sacrifice all their improvements because they were not notified in any way that this condemnation was taking place. Most of the people had no definite place to go. Indian people streamed out of the bombing range in all directions and they often moved their belongings just outside of where they thought the line was to be and dumped them, not knowing what else to do, but trying to comply with the Government's orders. No advice was given these people as to what they could do to protect themselves in any way.

Just before these people started moving from their homes, a team of Government appraisers visited each location and took photographs of the buildings. These appraisals often took ten minutes or less and the land-owners were not allowed to discuss the value of their land or improvements with the Government appraisers. In many instances the eviction was much more of a hardship than it appears to be on paper because in the usual custom of Indian people, many allotments were occupied by two or three families and they were all required to move. This made it impossible in many cases for the Indian people to move in with their relatives even temporarily, since all of them were being evicted.[43]

We have seven people in my family, and like a lot of the others, I had to camp with my tent wherever I could locate space to live temporarily. During this time I had to move my 18 head of cattle, 10 head of horses and 200 chickens, and had to leave 120 acres of good farmed land. I had to leave 20 acres of the best corn we ever raised on land that yielded 20 bushels to the acre. I lost two acres of potatoes, my whole winter's supply. I also lost all of the millet which I had raised to support my livestock through the winter. Many of the other families had hardships as bad as mine. As a result I lost eight milk cows that winter, as well as the 200 chickens I mentioned. I was finally able to lease some land and tried to build a house on it during the winter. I had no one to help me because my two boys were in Service at that time. The one in the Army was killed in action and the other one was in the Navy.[44]

I just figured up my total loss on the corn crop as $400, although the Government appraisers only allowed me $90. We were told not to harvest any crops because they belonged to the Government now and that we would be paid for them. Later on, someone told us we could go back and harvest them, but by that time they were destroyed or eaten by cattle, because I had removed the fence around it sometime earlier. I figured my moving expenses, together with the cost of building a new home, as $2,000, as well as $100 in labor in tearing down the original improvements on my land. I knew the other 126 other families who had to do the same thing I did, and they had similar expenses and similar difficulties.[45]

Many of the old people were extremely shocked by the news that they had to leave their homes within ten days. There was never any question about cooperating with the Federal Government. The Indian people never refused the Government use of their lands during the emergency, but the way it was handled not only caused hardships, but many of the old people took sick and died as a result of the sudden move.

My father-in-law had a stroke while he was packing his belongings, and died. At this time he lost his 320 acres and all his improvements for which the Government paid him only $1,600. He then had this stroke and was taken to the Government hospital at Pine Ridge where they cared for him a short while, and then notified the family to come after him, that there was nothing they could do to help. Shortly after that, he was moved to a private hospital and the $1,600 was used up in paying doctor and medical bills, and so that family lost everything.

One of the men even committed suicide after he had moved his wife and family into a house so poor that the roof leaked continually. His wife contracted pneumonia and died, and as a result, this man was so shocked that he took his own life.

Many of the old people who were evicted tried to get loans from the Government but were refused because they were so old the officials said they would not be able to pay back the loans, and in many cases the State of South Dakota dipped into the money which was paid for these lands and reimbursed himself in the amount of hundreds of dollars for old age assistance previously advanced to these people, thereby, reducing the price received for their lands to a point where it was ridiculous.

In all the terror and confusion many of the families had their belongings stolen or lost. These people today are scattered and most of them are still without permanent homes. Many are living in tents, in slum areas of towns and cities, and most of them are worse off physically and financially than they were when this land was taken, and many have died. We come here today to ask your help.[46]

19

"We Need a Boldness of Thinking" (1954)[47]

D'Arcy McNickle

Born and raised on the Flathead Reservation in Montana, D'Arcy McNickle (1904–77) was enrolled and allotted land as a citizen of the Confederated Salish-Kootenai Tribe. In 1935, John Collier hired him to work for the Office of Indian Affairs, where he served as a tribal relations officer. During this period, he helped found the National Congress of American Indians (NCAI) to provide a single voice on matters of shared concern. Established in 1944, the NCAI pledged to "enlighten the public toward a better understanding of the Indian race; to preserve cultural values; to seek an equitable adjustment to tribal affairs; to secure and to preserve rights under Indian treaties with the United States; and to otherwise promote the common welfare of the American Indians." Its mission became more urgent when the federal government moved toward abandoning the trust relationship. Consider how, in this address at the 1954 NCAI convention, McNickle countered the idea of termination by offering an alternative based on foreign aid. Why do you think McNickle invested such import in this parallel?[48]

Those of you who were at our first convention in Denver in 1944 will remember how we discussed our purposes in forming an all-Indian organization. We knew there was need for taking the step we planned, but we knew also that the step had been taken before; Indians had come together in plans for mutual assistance, and they had failed. Some of us thought it would be better not to try at all, than to try and add another failure to the record. All of us were agreed, however, whatever doubts we might harbor about our ability to create a successful organization, that Indians would never be adequately represented, their views would never be properly expressed, and they would never get full consideration of their needs, unless and until they were in a position to speak for themselves. Some things, cannot be left to friends and well-wishers, and though Indians have friends, the responsibility is still theirs. That, we know. . . .

The situation is dangerous, not just serious, but dangerous. Congress has been giving warnings for the past several years that appropriations for the benefit of Indians must come to an end. The Bureau of Indian Affairs must be abolished; the Indians must be "turned loose." Whether the abolishment of the Bureau would result in a net saving of moneys deserves our attention. Moneys appropriated by Congress for Indian affairs are used to purchase services, materials, equipment, which, for the non-Indian population are purchased and supplied out of other public moneys. Schools are financed generally out of State funds, with some forms of Federal assistance. Roads are built jointly out of State and Federal funds. Irrigation projects are constructed with Federal funds, and reimbursed out of earnings of the land over very long periods. Our national forests are managed with Federal funds. Hospitals, by and large, are supported privately, but in every city and in most counties health facilities for the indigent are provided out of public funds, and the public health nurse and sanitarians who work in the counties are paid for out of Federal funds.

Most of the activities which the Indian Service performs are counterparts of activities which the county, the city, the State, and the Federal Government provide and pay for with public funds of one kind or another for the non-Indian population. If the Bureau of Indian Affairs were abolished, the activities and the funds to pay for those activities would have to be provided by some other agency, State or Federal. The need for help would not be lessened, as you yourselves know from the conditions in which you live. No money would be saved, and it is open to serious doubt whether the Indians would get better services than they are now getting. The services might be considerably less, in States which are not economically able to take on the burdens now carried by the Federal Government.

These factors may not be weighed and balanced when the time comes to make a decision. And that is why I speak of a dangerous situation existing. In raising these grave issues, I have in mind that the Indians and this organization of Indians can bring about a larger concept of the Indian "problem" by taking action. Failure to take action and allowing events to drift from one fiscal year to another can only mean disaster. Appropriations may grow deceptively larger, while the basic jobs of attacking poverty and ill health and lack of education remain untouched. In time, Congress, out of impatience, will simply rid itself of responsibility by legislative fiat, destroying the trusts on your lands, curtailing appropriations and leaving you to your luck.

How then may individual Indians and tribes and the National Congress of American Indians, working together and working with other organizations, working with the Bureau as need be, and with your State delegations in Congress, bring about this enlarged concept? . . . Expressed in another way, how can this country, which needs the full production of its agricultural lands, which needs lumber and needs mineral wealth brought into useful form, how can this country afford to permit Indian resources to remain in their present substandard patterns of use? And how can the country afford to allow the human resources of the Indian people to remain undiscovered, unused, and unproductive?

WHAT I HAVE BEEN SUGGESTING IS, IN EFFECT, A DOMESTIC POINT 4 PROGRAM FOR OUR INDIAN RESERVATIONS, OUR UNDE-VELOPED AREAS.

What I am saying is that we need a boldness of thinking, a courage of decision, such as we have not yet had in the dealings of the Government with our Indian people. Years ago, Thomas Jefferson laid down the basis of a policy which, had it been adopted at any time within the last 100 years, would have made all the difference in the situation of our Indians. Jefferson wrote: "Encourage them to abandon hunting, to apply themselves to the raising of stock, to agriculture and domestic manufacture—the ultimate point of rest and happiness for them, is to let our settlements and theirs meet and blend together, to intermix, and become one people."

Today, on every hand, there is talk of assimilating the Indians. In the Senate a few days ago, a Senator mocked at the failure of Indians to become assimilated. He spoke disparagingly of Indians, as being unwilling to work. You and I know why Indians have been slow to assimilate. Some of the facts I have been discussing here today indicate clearly why a people haunted by poverty, by lack of education, by disease, and by lack of community acceptance, have held back from allowing their settlements to meet and blend with the settlements of the white man, from intermixing, and from becoming one people with the white men. I have also suggested how, through lack of material development of Indian resources, Indians have remained in communities apart, communities of rural slums.

I ask you to share with me again the thinking through of a program for our National Congress of American Indians. Let me now propose elements which I think should be part of that program. I offer them as a challenge to your thinking and to your desire to be leaders among your people. These proposals are not offered in any priority of importance, I set them down as they come to mind:

1. For each reservation there should be a master plan, based on complete surveys of all resources above and below the ground, including water

resources, and plans should be developed to obtain maximum family subsistence from the resources. . . .

2. For each reservation there shall be a Planning Commission (or Committee), authorized by Act of Congress to call upon the Departments of the Federal Government for assistance in gathering data and for technical advice, such Commissions to consist of representatives of the tribe or tribes residing on the reservation, to be selected in a manner prescribed by the governing body. No plans shall be submitted to Congress that do not have the prior approval of such Reservation Planning Commissions.

3. Requests should be submitted to Congress immediately for authority, if needed, and funds to carry out the necessary investigations and to prepare plans for Indian lands lying within the major river drainage basins. If actions to adjudicate Indian water rights are involved, such actions should be initiated.

4. Funds should be requested to carry out timber surveys on Indian forest lands and to prepare programs for the orderly harvesting of Indian timber. Indians should be encouraged to enter into commercial production of lumber.

5. An adequate revolving credit fund should be established to permit Indians to acquire livestock and farm equipment and to develop business and industry in their home communities, the amount of funds for any given reservation and the plans for use of such funds to be determined by the reservation planning commission.

6. An adequate land purchase fund should be made available to permit Indian tribes to buy up heirship lands and lands in non-Indian ownership where these are strategically located with reference to water and other Indian land holdings, with reimbursement to the United States on terms at least as favorable as those accorded farm tenants under existing law.

7. Action should be taken immediately to transfer to tribal ownership sub-marginal lands acquired with emergency relief funds for Indian use, and to restore to the tribes lands withdrawn from homestead entry but never preempted.

8. A program of on-the-farm and on-the-job training, comparable to the GI training programs with Federal financing, should be initiated.

9. A national policy with respect to the taking of Indian lands for public purposes should be promulgated.

I urge your most earnest consideration of the points I have offered. If adopted as the program of this convention and of the National Congress of American Indians, I think I can assure you that we will have work to do for many years to come.

PART III

DEMANDING CIVIL RIGHTS OF A DIFFERENT ORDER, 1954–1968

As the struggle for black equality gained momentum and national visibility through the 1950s and 1960s, it presented opportunities for and challenges to advocates of Native rights. The opportunities came in the form of increased attention and the opening of new spaces for dialogue about the rights of racial minorities. But riding on the coattails of the civil rights movement also presented challenges. For one thing, even well-meaning liberals often failed to distinguish the American Indian rights agenda from the African American one. If civil rights meant equality and equality meant sameness, as Standing Rock Sioux author Vine Deloria put it in his classic treatise *Custer Died for Your Sins*, Native nations wanted nothing to do with it.[1]

Even more dangerous was the agenda pursued by "terminationists" who wanted to end the trust relationship between tribal nations and the federal government, convert reservations into municipalities, and assimilate Indians into a narrowly constructed model of belonging. They routinely clothed their antisovereignty agenda, enunciated in House Concurrent Resolution 108 and operationalized through Public Law 280 in 1953, in the rhetoric of emancipation, freedom, and equality. While the former "named" tribes that were purportedly "ready" to assume "all the rights and responsibilities" of citizenship, and thereby handed Congress a legislative agenda, Public Law 280 was even more immediately perilous. It authorized several states to extend civil and criminal jurisdiction over tribes—whether or not they gave their consent—at their discretion. This was nothing short of a blatant assault on tribal sovereignty.

Members of Congress aggressively advanced termination legislation during the mid-1950s. In June 1954, the Menominees in Wisconsin, the Klamaths and sixty-one small tribes in western Oregon, the Alabama-Coushatta in Texas, and the Uintah-Ouray Utes and Southern Paiutes in Utah were all targeted. While pushback from the National

Congress of American Indians (NCAI) and other organizations stemmed the tide somewhat, the threat lingered through the 1960s. By the time of termination's repeal in 1970, more than thirteen thousand Indians in one hundred tribes, bands, and California rancherias had their legal relationship with the federal government severed. All of them would spend the next two decades fighting for restoration.[2]

During this period, an American Indian youth movement placed its mark on the national campaign for Native rights. It grew in large part out of an influx of American Indians on college and university campuses after World War II. Indian clubs provided a place for Native students to build a sense of community, and many of them, in turn, formed the Southwest Regional Indian Youth Council (SWRIYC). This coalition, founded under the auspices of the New Mexico Association on American Indian Affairs in 1957, created an important network for engaged students. But the politicization of young people took place in other contexts. The most important one proved to be the Workshop on American Indian Affairs, a six-week summer program for college students held first at Colorado College and later at the University of Colorado.

The workshops served as an intellectual training ground for a cadre of young people, many of whom formed an activist organization of their own, the National Indian Youth Council (NIYC). In August 1961, these optimistic youths met in Gallup, New Mexico, and committed themselves to building "A Greater Indian America." While much of their efforts involved giving talks on college campuses, attending meetings and conferences, and publishing editorials in their newsletters *American Aborigine* and *Americans before Columbus*, NIYC members increasingly became involved in confrontational politics. Over time, the organization embraced direct action by pledging its support for and becoming involved in the Pacific Northwest fishing rights struggle, picketing the White House, and supporting demonstrations within tribal communities.[3]

At the same time, the politics of poverty also served as an unanticipated means of countering termination. The War on Poverty, launched by the Economic Opportunity Act in 1964, operated on the assumption that people living in economically deprived circumstances needed empowerment. Its most contested innovation, the Community Action Program, called for "maximum feasible participation of the poor" and "local initiative" in the planning and administration of programs that affected their lives. Tribal leaders, seeing its guiding principles as a much-needed antidote to the Bureau of Indian Affairs' paternalism, immediately used it to their advantage. Mississippi Choctaw leader Phillip Martin, for instance, reported in 1973 that the Office of Economic Opportunity was "the primary support for Indian governments attempting to achieve Self-Determination and self-development."[4]

Chapter 3 highlights two critically important themes in Native activism. First, it shows how Native activists drew parallels to and forged alliances with organizations involved in the struggle for black equality. As racial politics grew more acrimonious, for example, Vine Deloria used his leadership position in the National Congress of American Indians to position Indians as a "safe minority" that politicians could champion without fear of white backlash. The NIYC, on the other hand, supported the black freedom struggle, and individual members participated in the March on Washington in 1963, the Selma march in 1965, and the Poor People's Campaign in 1968.

A second and related theme revolves around the parallels Native activists drew with international politics and decolonization, a movement that gained momentum after World War II. These connections, as D'Arcy McNickle's address in chapter 2 intimated, proved central to articulating a paradigm for asserting a vision that he referred to as "civil rights of a different order"—one built on the idea of nation building. But drawing these parallels and deciding how to act on them proved complex and controversial. Both veteran activists and newcomers were influenced by personal experience and local politics, concerns over modernity and loss of identity, movements for participatory democracy, struggles for racial and economic justice, the Cold War, and global decolonization. But they made sense of the connections in variegated, complex, and at times contradictory ways. While Native activists intended to take clear stands on citizenship, civil rights, and sovereignty, the documents in this chapter reveal that they were, in reality, engaging in delicate ideational dances and precarious political balancing acts that conveyed uncertain meanings and carried unknown repercussions.[5]

20

"We Are Citizens" (1954)[6]

National Congress of American Indians

In August 1953, House Concurrent Resolution 108 and Public Law 280 announced the federal government's intentions of terminating its special relationship with tribal nations and empowered certain states to begin arbitrarily extending civil and criminal jurisdiction on reservations. The National Congress of American Indians (NCAI) took issue not only with the negation of tribal sovereignty but also with the language used to justify it. In late February 1954, the organization called an "emergency meeting" in response to a spate of termination bills. Led by President Joseph Garry (Coeur d'Alene), who served in World War II and Korea, the organization took aim at terminationists, such as Utah senator Arthur V. Watkins, who likened termination to a "freedom program" that promised to "emancipate" Indians from slavery. Consider how this document related citizenship and American values to reservation lands and tribal sovereignty. In what ways do the ideas mark a departure from those articulated in earlier documents? How might they be seen as part of a continuing American Indian intellectual and political tradition?[7]

A Declaration of Indian Rights

Representatives of 183,000 American Indians gathered to consider the emergency created by numerous bills now pending in the Congress make to their fellow American citizens the following declaration:

American Indians seek for themselves only those things that are promised to every American citizen by our National charters, the Constitution and the Declaration of Independence: Life, liberty, and the pursuit of happiness; and enjoyment of the rights of citizenship which it is the duty of Government to secure to all.

The Government of the United States first dealt with our tribal governments as sovereign equals. In exchange for Federal protection and the promise of certain benefits our ancestors gave forever to the people of the

United States title to the very soil of our beloved country. We have never asked anything except that this protection be continued and these benefits be provided in good faith.

Today the Federal Government is threatening to withdraw this protection and these benefits. We believe that the American people will not permit our Government to act in this way if they know that these proposals do not have Indian consent; that these proposals, if adopted, will tend to destroy our tribal governments; that they may well leave our older people destitute; and that the effect of many of these proposals will be to force our people into a way of life that some of them are not willing or are not ready to adopt.

We feel that many of our fellow Americans do not know that we are citizens, free to move about the country like everyone else. We fight for our country, and we pay taxes like everyone else, except on the land and property our ancestors retained by agreement with United States Government.

Some of our fellow Americans think that our reservations are places of confinement. Nothing could be farther from the truth. Reservations do not imprison us. They are ancestral homelands, retained by us for our perpetual use and enjoyment. We feel we must assert our right to maintain ownership in our own way, and to terminate it only by our consent.

If the Federal Government will continue to deal with our tribal officials as it did with our ancestors on a basis of full equality; if it will deal with us as individuals as it does with other Americans, governing only by consent, we will be enabled to take our rightful place in our communities, to discharge our full responsibilities as citizens, and yet remain faithful to the Indian way of life.

21

"This Resolution 'Gives' Indians Nothing" (1954)[8]

Helen Peterson and Alice Jemison

Following close on the heels of House Concurrent Resolution 108, Public Law 280, and legislation targeting specific tribes, members of Congress introduced Senate Joint Resolution 4, a proposal to amend the Constitution's "commerce clause" (Article 1, Section 8) by removing the words "and Indian tribes." Its advocates argued that doing so would "restore the same rights to Indian tribes which are enjoyed by all other citizens of the United States." Critics argued that it meant to repeal the legal foundation for all of the services provided to Indian Country. In the following document, National Congress of American Indians executive director Helen Peterson (1915–2000), an Oglala Lakota, and Seneca activist Mary Jemison (1901–64) offered opposing views on termination and the joint resolution. Consider which position would be best characterized as nationalist and which one most threatened to obfuscate the distinction between civil and treaty rights. What meanings do they assign to citizenship, belonging, wardship, trust, and incorporation?[9]

Mrs. Peterson: My statement is on behalf of the National Congress of American Indians. . . . I am instructed by the President and Vice President of our organization and by a number of Tribes to oppose Senate Joint Resolution 4. . . . We understand this resolution, if passed, would take from the Federal Government the authority to regulate commerce with Indian Tribes in the United States. We further understand this constitutional authority is the only express basis for most of the Federal legislation to provide protections to Indians and their trust property, and that if passed, this resolution would render invalid substantially everything in the Code of Federal Regulations having specific reference to Indians and most of the statutes relating to Indian tribes.

With regard to this resolution, and some other legislation, Indians have repeatedly expressed bitter resentment at the trickery and unfairness of employing such words and phrases as "restoring the same rights to the Indian tribes which are enjoyed by all citizens of the United States" which purport to give Indians something that they do not already have. The use of such words and phrases is misleading to many Indians who lack education and to unsuspecting good citizens who want justice for American Indians. We want to make it unmistakably clear that we know Indians have been citizens since 1924 and already have the rights of citizens. This resolution "gives" Indians nothing; on the contrary, it would take from Indians protections they are properly entitled to and want to keep......

Mrs. Jemison: I am Mrs. Alice L. Jemison. I live at Mumford Park, Herndon, Virginia. I am the editor and publisher of "The First American." To qualify myself, I would say that I am an enrolled member of the Seneca Nation of Indians of New York State; that I have been engaged in national Indian affairs since 1933.

I wish to thank the committee for this opportunity to appear here in support of Senate Joint Resolution No. 4. In my estimation this is the only method by which Congress can ever fully free the Indians from the status in which they are now held. While there has been testimony here relative to the authority of Congress and where it stems, perhaps it is well to go back to the origin of this matter and look at what has been done. When the Constitution of the United States was adopted, the infant country was not dealing with a subject people in dealing with the Indians; they were dealing with tribes which were well-organized, had their own forms of government and held vast sections of territory for themselves.

In writing the Constitution, Article 1, Section 8, gave to the Congress the right to govern trade and intercourse between the states, foreign nations, and Indian tribes. However, Article 3, Section 2, which confers judicial jurisdiction upon the courts over these matters, neglected or did not include the words "and Indian tribes." It can probably be assumed that those who framed the Constitution did not think that the Congress of the United States would ever presume to legislate for these Indian tribes because they were foreign nations and were to be dealt with as foreign nations. That probably explains why the words "and Indian tribes" were omitted from Article 3, Section 2.

As a result of that, the Supreme Court of the United States has consistently held that Congress has paramount and plenary authority over tribal Indians and their property, which can neither be denied nor controlled by the judicial branch of the Government. . . . As long as the Indians remain in a tribal status, irrespective of the fact that they were made citizens under the Act of 1924, they are still subject wards of the Congress of the United States, and the Congress can take whatever action it sees fit. The good intentions of one Congress can be utterly destroyed by whatever action is taken by a subsequent Congress. It had been the policy of the United States Government, the Congress, to make citizens of the Indians. That was the determining policy in setting up the Bureau of Indian Affairs in 1824 under the War Department. The money was appropriated for the purpose of "civilizing and Christianizing" the Indians and fitting them to take their place as citizens of the United States. . . . As we all know, such is not the case. The money has been spent, but the Indians are poor. A great many of them are poor. The Indians are ignorant. The Indians are uneducated.

This will continue as long as the Congress continues the Indian Bureau, which has such arbitrary powers over the Indians of the United States. It is fundamentally wrong. I ask you, supposing the framers of the Constitution had said that whenever any immigrants come to this country we will put them on a reservation and have a special department of Government for each nationality that comes here. How many of the men who sit in Congress today would be sitting here if such a thing had been done? The immigrants came here and had freedom to develop as individuals under the American system of government. They had to work hard. They could not speak English. I know. I have worked with them. But they worked and they took advantage of America's idea of equal opportunity. They made good. I say that my people could have done the same had they been free.

This Congress has taken one of the greatest steps forward that has ever been taken in Indian affairs due to the adoption of House Joint Resolution 108. That is a very good measure and a forward-looking step. It provides for termination of Federal authority over certain Indian tribes. The legislation, however, that is proposed, provides these Indians may, if they choose, remain in a tribal status. The Congress of the United States will not be ridding itself of any responsibility for these Indians as long as they or their property remains in a tribal status.

So while the measures that have been proposed are good measures and I favor them, they are still not good enough to free the Indians. They will never be good enough to free the Indians until legislation such as Senate Joint Resolution 4 has been adopted. That is the only method by which Congress can free itself of the responsibility for the Indian.

The argument is made that if this resolution is adopted that all the legislation that has been passed will go by the board; that Congress will no longer have authority over Indian affairs. Well, Congress adopts special legislation for veterans. They adopt special legislation for farmers, or we would not have all these parity prices. I see no reason why they cannot adopt special legislation for Indians if those Indians need something, and I agree that many of them do. I see no reason why the Congress of the United States cannot continue to legislate for the benefit of the Indians of the United States with this exception: In those cases where legislation violates any constitutional rights which the Indians may have, the Supreme Court can then pass upon the constitutionality of that legislation which it cannot do at the present time and which is the reason that the Indians are in the condition that they are today.

22

"We Are Lumbee Indians" (1955)[10]

D. F. Lowry

The debate over termination and the extension of state jurisdiction was not simple or straightforward. Some communities divided internally, at times because of the machinations of outsiders; others supported termination until the consequences became apparent.[11] For its part, the National Congress of American Indians supported self-sufficiency but rejected House Concurrent Resolution 108 and Public Law 280 as means of achieving it. The era becomes even more complex when viewed from the South. Despite meeting with frustrations during the 1930s, the Lumbees continued to press for federal recognition. The following exchange between Lumbee leader D. F. Lowry (1881–1977) and members of Congress in 1955 provides a window into the complicated politics of race, class, citizenship, and sovereignty in the Native South.[12] Why do you think the representatives expressed so much concern over land ownership, the work ethic of Lumbees, and civic engagement? After reading this document, consider whether you are surprised that the resulting Lumbee Act of 1956 acknowledged the Lumbees as an Indian people but denied any federal relationship with or obligations to them.

Mr. Carlyle.[13] Now, the purpose of this bill is to designate a very fine group of citizens of my home county as Lumbee Indians of North Carolina. . . . I should like for you to recall that there is nothing in this bill that requests one penny of appropriation of any kind. There is nothing in this bill that would call for any upkeep or expenditure. It just simply relates to the name of these people. . . . They have their own schools. They are interested, of course, in their churches. They dot practically every hill in my country. The Indians are good farmers. They are good merchants. They are interested in civic affairs. They are interested in their politics; they take an active interest in our public officials. Some of them are public officials in our county. . . .

Mr. Aspinall.[14] What benefit would they expect to get from this? Just purely the name "Lumbee Indian Tribe" does not appear to me to give too much importance to it, unless they expect to get some recognition later on as members of some authorized tribe, and then come before Congress asking for the benefits that naturally go to recognized tribes.

Mr. Carlyle. No one has ever mentioned to me any interest in that, that they had any interest in becoming a part of a reservation or asking the Federal Government for anything. Their purpose in this legislation is to have a name that they think is appropriate to their group. I do not know that they refer to themselves as a tribe. They are citizens who belong to the Indian race and they were interested in having a name that would have, they think, some significance.

Mr. Aspinall. The difficulty there is this: Some of them may have some Cherokee blood in their veins. They surely would not want to get rid of their relationship to the famous tribe of Cherokees in order to become members of another tribe, any more than I might go back and pick up my mongrel ancestry and disclaim some of it for something else, which does not mean anything except maybe the place where I come from. . . .

Mr. Carlyle. Well, I just do not know of any particular tribe of Indians in this country that they claim to be associated with. Now, I may be in error there. I do have a member of that race here who could answer that question, I feel sure. There is a good bit of merit in your suggestion that it does not make much difference what you call a person or what the name might be, but this is their idea and they are well organized and they have requested it. . . .

Mr. Haley.[15] Our next witness will be Reverend D. F. Lowry. . . .

Mr. Carlyle. Have you made some study of your race?

Reverend Lowery. I have.

Mr. Carlyle. . . . What is the main purpose that the Indians of Robeson County have in asking that their names be designated as Lumbee Indians of North Carolina?

Reverend Lowery. Since the Indians of Robeson County are mixed, an admixture of seven different tribes of Indians, including the Cherokee, Tuscarora, Hatteras, Pamlico and Croatan—about seven different tribes were mixed with them and intermarried with the first colonies. If we get the name "Lumbee" we can . . . pick up the Act of the Legislature and pick up the bill and read that the Lumbee Indians are descendants of the seven tribes of Indians that settled on the Lumbee River, and are Lumbee Indians just like the Hatteras and Mississippi Indians. Then they would have no trouble telling the people, "We are Lumbee Indians." They could look us up and find we are in the law, in the books at Raleigh, and therefore we are honest in their eyes. That is No. 1. . . .

Mr. Aspinall. How many of your Indians who wish to come under this designation are there?

Reverend Lowery. . . . We had a referendum put on by the county commissioners. Here is a statement from the attorney of the county commissioners: The 1951 General Assembly Resolution No. 38, Section 2, Sheet 4 of referendum for an election says,

> "At such election the choice of a Name for the Indians of Robeson
> and adjoining counties shall be determined by the greatest number
> of votes cast in favor of a particular name or designation, and
> upon such choice being determined the name shall be certified
> by the Board of County Commissioners of Robeson County to
> the 1953 General Assembly of North Carolina for its consideration
> and action. The election was held under rules and regulations
> unanimously adopted by the Board of County Commissioners of
> Robeson County, and the results were 2,169 votes for "Lumbee
> Indians of North Carolina," 35 votes to remain "Cherokee Indians of
> Robeson County."

Mr. Aspinall. Do you think that all of those who were entitled to vote voted?

Reverend Lowery. No. They never do that. But we had as big a vote as we had when we elected the president, or the governor.

Mr. Aspinall. I do not know just how that would be in your area. At different times in my area it might be one thing, and at other times it might be something else.

Reverend Lowery. I have the rules of the election, if you would like to see a copy of that, which was carried on, and it said every person would have a right to vote.

Mr. Aspinall. Do you have any tribal organization?

Reverend Lowery. Yes, sir; we have the Lumbee Brotherhood, with 4,000 members. This was organized, you know, along with this move.

Mr. Aspinall. Do you own any communal property?

Reverend Lowery. I did not understand?

Mr. Aspinall. Do you own any communal property? Is there any property held in common among the Indians, or do you have individual ownership.

Reverend Lowery. No, sir. The members own land, but this is just a cooperative move, a brotherhood.

Mr. Aspinall. Do you desire or do you think that any members of your organization would desire to have a reservation?

Reverend Lowery. No, sir; not that I know of. If there is, it is a man that has not got any land, and he does not want to work for anything, and he thinks the Government might give him a little.

Mr. Aspinall. Do you or any members of your organization anticipate that after you might receive this designation you would come to Congress and ask for any of the benefits that otherwise go to Indian Tribes?

Reverend Lowery. No, sir. We would leave the county before we would come under a reservation or anything like wards of the Government. We are citizens and always have been citizens. We would leave before we would come on the reservation. . . .

Mr. Carlyle. Let me add one thought in answer to your question. The subject of a reservation does not meet with the approval of the Indians of Robeson County at all?

Reverend Lowery. No, sir.

Mr. Carlyle. They are land owners, large farmers, and they are engaged in the mercantile business extensively. They are good businessmen. They are not interested in a handout.

Mr. Aspinall. How many of them at the present time are on the Public Welfare rolls?

Mr. Carlyle. I would not know that, but I would say no larger a percentage than you would find among the other races.

Mr. Aspinall. You mean no more than you would find among the non-Indians?

Mr. Carlyle. That is right. I would say that those who are on the welfare rolls would not exceed the number, percentagewise, you would find among the Negroes and the white race.

Reverend Lowery. We are all working Indians. I am a retired rural letter carrier. I drove the mail for thirty years. I am a retired minister. I preached for forty years before I retired at the age of seventy-two. So we work.

23

"The Mississippi Choctaws Are Not
Going Anywhere" (1960)[16]

Phillip Martin

Like the Lumbees, the Mississippi Band of Choctaws met with frustration
when they attempted to organize under the Indian Reorganization Act.
Unlike the Lumbees, however, they eventually succeeded in gaining recognition in 1945. But the challenges they faced were far from over. Whites
typically defined Choctaws as "colored," and the latter found themselves,
along with African Americans, on the wrong side of the color line. Place,
shared language, kinship ties, churches, and social gatherings helped communities endure in Mississippi as in North Carolina. By 1960, however, as
this letter from Chairman Phillip Martin (1926–2010) to Interior Secretary
Fred Seaton attests, the Mississippi Choctaws had had enough of racism
and discrimination and pressed the government to take action. In so doing,
Martin deployed concepts familiar to the black freedom struggle, such
as equality, citizenship, segregation, integration, discrimination, and civil
rights. But did he invest them with the same meanings? Consider whether
the present state of the Mississippi Band affirms or qualifies the solutions
he proposed. What does this tell us about continuity and change in regard
to his conception of integration and nationhood?[17]

Dear Secretary Seaton:

The Business Committee of the Mississippi Band of Choctaw Indians has
authorized me to appeal to you as the highest official in the United States
concerned with Indian people. This is not our first appeal to your Department to help us win recognition of our equality as citizens of Mississippi
and America. We have appealed to our Superintendent, our Area Director,
the Commissioner of Indian Affairs and other Washington officials of the
Bureau, and your former Assistant Secretary of the Interior Roger Ernst.
As I said, this is not our first appeal, but it is our last appeal to the Interior
Department to help us before we try to help ourselves by action in the courts.

The situation which we have endured too long and can no longer endure is this. We 3,000 Mississippi Choctaws live in three counties side by side with white people who discriminate against us because of our color. They will not let our children attend the public schools. They will not let us eat in the restaurants they patronize. They force us to use segregated restrooms. The hearts of our old people grow heavier every day, because they hoped for a change in their lifetime.

The Bureau, from our Agency straight up to Washington, says, "there is no future for your people in Mississippi. Send your children to Oklahoma to school. Relocate."[18] Some of our people will send their children far away to school. Some will relocate in the big northern cities, looking for equality in a slum. But most of the 3,000 will remain and multiply. History and statistics show that the Mississippi Choctaws are not going anywhere. We did not go when the other Choctaws allowed themselves to be herded out of their homeland into Oklahoma. The numbers that relocate will never keep pace with the numbers that come home again, and the numbers that are born. For better or for worse, nothing will drive the Mississippi Choctaws from the place where they are. Nothing will drive our people away, but the shame of our people's condition has driven us, their elected Council, to desperation.

The Bureau of Indian Affairs and we Choctaws agree that our situation is tragic and no self-respecting human beings should be expected to go on living in it. Our agreement ends there. Our Choctaw goal is to change the situation. The Bureau's goal for the Choctaws is for us to remain away from it. We do not think the Bureau of Indian Affairs should be allowed to substitute their goal for ours. That is termination against our will, the policy you said should not be forced on any tribe.[19]

The Bureau in Washington, the Area office and our Agency, gives these excuses for substituting their goal of termination for our goal of integration. They say that the Supreme Court decision on segregation antagonized the Southern whites so much that the Choctaws' chance for assimilation was set back one hundred years. For a reason I shall explain, the Bureau never worked wholeheartedly for our assimilation in the past, and there is no real difference now that they are not working for it at all.

Before I explain why the Bureau tries to make us run away when we want to stand, I should say that we Mississippi Choctaws think Relocation is a generous answer to the problems of some of our people, even though it will never answer the problem of the tribe, and our Relocation Officer is a trustworthy man. I should also say that the Reservation Superintendent in charge of our Indian schools is a capable, understanding administrator, and a few other members of our Agency staff are as friendly as they dare to be with their jobs at stake. Further I should say that our Superintendent is cooperating with the Washington Office and our Business Committee to bring in industry to our area to make employment for Choctaws. (The demand for this industry came from the Business Committee, and the funds to attract it are Choctaw funds.) I have mentioned these satisfactory things here, because I do not want the Bureau to refer to them later as proof that our situation is better than we say. Each one of these things is excellent by itself, but does nothing to end the racial segregation that makes the good things of life like ashes to us.

Now I shall explain why I said the Bureau never worked whole-heartedly with us to change our situation and never will unless an official as high as you orders them to or we go to the courts. I do not like to state the reason, because it concerns our Superintendent and members of the Agency staff, and we are sorry to make these people suffer. They are average human beings, timid but not bad, and it is pitiful that their fate put them in a job they do not have enough courage to do. These unhappy people have the power to tell their superiors in Washington that equality for our people is impossible, and the power to make it impossible. We call them unhappy people because they themselves believe in and practice the racial segregation it is their duty to combat as representatives of the Government of the United States. They are part of the situation which must be changed, and may God help them, for juster Mississippians than they are, and the situation will be changed.

Several months ago a tribal delegation went to Washington. Our Area Director and Superintendent accompanied us, and stayed with us closely, and we had to ask the Association on American Indian Affairs to arrange a private appointment with your former Assistant Secretary. We told him, in front of Mr. Newton Edwards of your Department and Miss LaVerne Madigan of the Association, everything I have told you in this letter.[20] We told him that our people's goal is gradual assimilation, a goal the Bureau in Washington recommends for all Indians. We told him the Bureau's plan of Relocation as the only answer to discrimination against Choctaws is unacceptable to us. We said we want the Bureau to adopt a policy that will make it mandatory for our Agency to help us work out and carry out a long-range race-relations program. We said we wanted this program to start immediately with honest cooperation to help us place our best high school students in Mississippi public high schools that will accept them, and place our first-grade students in the public schools of the counties where we live. We said that we were officially requesting a new Superintendent who would be capable of carrying out this program and would want to carry it out.

Mr. Ernst gave us his solemn word that our problem would be worked out, and he asked us to be patient while this was being done. Then and again after our conference Miss Madigan urged us to wait quietly, because promises to Indians have been kept since you became Secretary of the Interior. . . . Recently we invited her to visit us in Mississippi, and when she came we told her to tell the Department that another school-opening was over and our children were still segregated and our Superintendent was still saying nothing could be done, and we can not wait any longer for the help we have a right to expect from our own Federal government. Miss Madigan telephoned from New York a few days later and told us that Mr. Ernst is no longer with the Department.

We asked if the Association would help us when we take court action. Miss Madigan said the organization could not refuse that request, but she asked us not to make it until she has a chance to talk to you about this and other Indian problems she knows you would want to solve. We agreed to delay our request that long.

We hope that you will read this letter before you talk to Miss Madigan. It is not that we do not trust her and Mr. Newton Edwards to report truthfully on our situation. It is that we want it on record that we spoke out as Choctaws.

24

"A Human Right in a Free World" (1961)[21]

Edward Dozier

Hundreds of American Indians from across Native America gathered at the University of Chicago in June 1961 for the American Indian Chicago Conference. Working in small committees and plenary sessions, they refined a document that had been six months in the making, the "Declaration of Indian Purpose." This important statement intended to convey a shared vision of the future to President John F. Kennedy and to turn the page, once and for all, on termination. Little attention has been paid to other aspects of the conference, such as this keynote address by University of Arizona anthropologist Edward Dozier, a Santa Clara Pueblo who served in World War II and earned a Ph.D. from UCLA in 1952. Consider how Dozier invoked concepts such as second-class citizenship and integration but distinguished what they meant in Native America versus other contexts. How did he counter misconceptions about the federal trust relationship and assuage the anxieties regarding diversity, pluralism, and multiculturalism that pervaded the majority society during the era of the Cold War?[22]

This is an historic and memorable occasion. We have here a gathering of Indians from many tribes and from vast areas of the American continent to discuss problems that affect us all. This is not simply a gathering of reservation Indians, but also of Indians now living in off-reservation locations as well as of Indians who have lived for many years without federal recognition. And I might add for those Indians without such recognition, that federal supervision has not been a bed of roses. Through the years the Bureau of Indian Affairs has groped and stumbled along. It has advanced and progressed under well-intentioned and far-sighted administrators and retreated and floundered under lax and selfish bureaucrats. . . .

The importance of this conference cannot be minimized, as Indians and citizens of this great country, we can bring benefit to ourselves and contribute to the progress of our nation. From a gathering such as this, good ideas and sound proposals are bound to come.

We don't want a free ride—we want assistance which many of us need badly. We will meet the government more than half way in our cooperation. We ask only for the aid to enable us to build and revitalize our communities and enrich our ways of life for a better America. I am sure that we go along with our President and ask: "Not simply what can our government do for us, but what can we can do for our government?"

One of the important characteristics of us as American Indians is our enormous diversity. One has merely to look over this congregation to realize the fact and when we examine the groups from which we come, the diversity is compounded. Yet, despite this variation, Indians have and continue to share a common situation. The very fact that there was an enthusiastic response to this general meeting of Indians is indicative of this commonality.

The common situation which we now face is largely the result of contact beginning from the very earliest days of European colonization and continuing until the present time. Indians as groups and as individuals have been affected by this contact in different degrees and at different rates. For most of us here, our relationship to the federal government is of two fundamental types: The first involves special Indian status stemming mainly from the ownership of land—reservations and grants—and the income therefrom held in trust and tax exempt. Allied to this is a limited sovereignty or home rule and exemption from state laws within reservation boundaries. Also a part of this general relationship is the federal responsibility for local services such as education and health among others. The second type of our relationship with the federal government is more specific and involves particular kinds of pacts or treaties which specific Indian groups have made with the federal government.

Both categories of relationships are contractual in nature and were made to adjudicate and/or compensate Indians for lands or natural resources alienated to the non-Indian population. While these are couched in legal terms there is a moral as well as a [contractual] aspect to our relations with the federal government. It may be said that the government has a moral obligation to assist Indians and that we in turn have the obligation to better ourselves and our communities. For perhaps the majority of us here, it is this rather special position of the American Indian with respect to the federal government that we must bear in mind when we consider the recommendations and proposals during this Chicago conference.

Many among us here are Indians whose tribal ties have been broken and may have been non-existent for a long time. Yet, as Indians, we may be entitled to the special obligations and services which the federal government provides other Indians. Government responsibility for Indians does not apply solely to reservation Indians nor do they end there. . . . Others of us have never or only sporadically received federal government aid and our voices need to be heard and our cases considered.

For all of us there has always been the problem of "second class citizenship." This has expressed itself in the deprivation of full rights as citizens and the nagging and vexing problem of discrimination. Here our problems are not unique for we share them with other ethnic minority groups and many others sympathize and understand these problems. We may work here with other minority peoples, particularly in the area of racial or religious discrimination. For many other problems, however, our problems are different and demand different solutions since they arise out of our historical occupation and attachment to the American soil and its ancient heritage.

We recognize that we also have responsibilities and obligations—the burden is not only on the side of our government. The assistance we desire is to be put on our feet so that we may take over and build strong communities and as individuals face the world with pride and dignity. Our communities will not be blue print copies of one another nor will they necessarily resemble those of the dominant American society. As Indians, we have different backgrounds and different heritages and we are all proud of this ancestry. In our diversified nation, our communities can grow and change separately and together to give our nation its strength and vitality.

Such important developments as the passage of laws terminating the Indian status of several tribes since 1953 and the Supreme Court decisions outlawing segregation have focused attention on the rights of minority groups. While many of the factors which infringe on the rights of minority groups also affect the Indian, fundamentally the problems we are concerned with here are the contractual aspects of American Indian relations with the federal government. In view of this, such statements as "give the Indians freedom" and slogans like "termination" and "integration" have little or no relevance to Indians and the Indian problem.

The question of integration does lead us, however, to a consideration of the place of Indians in the dominant American society and this in turn to fundamental scientific and policy questions. Must Indians lose their distinctive identities in order to be "Americans?" Or expressed more broadly, what is the nature of the unity of a mobile and complex society like the United States? Is it possible to maintain the unity necessary to a society while permitting a wide range of cultural values and group allegiances? Most social scientists are convinced that it is possible. Indeed, they are likely to declare that not only is it possible but that even more emphatically ONLY by the maintenance of freedom for cultural variation can a heterogeneous society keep conflict at a minimum, preserve the flexibility necessary in a time of rapid change, and support the cultural value, so widely shared, of individual freedom.

In our diversity and, of course, in being the original inhabitants of this continent we American Indians are truly American. Ours is a nation of intense diversity and American Indians no less so than others. It is the inherent right for Americans to be different. Our free nation can no more insist that Jews stop being Jews, and that Catholics give up their religion than it can insist the Indians stop being Indians. Of paramount importance is that American Indians can be integrated into the total American society without giving up the inherent right of human beings to be different. Freedom to be completely assimilated as individuals is always a live option, but freedom to be related to the total society as culturally differentiated groups is also possible.

The struggle for individual freedom, whether of the individual or of groups, is at present being manifested in many parts of the world. The situation in Africa, in Southeast Asia and elsewhere are examples. In our own complex American society the various American Indian societies contribute toward the strength of the whole by providing the checks and balances so essential in a free society. There is no greater and emphatic example to the world of the effectiveness of a truly democratic society than the diversified Indian societies of America.

Our purpose in this conference is to compile a series of suggestions and recommendations. Here we must unite for it is the commonness of purpose that brings us together. While we differ as groups and as individuals our problems have a commonality. Pooling our efforts toward policies of greater benefit for ourselves is our goal. We believe that these proposals will receive the careful attention of Congress, the present administration, and the American public. We want to work toward fashioning a better world for ourselves and we want to do it with the dignity and respect due us as individuals and as groups. Above all, we do not want to be urged to give up something about ourselves which may be different in order to obtain assistance which will benefit us all. To remain Indians and yet Americans, we believe to be a democratic principle and a human right in a free world. With consultations and joint agreements with our government, we believe that we can work together to develop a strong, unified and vigorous America.

25

"This Is Not Special Pleading" (1961)[23]

American Indian Chicago Conference

The Declaration of Indian Purpose's proposals for reclaiming a future ech-
oed calls for an approach to federal-Indian relations modeled after the Point
Four program for international development. This was no coincidence,
given that D'Arcy McNickle, working with other members of the National
Congress of American Indians, drafted the initial version in December
1960. During a series of regional conferences over the next several months,
Native people across Indian Country read, critiqued, and proposed revi-
sions to the document. Challenges came from conservatives who feared
its critical edge would be seen as un-American and ardent nationalists who
believed that it did not go far enough in demanding sovereignty. The latter
position anticipated future conflicts as patriotic parallels to modernization
and development gave way to calls for decolonization and national liberation. Consider whether the following excerpts from the Declaration of
Indian Purpose should be read as blatantly milquetoast or latently radical
and how the authors attempted to transform Indian politics into a Cold
War imperative.[24]

CREED

WE BELIEVE in the inherent right of all people to retain spiritual and
cultural values, and that the free exercise of these values is necessary to
the normal development of any people. Indians exercised this inherent
right to live their own lives for thousands of years before the white man
came and took their lands. It is a more complex world in which Indians
live today, but the Indian people who first settled the New World and built
the great civilizations which only now are being dug out of the past, long
ago demonstrated that they could master complexity.

WE BELIEVE that the history and development of America show that
the Indian has been subjected to duress, undue influence, unwarranted
pressures, and policies which have produced uncertainty, frustration, and

despair. Only when the public understands these conditions and is moved to take action toward the formulation and adoption of sound and consistent policies and programs will these destroying factors be removed and the Indian resume his normal growth and make his maximum contribution to modern society.

WE BELIEVE in the future of a greater America, an America which we were first to love, where life, liberty, and the pursuit of happiness will be a reality. In such a future, with Indians and all other Americans cooperating, a cultural climate will be created in which the Indian people will grow and develop as members of a free society. . . .

TREATY RIGHTS

It is a universal desire among all Indians that their treaties and trust-protected lands remain intact and beyond the reach of predatory men.

This is not special pleading, though Indians have been told often enough by members of Congress and the courts that the United States has the plenary power to wipe out our treaties at will. Governments, when powerful enough, can act in this arbitrary and immoral manner.

Still we insist that we are not pleading for special treatment at the hands of the American people. When we ask that our treaties be respected, we are mindful of the opinion of Chief Justice John Marshall on the nature of the treaty obligations between the United States and the Indian tribes.

Marshall said that a treaty ". . . is a compact between two nations or communities, having the right of self-government. Is it essential that each party shall possess the same attributes of sovereignty to give force to the treaty? This will not be pretended, for on this ground, very few valid treaties could be formed. The only requisite is, that each of the contracting parties shall possess the right of self-government, and the power to perform the stipulations of the treaty."

And he said, "We have made treaties with (the Indians); and are those treaties to be disregarded on our part, because they were entered into with an uncivilized people? Does this lessen the obligation of such treaties? By entering into them have we not admitted the power of this people to bind themselves, and to impose obligations on us?"

The right of self-government, a right which the Indians possessed before the coming of the white man, has never been extinguished; indeed it has been repeatedly sustained by the courts of the United States. Our leaders made binding agreements—ceding lands as requested by the

United States; keeping the peace; harboring no enemies of the nation. And the people stood with the leaders in accepting these obligations.

A treaty, in the minds of our people, is an eternal word. Events often make it seem expedient to depart from the pledged word, but we are conscious that the first departure creates a logic for the second departure, until there is nothing left of the word.

We recognize that our view of these matters differs at times from the prevailing legal view regarding due process.

When our lands are taken for a declared public purpose, scattering our people and threatening our continued existence, it grieves us to be told that a money payment is the equivalent of all the things we surrender. Our forefathers could be generous when all the continent was theirs. They could cast away whole empires for a handful of trinkets for their children. But in our day, each remaining acre is a promise that we will still be here tomorrow. Were we paid a thousand times the market value of our lost holdings, still the payment would not suffice. Money never mothered the Indian people, as the land has mothered them, nor have any people become more closely attached to the land, religiously or traditionally.

We insist again that this is not special pleading. We ask only that the United States be true to its own traditions and set an example to the world in fair dealing.

CONCLUDING STATEMENT

To complete our Declaration, we point out that in the beginning the people of the New World, called Indians by accident of geography, were possessed of a continent and a way of life. In the course of many lifetimes, our people had adjusted to every climate and condition from the Arctic to the torrid zones. In their livelihood and family relationships, their ceremonial observances, they reflected the diversity of the physical world they occupied.

The conditions in which Indians live today reflect a world in which every basic aspect of life has been transformed. Even the physical world is no longer the controlling factor in determining where and under what conditions men may live. In region after region, Indian groups found their means of existence either totally destroyed or materially modified. Newly introduced diseases swept away or reduced regional populations. These changes were followed by major shifts in the internal life of tribe and family.

The time came when the Indian people were no longer the masters of their situation. Their life ways survived subject to the will of a dominant sovereign power. This is said, not in a spirit of complaint; we understand that in the lives of all nations of people, there are times of plenty and times of famine. But we do speak out in a plea for understanding.

When we go before the American people, as we do in this Declaration, and ask for material assistance in developing our resources and developing our opportunities, we pose a moral problem which cannot be left unanswered. For the problem we raise affects the standing which our nation sustains before world opinion.

Our situation cannot be relieved by appropriated funds alone, though it is equally obvious that without capital investment and funded services, solutions will be delayed. Nor will the passage of time lessen the complexities which beset a people moving toward new meaning and purpose.

The answers we seek are not commodities to be purchased. Neither are they evolved automatically through the passing of time. The effort to place social adjustment on a money-time interval scale which has characterized Indian administration, has resulted in unwanted pressure and frustration. When Indians speak of the continent they yielded, they are not referring only to the loss of some millions of acres in real estate. They have in mind that the land supported a universe of things they knew, valued, and loved. With that continent gone, except for the few poor parcels they still retain, the basis of life is precariously held, but they mean to hold the scraps and parcels as earnestly as any small nation or ethnic group was ever determined to hold to identity and survival.

What we ask of America is not charity, not paternalism, even when benevolent. We ask only that the nature of our situation be recognized and made the basis of policy and action. In short, the Indians ask for assistance, technical and financial, for the time needed, however long that may be, to regain in the America of the space age some measure of the adjustment they enjoyed as the original possessors of their native land.

26

"I Can Recognize a Beginning" (1962)[25]

Jeri Cross, Sandra Johnson, and Bruce Wilkie

The Workshop on American Indian Affairs served as an intellectual training ground for a generation of activists.[26] Over six weeks, scholars, lawyers, political figures, and tribal leaders introduced students to social scientific theories regarding race, folk and urban societies, culture and personality, marginality, inner- and other-directedness, pan-Indianism, nationalism, colonialism, and the history of Indian-white relations. Cherokee anthropologist Robert K. Thomas (1925–91), one of the curriculum's primary architects, wanted young people to liberate themselves from the "old bugaboo of race," the "bullshit dilemma" of supposedly having to choose between "being Indian" or "being white," and the system of colonial oppression that lay at the heart of the real "Indian problem." Consider how the following excerpts from essays written during the 1962 workshop lend insight into the different kinds of "awakenings" students experienced—about themselves personally, about the possible futures of their communities, and about the structural causes of disempowerment. You will find additional information about the authors and the questions to which they responded in the notes.[27]

Jeri Cross, "A Thought"[28]

With all the wisdom of a sixteen-year old whose observations of life's complexities though limited were very concrete, I asked my mother why didn't she raise my younger sisters and brothers as whites. She smiled (I remember the smile—a sheepish one) and she said, "I tried that on you four older girls." Her philosophy—to inject as much white or European thinking into her children and to discourage Indian ways in them—was not a surprising one considering the public school situation to which we were exposed and also the "lazy" Indians with whom (we were continually being reminded) we lived.

Since my mother is the most wonderful person in the world, I quite easily acquired her viewpoint. However, a mother's medicine isn't in any

Robert K. Thomas considered the 1962 Workshop students to be some of the best he had ever taught. Among them were Bruce Wilkie (back row, fourth from left); Jeri Cross (back row, sixth from left); and Sandra Johnson (front row, fifth from left). Also in this photo are Fran Poafpybitty (to the right of Cross, noted in Document 29), Thomas (back row, second from right); and Clyde Warrior (back row, far right, Document 27). D'Arcy McNickle Papers, Ayer Modern MS, The Newbery Library, Chicago.

way as potent as powwows, forty-nines and stomp dances. And smooth-faced, non-hairy chested Indian boys effortlessly and unanimously won the case for Indians for us girls.

Two conflicting social opinions existing in the mind of one person do not encourage a restful night's sleep (or nights' sleep). Trying to uphold two separate and I mean separate—social circles is a job for Superman; he alone can ably cope with two identities and remain a sane person. To me assimilation was best for all concerned (especially us) in the long run. It became my duty not only to Americanize myself but to drag (?!!!) others with me. Always a conscientious, duty-bound conformist, I complied, and then I literally played Indian against white in a cat and mouse game which neither one could possibly win. What an encouraging catharsis to know it's possible to be myself. To suggest a drastic turn over in my thinking is far from true, but I can recognize a beginning.

Sandra Johnson, "What do you hope your community will be like 20 years from now and why?"[29]

Twenty years from now I would like our community to be self-supporting and responsible. I would like to see a few businesses controlled by Indian people and those white people who do own businesses—I would like to see a corporate tax placed on. An effective, efficient tribal government would be wonderful to visualize. As for the physical features—I would like to see a sewage system, paved streets, and an adequate housing program—a clean up the town campaign would be needed. Law and order are the big questions. I would like to see local effective law and order or an outside appointed policeman. I do not think it desirable to grow up in a community where everything is allowed—where drinking is the rule and not the exception. The local parents also express this view, although they never bring it up at the meetings. I would like to see this, because I consider these goals all desirable. Furthermore, I believe most local people want this and although I have made no scientific survey—the general consensus seems to be "It would be nice, but it'll never happen"—a real fatalistic non-trying point of view—although it's understandable.

Being realistic, I would say that it will all start with a few individuals— to get the ball rolling. If Bruce [Wilkie] gets the chairman's position—that will be a big start. From there the most helpful information has been the [Area Redevelopment Administration]. To get the council's approval will be the difficult part. Every change will be slow and will be by individuals. A college education will be necessary for some of our tribe and a growing ambition—I have no concrete answers other than to go into the community, find out if their "wants" are like mine, and try to accomplish it. Much study on my part will be necessary and thanks to the workshop—my interest has been aroused.

Bruce Wilkie, "Describe the consequences for the world and social relations of a folk people under a colonial administration"[30]

Under a colonial administration, like that of the Bureau of Indian Affairs, responsibility of self-government is withheld from the people. All matters concerning the Indian community must meet the approval of the Indian Bureau. Although an Indian council may be elected by popular vote every one of its actions must meet the approval of the Indian Bureau. In essence decision-making is taken out of the hands of the people concerning their community as a whole.

The consequences of this colonial structure on the Indian community is general apathy concerning Indian affairs. With responsibility and decision-making taken away from them, the Indian people have little or no faith in the system of government imposed upon them. The Indian council is, in reality, a figurehead body providing a buffer between the Indian people of the community and the colonial administration (the Indian Bureau). Widespread suspicion prevails among the Indian people concerning the Indian Bureau and Indian council. Most programs designed to aid the Indians, initiated by the Indian Bureau, meet with little success because the Indian people for the most part, want to do things their way. Such a program fails because the Indians have very little, if any, enthusiasm for any programs not originating within their own group. . . .

The Indian people, concerning matters of government, foot it for themselves. No form of governing agency is going to tell the Indian to do anything against his wishes—because, in effect, he did not put the governing agency in its position. . . . The worldview becomes very narrow emphasizing skepticism on most institutions which are not "Indian." Social relations are strained not only between whites and Indians but also among Indians themselves. Whites feel the Indians incompetent because they appear not able to handle their own affairs. Indians are suspicious of whites and relations are strained among Indians because they are denied the right to handle their own affairs. Group dignity appears lacking because the Indians are not allowed the prerequisite to group dignity—self-government. . . .

In twenty years my hope for my community is one of complete self-government, group dignity, and individual participation in the welfare of the community. In order to achieve this end, a major change in governing structure must take place. The Indian Bureau will have to return the responsibility and decision-making of government to the people. Federal obligations must be continued in the form of assistance, protection—but the assistance must be administered by the Indian people themselves. The present form of tribal government must be revised to a form which would return power to the people. The Indian people will have to make their own mistakes and learn from them. . . .

27

"To Survive as a People" (1964)[31]

Clyde Warrior

The National Indian Youth Council (NIYC) emerged from a nucleus of Native men and women involved in the Southwest Regional Indian Youth Council, the Workshop on American Indian Affairs, and the American Indian Chicago Conference. Through the 1960s, its members engaged in consciousness-raising campaigns across Indian Country, supported fishing rights demonstrations in the Pacific Northwest, lobbied against anti-Indian legislation, promoted community self-determination in education, and participated in interracial alliances for economic justice.[32] Clyde Warrior (1939–68), a Ponca from Oklahoma and former Workshopper, was one of the organization's most outspoken figures, and his essay "Which One Are You?" is a classic statement on Indian identity.[33] While that piece has been reprinted many times, the following essay, though equally significant, has not. Consider how Warrior situated his response to the criticism that NIYC lacked a "reasonable policy or viewpoint" in larger domestic and international contexts. What does the essay reveal about the state of the Native rights movement in the mid-1960s? And how might Warrior's words be read as a "radical" example of what political scientist Kevin Bruyneel refers to as postcolonial refusal?[34]

The National Indian Youth Council has been the victim of undue and unjust criticism from uninformed and irresponsible people both Indian and non-Indian. The harshest criticism coming from prominent Indian leaders. Criticisms have ranged from saying that NIYC consists of ignorant little kids to foolish radicals with no reasonable policy or viewpoint.

FOR SELF-GOVERNMENT

The NIYC is very much in favor of Indian self-government, real, not fictional self-government, and self-determination. Also, NIYC feels that the greatest hindrance to the realization of true self-government of Indian tribes is that hard powerful bureaucracy created by Congress to bring about the very self-government that [it] is hindering. Further, NIYC feels that this bureaucracy is actively using all its resources and manipulating powerless tribal governments against their own communities to cause dire social and economic conditions. In none of the social and economic "programs" do Indians have any voice, and implicit in these "programs" is the goal of breaking up the Indian community as a living community of people who are also citizens of this country.

CONFUSE PEOPLE

These programs may be carried out with the best of intentions, but they only serve to divide and confuse a helpless people. Even the people of Angola, under the Portuguese, or Zulus of South Africa or the Negroes of Mississippi do not have to suffer this type of discrimination. Segregation and exploitation are enough of a cross to bear, but the Indian is attacked in his own home and community as no other American citizen is. Even the educational system on reservations (over which Indians have no control) is explicitly aimed at breaking up the Indian's family and community. Furthermore the few rights guaranteed by treaty that the Indian has left, the last sign that he might be able to survive as a people are being eroded away by high-handed action on the part of state governments, and unwittingly, we believe, by unilateral action on the part of Congress.

This system under which Indians live, a horrendous combination of colonialism, segregation, and discrimination has been going on for over 100 years. The result is that Indians are not only uneducated and poverty-stricken, helpless and without hope, divided among themselves, but also confused and threatened beyond belief. NIYC feels that there must be some drastic steps in the way of legislation to ameliorate the current American Indian situation.

LIST THREE THINGS

NIYC feels that three things must be done:

1. Decision-making power over the lives of people in an Indian community must be legally taken out of the hands of a federal bureau and put where it belongs in the hands of the people, and the community. America cannot afford to continue a system of repressive internal colonialism which parallels the Soviet treatment of its national minorities. This does

not mean we are advocating the elimination of the Bureau of Indian Affairs. Certainly, the Indians need the advice of competent technical experts as there are in the bureau, but the bureau is needed for technical advice and administrative help, not to rule Indian communities, not to promulgate ineffective education and economic programs implicitly aimed at breaking up Indian communities and which also serve to threaten, confuse, and further divide Indians and compound the problem. Indians need at least the self-determination that other American communities have. Indians must have real self-government.

2. Indians are not large and politically powerful, but NIYC does not feel that this gives state or federal governments the right to disregard and violate existing treaties. These treaties were made by the United States as a small emerging nation and world power to survive in the early days of their struggle upward. Now because the United States is a powerful nation and Indian tribes are weak does not justify the blatant violation of these time-honored agreements. If the United States is to be the moral force in the world which she has aspired to be, morality must begin at home. We only ask the American people to honor their word. Unilateral action by Congress or state governments in regard to Indian treaties is immoral. Indian consent not "consultation" is needed in any restructuring of the relationship, spelled out in treaties and statutes, between the Federal government and Indian tribes.

3. A drastic and revolutionary economic and education program in which Indian communities make the basic decisions with the BIA in an advisory capacity, is needed to amend the century of discrimination which has caused the present conditions of American Indians. The trend must be reversed and Indians must be able to lead a decent life in their own communities. However, under the present discriminatory system any program would only further discrimination. These programs must not once again be used to coerce the Indian community, break up community life and bring discord again into the Indian family and home. The BIA must be in an advisory capacity with the community making the necessary decisions if we are to reverse this downward trend.

If this system continues, the Indian will be destroyed as a people. America cannot unwittingly let this happen. Colonial rule and deception of Indian communities must not be allowed to continue.

The indignity of Indians with hats in their hands pleading to powerful administrations for a few crumbs must be removed from the American scene.

The indignity of a school system which is calculated purposely to turn children against their parents is an aspect of state control as only seen in Nazi Germany, Communist China, and American Indian reservations. This kind of discrimination is an indignity that no other ethnic group has to suffer.

The indignity of a man's family being turned against him in his home and community, while he is powerless by law to oppose it, or because such opposition would cause him dire economic deprivation and literal starvation is a national disgrace.

Disgrace against the Indian in his own home and community is intolerable. It is inconsistent with American Ideals. The perpetual threat that his treaties will be disregarded and his community broken apart is eroding the Indian character and sapping his very life blood. These indignities must be wiped away and the Indian, like any other American, must be able to lead a decent life in a free community.

FAITH IN AMERICANS

The NIYC knows that all well-meaning Americans want to act morally and decently in regard to American Indians. NIYC feels that once the American taxpayer realizes the current situation of the American Indians he will no longer allow his tax dollar to be used to continue such a deplorable situation. This is the position of NIYC and their overall attitudes in respect to ameliorating the current situation of Indian communities.

With respect to our critics and our views on Indian Affairs the members of National Indian Youth Council state: "We as members of NIYC have to ask ourselves constantly and very clearly which are the things in the past which we mean to carry forward in our children's life and which are those we shall leave behind."

NIYC is often told we spend too much time talking of the "old days." But we feel that talking about the past means talking about the future. NIYC has made mistakes. But we were the first to hold our annual meeting in the tradition of our forefathers, the open "council." Also the first to hold a successful demonstration of protest against abrogation of treaties. Perhaps our mistakes were made in order that they should not be repeated by us and others.

Recently a few members of NIYC were talking with a young Indian student who obviously was not a credit to his forefathers. He said "I'm for helping Indians, but I just don't have time and besides what good will it do me." We felt sorry for this misguided young soul. He is like many, he wants his future served to him like breakfast in bed on a silver platter, everything to his liking and perfection; then perhaps he may take a bite.

As members of the NIYC we are trying to make the future better ourselves. Working with limited resources, meeting frustrations, mistakes, successes, but we as Indian people are doing it ourselves. We are proud not to be onlookers but to be taking part with our people in a brave struggle for a better future. As members of NIYC we believe that everything is still ahead for us.

The history of our people is not over.

28

"We Were Here as Independent Nations" (1965)[35]

Vine Deloria Jr.

Vine Deloria Jr. (1933–2005) did not intend to be central to the political history of Native America during the 1960s. When selected to serve as the executive director of the ailing National Congress of American Indians (NCAI) in 1964, he had recently earned degrees at Iowa State University and the Lutheran School of Theology in Illinois and was recruiting students to attend elite preparatory schools for the United Scholarship Service. Nonetheless, Deloria immersed himself in politics and law, revived the NCAI, and devised effective strategies to advocate for Native rights during his three-year tenure. He also mastered the art of drawing parallels and analogies to convey ideas about Indians that would otherwise have been lost on non-Indians he needed as allies. In this testimony given before a Senate committee on constitutional rights, Deloria put his skills on display. The committee had completed a survey of the "serious constitutional problems confronting" Native people and now proposed several pieces of legislation "to provide our Indian citizens with the rights and protections conferred upon all other American citizens." Consider how Deloria defended tribal governments and courts, critiqued Public Law 280, and rejected the citizenship of sameness.[36]

Mr. Deloria. The National Congress of American Indians endorses S. 963, S. 965, S. 967, and S. 968 as basically good bills which will provide for a more adequate protection of the constitutional rights of American Indians. S. 961, as presently written, does not spell out exactly what rights and responsibilities guaranteed by the U.S. Constitution would be applicable to either tribal governments or individual Indian citizens in relation to their tribal governments. Since many tribes have written a basic bill of rights into their tribal constitutions based upon the provisions of the U.S. Constitution, we feel that this bill, in most cases, is not needed. Until definite rights and responsibilities can be defined, we believe that this bill should not be considered further.

We believe that S. 962 should not be considered as many tribes have or soon will have provisions for appellate procedures based upon their own needs and customs. We would like to comment specifically upon the provisions for a model code as contained in S. 964. A uniform model code would not, in all cases, promote justice as many tribal laws are built upon tribal customs, and all tribal customs are not the same. We would suggest that S. 964 be amended to provide only for the training of judges and to appropriate such sums as necessary to carry out a training course in legal procedures for Indian judges. It is more important for judges to receive continuing training in judicial procedures for the administration of tribal courts than for a uniform code to be introduced for the tribes.

We wholeheartedly endorse S. 966 [which called for the repeal of Public Law 280 and would allow the exercise of state civil and criminal jurisdiction in Indian Country only with tribal consent] and suggest the following amendment: "The extent of such jurisdictions, either civil or criminal, shall be as agreed upon from time to time by the State and the tribe concerned, and may be extended or retracted by agreement of both the State and the particular tribe as experience proves practicable and planning may indicate to them advisable." This amendment would allow for greater flexibility and common understanding of the problems involved in all areas in the relations between tribes and State governments.

We are aware that this country is presently groping for new forms of social understanding and participation. Governor Collins has called this the formation of the American soul.[37] We feel that the passage of S. 966 would be a most significant step in the formation of a greater society. . . . Tribal customs can best handle most of the problems that occur on the reservations and within the tribe. Passage of S. 966, with the amendment proposed, would allow tribes to continue to provide for their own people until there is sufficient understanding by all parties concerned to provide for Indian people under another legal and social system. . . .

Much has been made of the so-called transitional nature of tribal government. We feel that tribal groups are indeed in transition, but to a new form of social understanding which, if understood by other people, would help solve some of the pressing social problems of today. We suggest that tribes are not vestiges of the past, but laboratories of the future. As we see the larger society beginning to adopt Indian social forms, we feel impelled to suggest that tribes be allowed maximum flexibility in developing their own economic, political, and human resources so that they might bring the best of the Indian understanding of life to the rest of this country. We urge passage of S. 966 with amendment as a good constructive beginning and as the application of the first principle of government—the consent of the governed.

Mr. Creech.[38] Mr. Deloria, the representatives of the Department of the Interior have defined the system of law and order now existing among the various Indian tribes as being transitional. Do you visualize the Indian court system as being transitional?

Mr. Deloria. I think you have to look back at the way policies have been made for the Indian. It was always assumed that if you had the best social, economic, and political knowledge and applied this to the Indian, he would soon assimilate. And so, basically, it was to turn Indians into ordinary American citizens without regard to the fact that Indians have always been here and have always conducted their societies according to certain social forms. Now, in the 1887 Allotment Act you have the idea that if you give each Indian 160 acres, that he is going to be a farmer and pretty soon there will be no Indian problem. Again in the 1950s, with the idea of termination you have the idea if you make the American Indian a businessman that pretty soon he will assimilate, and there will be no more Indian problem. But in the time intervening the American society has been coming closer to Indian forms.

For instance, you have the rise of the conservation movement just about the time of the Allotment Act in which America begins to appreciate, in the same sense the Indian does, the beauty of the land and the respect you need for it. Now I think since World War II this society has been coming around to a society that is socially concerned about itself and about its citizens. If you look at the way your average Indian tribe operates, with your kinship system, and with Indian social patterns, you find that this is the type of society Indians have.

In reference to S. 961, it has been continually noted throughout these hearings should we spell out certain things, and quite often they are things spelled out in the Constitution. I believe that Indians not only do not understand this but it would be detrimental to spell some of these things out, because, for the most part, you have these rights naturally as your customs. In other words, no one prevents you from free speech. No one prevents you from assembly, because Indian society is simply that way. . . . [W]here you originally have the rights inherent in the Indian customs and in Indian society, I do not think it is necessary to spell these out. So, Indians are transitional in these ways. . . .

S. 966 which will correct the idea that somebody else should be planning for these Indians, you see. Not only will we have consent of the governed if we get S. 966 passed, but we can have the opportunity then to be released from this psychological fear on the reservation of having the whole culture run over. Now, when you do not understand a State law, this becomes something that is basically outside. What you really have is submission, you see, because you do not understand your rights, you do not understand your responsibilities, and so you have these people caught in this tremendous psychological trap. As long as the law stands with no consent, you have a basically paralyzing fear that you will be thrown under a system which you do not understand, and this is not justice at all. . . .

Mr. Baker.[39] As near as I can determine from your remarks, the position you are taking is that there should be an upgrading on the reservations to develop their—for lack of a better word—legal sophistication so that their internal system will operate more effectively, is that a reasonable paraphrase?

Mr. Deloria. That is correct.

Mr. Baker. I would assume that the thrust of that then would be the maintenance of a perpetual separateness. In other words, the integrity of the tribe would be maintained and there would be a parallel system adopting the best of our system and maintaining the best of the existing system. Is that also an accurate paraphrase?

Mr. Deloria. I think there can be adaptations all the way along. What I would like to refer to in terms of assimilation is what we find in the Old Testament. The Hebrews were down in Egypt for 400 years. I am sure there was continual pressure on these people to assimilate. But the fact that they held their culture and they continued their religious traditions, in effect they continued to be one people, is the reason we have the great religions stemming out of these people. Now, I would draw this analogy to American Indian tribes basically. That we can contribute in a great many ways, provided we are allowed to remain Indians. And so I do not see it as an either/or proposition, you see?

Mr. Baker. I think there have to be certain profound philosophical problems involved there, since each one of us in this room has come from a somewhat diverse background, and the common good has dictated that we, rather than remain separate, have worked to minimize our differences to provide the best for the greatest number. The economic status of the Indian now on the reservation would indicate that some progress has to be made to assist him, and our system contemplates that this progress normally is made through the law. . . .

Mr. Deloria. This is true, but I do not see ever any reason for assuming the disappearance of Indian tribes, according to some type of sociological doctrine.

Mr. Baker. You think the maintaining of this little island of culture, with what small dissemination it will have through the culture that surrounds it, will have a better effect both for the Indian and the surrounding culture than a gradual assimilation into one melting pot society.

Mr. Deloria. Right, and there is a current sociological study out called "Beyond the Melting Pot," in which it examines ethnic groups in New York City, and it points out that these groups, over three generations, have adapted but have not really assimilated. So there are a great many things each of us can contribute.[40] The thing that the Indian has always feared is that an economic and a political system that he did not understand would be thrust upon him.

Mr. Baker. I would assume that each immigrant who came to this country had the same fears. He is coming from one culture into a completely foreign culture, by and large, unless he was Anglo-Saxon.

Mr. Deloria. That is right, sir, but they came over as individuals, and we were here as independent nations, and treaties were made with us, and we each have traditions. And, in fact, there is a great deal of talk about Indian unity, but, in fact, the tribes have independent relations to each other. This organization I run is kind of a miniature United Nations with everybody taking his shoe off and hammering on the desk. There are different traditions there. The migrations from Europe come individually fleeing from some things and seeking opportunities in others, while the tribes for the most part are, or have been, independent nations owning their own lands, having their own traditions, religions, et cetera. So you cannot really compare the two. In fact, you cannot take the Indian out of his tribal tradition and compare him to an individual immigrant coming over, you see. But I would point out that as they come over now they are trying to set up new Swedens and new Englands and these things. . . .

Mr. Baker. The problem that I see is that you are saying that there is this pathological fear that a foreign or unknown system is going to be imposed upon them, and all you are doing is perpetrating this system by maintaining a complete separateness rather than a gradual dissolution of the differences.

Mr. Deloria. There is a gradual dissolution of the differences. However, when things occur like the jurisdiction in South Dakota where this is a sudden and sharp chopping off, this is not justice. It is not reasonable. It is not even rational. Now my county, my reservation that I come from is over 100 miles long, and there are no provisions to put any law enforcement in. . . . And so all we basically ask is justice, the consent of the governed, time to develop what we think should be developed in our own way. You cannot get a contribution to this society from Indians if you try to turn the Indian into a white man or into anything else, you see.

But we are making a great many contributions, I would feel, and we can continue to. But where Public Law 280 presently stands, there can be unilateral action. It will be unilateral action basically against tribes, and I think this would cause pathological fear in anybody. . . . Suppose a State wanted to take jurisdiction over a tribe. I would think the proper way to go about this is for the people on the reservation would petition their tribal council to hold a referendum, and on the basis of that referendum, then the tribe would apply to the State for jurisdiction in a certain matter. Otherwise this Public Law 280 can be used as a very deadly weapon if it wants to be. . . . So putting a consent clause in here and allowing great flexibility, I think, would provide for a great deal of understanding. I think this is the basis as I was saying earlier, that laws become customs and customs become law, and only in this sense do you have justice.

29

"Is It Not Right to Help Them Win Their Rights?" (1965)[41]

Angela Russell

Vine Deloria and the National Congress of American Indians made it clear that they supported African American demands for social and economic justice. But the National Congress of American Indians stopped short of forging an actual alliance, pointing to philosophical and tactical differences. The National Indian Youth Council (NIYC) tentatively explored ways of working with the black freedom struggle, which ultimately led to the organization playing a key role in the Southern Christian Leadership Conference's Poor People's Campaign. Before that time, however, individual NIYC members participated in civil rights efforts, including the March on Washington in 1963 and the Selma-to-Montgomery March in 1965. The following document, written by Angela Russell, a citizen of the Crow Nation who would go on to become a tribal judge, offers a rare personal insight into Native involvement in the civil rights movement. Consider why she felt being involved in the Selma march was so important and how she connected it to Native rights.

Since that big day in March when one of my friends and co-workers, Fran Poafpybitty, and I went down to Alabama to march on the final day of the Selma-to-Montgomery March, I have been asked by countless friends, tribal leaders and even relatives the reason I went. "Why did you go?" many have asked. Let me caution those of you who firmly believe that protesting of any sort, whether it be demonstrating, picketing or petitioning, is below the dignity of any American Indian, to stop here. But, if you are part of that group who feels that we, as American citizens, have the right to publicly protest when we believe that our rights, or those rights of a select minority in our country, are being violated, then continue. Some of you may change your mind in the process, but as is often said, "One learns something from every experience."

Fran and I went down to Montgomery, not representing any particular organization, but as interested and concerned individuals—American

Indian individuals! . . . The trip down [from Denver] was long and hectic! None of us were consciously aware of any type of physical danger that we might have met there, in fact, we did not realize that there was anything to fear, until we got further South. (We were the first chartered bus of marchers to arrive in Montgomery.) It was in southern Missouri and Arkansas that we first experienced the strong negative reaction of the townspeople toward our group. . . .

We changed bus drivers periodically on the thirty-six hour ride to Montgomery. We could tell, as we got further South, that our bus drivers were getting a little tense and scared. . . . We arrived at the Catholic City of Saint Jude outside Montgomery's city limits bright and early [Thursday] morning. It was a hazy day, but already the camp was filled with much activity and excitement. The Selma marchers had arrived there the previous night and some were still lying there sleeping in their sleeping bags, on old blankets, on cardboard boxes, or just on the bare wet ground.

By 9:00 A.M., there were about 3,000 marchers convened at Saint Jude. . . . The trek into the city was long but interesting. As we marched along one of the Negro sections of town, we were cheered and hailed by old and young alike. As we marched hand-in-hand we sang freedom songs as "We Shall Overcome," "Which Side Are You On," and "Ain't Gonna Let Nobody Turn Me Around." It was a wonderful feeling being a part of this group. As one gazed around at the marchers, one was struck by the diversity of people and age groups. There were a number of things, though, that we all had in common: loud singing voices, firm hand grips, tears streaming down our cheeks, and membership in the human race.

As we entered the business district, and neared the Capital, we found the white citizenry abusive and angry. . . . The Capitol was white, massive and very impressive. Over the Capitol were flying together the Confederate and Alabama State flags! I was struck to see the Confederate flag towering over the United States flag which was placed just outside the entrance to the Capitol. As we reached the Capitol, each of us looked for a place to sit on the hot, smelly street. It had taken us almost three hours to reach this point—our destination. The afternoon had gotten steadily hotter and the humidity was high. We were roasting from the heat and the hike! Yet, our spirits were high and we were ready for more. Only the Federal Troops, who were protecting the marchers, stood dead-still like wooden soldiers.

The speakers' podium was set up in front of the Capitol. After much hustling and bustling, the program started. The podium was packed with many of the top leaders of the civil rights movement including those from the Student Non-violent Coordinating Committee, the organizing sponsor of the march, the Southern Christian Leadership Conference, clergymen from all parts of the United States, distinguished government officials, show celebrities and the noted author, James Baldwin.

After the "sing-out" led by Harry Belafonte with Joan Baez, the Chad Mitchell Trio, Odetta, and many other famous singers and entertainers, the series of speeches began. Speakers included Dr. Ralph J. Bunche, UN Undersecretary for special political affairs, Rev. Ralph D. Abernathy, King's top aide, Martin Luther King, Jr., James Baldwin, Mrs. Rosa Parks, known as the mother of the civil rights movement, and others. The things these men and women said concerned their struggle and progress in the civil rights movement. They were short but moving speeches.

Dr. Martin Luther King had said at the beginning of the march in Selma, "You will be the people that will light a new chapter in the history books of our nation. Those of us who are Negroes don't have much. . . . Because of the system, we don't have much education. . . . But thank God we have our bodies, our feet and our souls. Walk together children . . . and it will lead us to the promised land. And Alabama will be a new Alabama, and America will be a new America." There, again in Montgomery, we felt the full force of similar statements. The people were drawn together in a close unity as I have never experienced before! I thought to myself how great it would be if American Indians could unite in this way for a good, purposeful cause!

The last speaker was Mrs. Rosa Parks, the mother of the civil rights movement. She appeared to be a small woman but when she started talking, it was with real force and sincerity. I thought to myself how courageous this woman was to defy the unwritten laws of her community and state. She had refused to yield her bus seat to a white man in Montgomery and for this she was jailed. This was the impetus that set off the civil-rights demonstrations led by Martin Luther King. . . .

By 4:00 that afternoon, the program ended. Martin Luther King asked the out-of-town marchers to get out of the city before dark. There was a mass exodus out of Montgomery—we were exhausted, but down deep we felt a certain satisfaction. It was only the next morning that we learned of the tragic death of Mrs. Viola Liuzzo, a white civil rights worker, from Chicago. She had been shot to death the night before while driving some of the Selma marchers home. It was sad and disheartening to learn that our peaceful demonstration had ended with this tragedy.

Each of the 3,000 and more participators in the Selma-to-Montgomery March, no doubt, had their own special reasons for going South. Some may have gone down to transmit goodwill, others to lend support to the movement, and still others for a new experience. Yet, I believe that along with various personal reasons, we all went protesting the denial of voting rights to a certain segment of our population.

This was certainly not the first time Indians have been involved in a demonstration. Clyde Warrior, a Ponca from Oklahoma and a member of the National Indian Youth Council, took part in the March on Washington, D.C., in August of 1963. Many feel that this march gave much support to the passing of the Civil Rights Bill in July, of 1964, as did the Selma-to-Montgomery March for the second Civil Rights Bill passed in July of this year.

Recent Indian protests include the Fish-In by the Indians of Washington state in protest of violation of their fishing rights (Olympia, March, 1964), a demonstration by the Indians of Maine at the United Nations (New York City, a few years ago), a demonstration sponsored by the Minneapolis Urban American Indian Committee for unfair practices of the Bureau of Indian Affairs (Minneapolis, fall, 1965), and numerous small demonstrations again this fall in Washington state for fishing rights.

In fact, one young Indian writer asserts that it was the Indians who probably originated demonstrating and public protesting. He claims that when Osceola of the Seminoles was captured and imprisoned, his fellow Seminoles demonstrated outside his jail cell. And, the Northern Cheyennes demonstrated their refusal to be confined to Indian Territory (now Oklahoma) by walking all the way back to their homeland in Montana and Wyoming. There are countless other examples in Indian history of demonstrations and protests.[42]

Just as American Indians want their treaties respected, the American Negros want their rights as citizens respected and not violated in this country. Is it not right for us to help them win their rights? I'm reminded of the words of one of our great presidents, Abraham Lincoln, who said, "To sin by silence when they should protest makes cowards out of men."

30

"We Will Resist" (1965)[43]

Nisqually Nation

To workshop instructor and Cherokee anthropologist Robert K. Thomas's delight, the National Indian Youth Council (NIYC) expressed its admiration for the civil rights movement's use of direct action and launched its "Campaign of Awareness" in support of Nisqually, Puyallup, and Muckleshoot fishing rights in the Pacific Northwest in late 1963. All of these communities were being harassed by state law enforcement agencies for exercising the right to hunt, fish, and gather in their "usual and accustomed places," which they reserved in treaties signed with the United States during the mid-nineteenth century. When NIYC provided organizational support for a major demonstration in Olympia, Washington, in the spring of 1964, it brought public attention to a long-standing grassroots movement with strong ties to Frank's Landing, located along the Nisqually River. In the 1970s, the federal courts finally ruled in favor of the tribes, though the battle was far from over. Consider how Nisqually people justified their decision to take direct action and, in so doing, deployed powerful symbols to defend the sovereignty of a river at a place known as the "moral center of the tribal sovereignty movement."[44]

During January and February 1965 the Nisqually Indians of central Washington State wrote a series of letters and staged a series of very significant demonstrations. The six letters, which were a combination of complaints and petitions pertaining to basic Constitutional issues and flagrant violations of law committed by government officials, were sent to Washington State Superior Court Judge Cochran, Governor Dale Evans and the U.S. Attorney General Nicholas Katzenbach, with copies to President Johnson, Mexico, Panama and interested parties.

The demonstrations were made to promote unity amongst Nisqually people, neighbors of the Puyallup fisherman whom Marlon Brando and Mad Bear[45] helped to publicize in 1964, and to dramatize the principles

involved in their stand for fishing and other treaty rights and responsibilities as opposed to the new and treaty-violating (and therefore un-
Constitutional) laws and policies of Washington State. The most notable
demonstration was the raising of a "Flag of Distress" with accompanying
"Declaration of Facts" or Proclamation.

The above mentioned letters reject jurisdiction of a State court in matters pertaining to US treaty issues, call upon [the] US Attorney General to
defend Nisqually and US treaty rights and also call upon [the] Governor of
Washington State to correct or punish his officials for "unlawful exercise of
police power." These and similar charges are substantiated by ample and
convincing references to law but have received no adequate response from
state or federal officials to date. Nisqually Indians have no attorney and no
funds with which to hire one. Nisqually Indians do not have a public relations
expert to help them find an attorney who is willing to work for free to defend
the US Constitution and a small group of penniless patriots. Therefore
Nisqually Indians cannot even file the papers which would "remand" the case
against them from State to Federal court, where they feel this case belongs,
let alone plead their case once it is even accepted by a Federal court.

Nisqually Indians therefore conducted a public "Flag Raising Ceremony" on the banks of their sacred river, and issued the [following]
Proclamation.

Proclamation or Declaration of Facts

Nisqually Nation, January 1, 1965

WHEREAS the Treaty of Medicine Creek and all other treaties with the
Indian people as one party and the United States as the other party was a
grant of rights and land from the Indians, to the United States Government.
The Supreme law of the land is the right to govern and tax all citizens
of the United States by the United States Government except the Indian
people. These self-governing rights were reserved by the Indian People.

WHEREAS the Bureau of Indian Affairs was created to protect the
rights and interests of the American Citizens, not the Indian People.

WHEREAS the citizens of the United States have consistently and persistently with force and coercion denied the existing reserved rights and
powers of the Indian people.

WHEREAS the United States Government has never, past or present,
honored or protected in any way or manner the rights of the Indian people.

Be it therefore resolved that we the undersigned Indians declare:

That as much as the citizens of the United States have denied the power and effects of said treaty they no longer have a legal right to reside, tax or hunt or fish upon said lands or waters, within the ceded areas of the treaties made with the Indian people.

Be it also known that as we are without power to enforce or expel said citizens from this land we nevertheless declare that said citizens have denied their own right to be here legally.

Be it also resolved that we will resist to the best of our abilities the continued attacks upon the Indian people.

We also declare that we are weary of being forced into pauperism upon our own land.

This flag is raised today as a distress signal to any or all nations, kindreds, and tongues, who believe that the Indian people also have God-given rights, upon this land. We say to these nations, kindreds, and tongues, that if the policies enacted by the United States government concerning the Indian people were examined under close scrutiny the similarities between them and Hitler's policies concerning the Jewish people would be self-evident.

We declare that this declaration is just and true with only God as our witness.

(Signed and subscribed to by 150 people.)

31

"I Want to Talk to You a Little Bit about Racism" (1968)[46]

Tillie Walker

Tillie Walker, a Mandan-Hidatsa from the Fort Berthold Reservation in North Dakota, directed the United Scholarship Service, an organization that promoted attendance in elite preparatory schools and provided scholarships to college students. In that capacity, she networked with many organizations involved in Native politics and built particularly strong ties with the National Indian Youth Council. In early 1968, Walker became immersed in organizing the Indian contingent of the Poor People's Campaign, a massive interracial coalition of the poor that intended to march on Washington in the spring and stay there until Congress took action on poverty and hunger. The devastating impact the construction of the Garrison Dam had on Fort Berthold served as one of the impetuses for her activism, and residents in that community turned out in large numbers for the campaign. Consider what this document, drawn from a presentation she made during a meeting with Interior Secretary Stewart Udall, reveals about the interplay between the politics of race and class during the 1960s.[47]

My name is Tillie Walker and I am from the Fort Berthold Reservation in North Dakota and I live in Colorado. I want to talk to you a little bit about racism. I was involved in the Poor People's Campaign since March 14, at the invitation of Dr. Martin Luther King. There were about 15 Indians invited to that meeting, so that all races across the country could meet together, and see what they felt about something called the Poor People's Campaign.

I called around when I got the invitation to see who else would come. And I want to tell you something about the response that I had, because it does involve you, and it does involve the people you have on the reservations and in the cities. I went to Fort Berthold reservation right after

March 14, my brother is the Community Action Director there, and I asked him to see whether the Tribal Council would be interested. I have many relatives on the Tribal Council and they said, yes, please come up.

On the way up, I stopped at the United Tribes meeting in Bismarck, North Dakota and when I told them about the Poor People's Campaign, one of their responses was, one member said, "You will never get a Tribal leader to come because they all have their hands in the pork barrel. You'll never get any tribal leader to be a part of this." But this didn't stop me. I went to Fort Berthold and talked to the Tribal Council and they voted unanimously to come. Before I talked to them, Mr. Secretary, one of my uncles told me the Superintendent of the Reservation told him there was too much to lose. "Indians don't act like that. Indians don't do things like that."

After this, I went to Standing Rock Reservation at the invitation of a former classmate of mine, and I found a lot of stone faces there. The response was good though, because they said, "we should be a part of that Poor People's Campaign." And my relatives there told me they had heard you from the Aberdeen office saying "Indians don't do things like that." And you know what they mean, Mr. Secretary? They mean that Indians don't work with Negroes in this country. That is racism. And I am angry. [Applause]

When I got back to Denver, I had a call from the head of the Relocation Office in Denver and he said to me "Who is this rabble-rouser up in North Dakota who wants to get involved with something about a Poor People's Campaign? Is his name 'Mad Dog?'"[48]

I said I was involved in the Poor People's Campaign because Indian people are poor and the poor know no color.

Before your men out in the field, Mr. Secretary, tell us things like this, and before we will talk to you anymore, you ask the Standard Oil Company to give up their oil taxation allowance, then we will talk to you about how much we have the lose. Before you have your men out there talk to us about too much to lose, have them go out there and live on the 320 acres I own and live off of that, with fifty cents an acre or a dollar an acre, for a year. You are welcome to come, too. [Applause]

Before they tell us that we have too much to lose, Mr. Secretary, in being a part of the Poor People's Campaign, let them tell us how much they earn, sitting on their reservations and telling our people that they should not be a part of this, because there are Negroes in it. I am tired of this kind of racism. And I won't stop recruiting. [Applause]

Native activists, including Tillie Walker (back row, seated fourth from right, Document 31), conduct a sit-in before the doors of the Supreme Court to protest the *Puyallup* decision during the Poor People's Campaign. Karl Kernberger Pictorial Collection, Center for Southwest Research, University of New Mexico, photograph 2000-008-0116.

We are tired of all the programs coming out of Washington. We are tired of all the conditions that are being set up. We are tired of our Tribal leaders being owned, and we are going to be back in Washington, even if it is just a handful who are here, and we are going to tell about what is going on. And don't tell me that I am a non-reservation Indian and I can't speak. Because my family lived in the Missouri Valley long before Columbus ever set his feet on these shores. [Applause & standing ovation]

32

"A Sickness Which Has Grown
to Epidemic Proportions" (1968)[49]

Committee of 100

If Angela Russell and Tillie Walker clarified what Native and African Americans had in common, the following statement emphasized what made Native rights "civil rights of a different order." Signaling a break with the National Congress of American Indians (NCAI), the National Indian Youth Council served as one of the organizers of the Native contingent in the Poor People's Campaign. Confrontation, if not violence, became its voice in May and June 1968, as thousands of poor people and their advocates descended on Washington, D.C., established Resurrection City, testified in Congress, and took to the streets. Mel Thom (Walker River Paiute), Hank Adams (Assiniboine), Tillie Walker, and Victor Charlo (Flathead), among others, prepared the way in late April as members of the Committee of 100, an interracial group that presented the coalition's demands to President Lyndon Johnson's cabinet. Compare the tone and core ideas of this statement to those found in the NCAI, Dozier, and Chicago conference documents. Does knowing that the Indian committee members sang "We Shall Overcome" with a diverse group of non-Indians on their way to this confrontation confirm or challenge the fear of having Native rights conflated with civil rights?[50]

We have joined the Poor People's Campaign because most of our families, tribes, and communities number among those suffering most in this country. We are not begging. We are demanding what is rightfully ours. This is no more than the right to have a decent life in our own communities. We need guaranteed jobs, guaranteed income, housing, schools, economic development, but most important—we want them on our own terms.

Our chief spokesman in the federal government, the Department of Interior, has failed us. In fact it began failing us from its very beginning. The Interior Department began failing because it was built upon and operates under a racist, immoral, paternalistic, and colonialistic system. There is no way to improve upon racism, immorality and colonialism; it can only be done away with. The system and power structure serving Indian peoples is a sickness which has grown to epidemic proportions. The Indian system is sick. Paternalism is the virus, and the Secretary of the Interior is the carrier.

Foremost, we demand to be recognized for what we are. Most of us are groups of tribal families. We are not white middle-class aspiring groups of people in need of direction. We do not understand why Indian tribes cannot select their own Superintendents. In fact, the need for a Superintendent can indeed be questioned. Why must we beg for administrative support for our communities? Why must we beg for lease money, per capita payments, and Indian Bureau Services, when they are rightfully ours?

American Indians have the political units, land bases, and are competent but we cannot use these resources because we are not allowed to control anything or to make any basic choices except to get out. That is no choice.

The political structure is systematically controlled by the government and special interest groups who exploit us. This must end. We do not understand why Indian tribes cannot tax railroads which cross their lands, or why we do not have the power to tax non-Indians living within the boundaries of our reservations.

We recognize that the Department of the Interior, more particularly, the Bureau of Indian Affairs, has taken some measures toward involving tribes in decision-making. We also recognize these measures for what they are—tokenism. The advisory committees, such as the National Indian Education Advisory Committee, Secret Task Forces, President's committees and commissions, are only convenient means to implement an already established policy.

We demand an end to racism in the schools, public as well as federal. The school system has been the beginning of racism for Indian children. Indian children are systematically told that they should relate to an Indian who is successful in the eyes of the white man rather than to his own family or tribe. Our Indian children are discouraged from understanding their families and communities as they really are. The Indian student dropout rate is as high as 60%, and no one is asking what is wrong with America's school system. They only ask and blame the Indian communities for this high dropout rate.

We need more than just Indians in teacher and counselor capacities. We must also demand that these teachers and counselors be directed by and responsive and responsible to the respective Indian communities. Besides being a demand, this is equally a just and practical measure to answer the problem that is baffled Indian educators since that became a field.

Some recognition has been given to the need for bicultural education. However, we are fearful that we have once again become victimized by paternalism. Let it be understood that we do not want our children being told by white or white-oriented Indian education experts what we were, what we are, and what we should be.

We do not understand why people from the Indian communities cannot speak to graduating Indian classes, from BIA and in public schools, where there is a majority of Indian students.

In conclusion, we make it unequivocally and crystal clear that Indian people have the right to separate and equal communities within the American system—our own communities, that are institutionally and politically separate, socially equal and secure within the American system.

We asked to be heard—not just listened to and tolerated. In World War I, World War II, and the Korean Conflict, American Indians had the highest volunteer turnout per capita than any other ethnic group in the country. Now some American Indians are becoming dissatisfied with rather than proud of their country and are going to jails rather than serving this country in battle.

The inequality and dissatisfaction that is evidencing itself cannot be taken lightly. The oppressed can only be oppressed for so long.

PART IV

DECLARING CONTINUING
INDEPENDENCE, 1969–1994

To deflect the "freedom program" of terminationists and avoid confla-
tion with civil rights from the 1950s through the early 1970s, Native activists developed a vocabulary to discuss Indian concerns that the majority
society could understand. Essentially, this amounted to connecting ideas
and issues in Native America to matters of pressing national and international concern to prevent them from being dismissed as unimportant
or obscure. In so doing, they endeavored to move American Indian politics from the margins to the center of the public sphere. Vine Deloria Jr.
referred to this art of drawing parallels, connections, and associations as
talking "the language of the larger world."[1] Though a master of the craft,
he was certainly not its lone practitioner. In fact, as the previous chapters
demonstrate, Deloria inherited an American Indian political tradition:
Lili'uokalani spoke the language of imperialism; the All-Pueblo Council
spoke the language of religious freedom; D'Arcy McNickle spoke the language of international development; and so it continued.

If the rhetorical strategy represented continuity, the ways in which it
manifested itself shifted with changing contexts and circumstances. The
linking of Native rights to decolonization, for instance, gained salience
and sophistication from the late 1960s to the mid-1990s. After occupying the abandoned federal prison on Alcatraz Island in November 1969,
for instance, demonstrators laid claim to "the Rock" on behalf of the
"Indians of All Tribes." Elaborations on the intellectual and philosophical connections between Native America and the indigenous world, as
well as the creation of mechanisms for shared political action, followed.
During the 1970s, the American Indian Movement (AIM), Women of All
Red Nations (WARN), and National Indian Youth Council (NIYC), for
instance, publicized crises in Latin America and built alliances with indigenous organizations.[2] Meanwhile, the Iroquois Confederacy and newly
formed International Indian Treaty Council (IITC) spearheaded efforts to

gain formal representation for tribal governments in the United Nations (UN). Like the League of Nations before it, the UN often did a better job of talking about decolonization and universal human rights than actually promoting them. Nonetheless, Native activists insisted on being a part of the conversation.[3]

Like Deskaheh before them, 1970s-era activists could not compel the United Nations to recognize tribal governments as equal members of the family of nations. The IITC did, however, set a precedent in 1977 by securing consultative status as a nongovernmental organization in the UN Economic and Social Council. By the 1980s, aggressive lobbying on the part of indigenous groups led to the establishment of the Working Group on Indigenous Populations within the UN's Subcommittee on the Promotion and Protection of Human Rights. The working group's efforts then culminated in the Draft Declaration on the Rights of Indigenous Peoples in 1993, an important statement that faced a difficult path to formal adoption—one that would take another decade and a half to travel.[4]

Activists simultaneously carried forward the struggle for sovereignty at home. The American Indian Movement emerged as the most visible force, spearheading the Trail of Broken Treaties and Bureau of Indian Affairs (BIA) occupation in November 1972 and the standoff against the federal government and Pine Ridge tribal council at Wounded Knee in the early months of 1973. AIM originated in the Minneapolis–St. Paul area in July 1968 and initially focused on discrimination and police violence in urban communities. Its scope soon broadened to include all Native— and ultimately all indigenous—peoples. Their Twenty Points, drafted in large measure by NIYC member and fishing rights veteran Hank Adams (Assiniboine) for the Trail of Broken Treaties, provided a clear articulation of the Native rights agenda, one founded on tribal sovereignty, treaty rights, and the restoration of nation-to-nation relationships.[5]

By the mid-1970s, the federal government abandoned termination in favor of an approach founded on the principle of self-determination. A flurry of legislation followed, including the Indian Self-Determination and Education Assistance Act (1975), the Indian Child Welfare Act (1978), the American Indian Religious Freedom Act (1978), the Indian Gaming Regulatory Act (1988), the Native American Graves Protection and Repatriation Act (1990), and the Indian Self-Governance Act (1994). In addition, the Taos Pueblos secured the return of their sacred Blue Lake in 1970; the following year, the Alaska Native Claims Settlement Act recognized title to 40 million acres of land, provided monetary compensation, and

The occupation of Alcatraz in November 1969 instantly became a symbol of indigenous survivance. It continues to figure significantly in resistance and rights movements. Photograph by Bill Wingell, used with permission.

established twelve regional corporations to promote economic development; and in 1980, Penobscots and Passamaquodies wrested an $81.5 million settlement from Congress for the illegal taking of what amounted to two-thirds of the state of Maine.[6]

These victories were, in reality, compromises—and not always satisfactory ones. What is more, throughout the period tribal nations had to deal with pendulum swings in Congress and the courts. It seemed as though a step forward in one area brought a step back in another. Congress produced its share of detrimental legislation during this period, and the courts delivered several stunning defeats in areas where victory seemed to have been secured. Among the most debilitating proved to be the *Oliphant* decision, which denied tribal courts criminal jurisdiction over non-Indians.[7]

The documents in this chapter chart a continuing tradition of asserting sovereignty through a vast array of strategies and techniques in contexts that ranged from the grassroots to the global. Whether demanding a place among the family of nations in Geneva, defending the use of a sacrament the majority society dismissed as a drug in Washington, D.C., or reminding federal legislators that tribal sovereignty predated that of the United States, American Indians offered a vision of what it meant to be citizens of enduring nations. But declaring continuing independence proved to be the easy part. Acting on it was another matter altogether. As tribal leaders and Native activists engaged issues of economic development, religious freedom, federal recognition, and self-government, they found that the ground they were gaining during the so-called era of self-determination remained uneven and contested.

33

"Our Children Will Know
Freedom and Justice" (1969)[8]

Indians of All Tribes

The Native activists involved in the Poor People's Campaign presented an uncompromising view of colonialism. But it was one thing to develop an intellectual critique and quite another to create a mechanism for dealing with it. While President Lyndon Johnson pledged his support for self-determination in March 1968, the Supreme Court handed down decisions detrimental to fishing rights, and Congress seemed adrift. Public attention returned to Native America in November 1969 when American Indian protestors occupied the abandoned federal prison on Alcatraz Island in San Francisco Bay. For nineteen months, the self-proclaimed Indians of All Tribes held "the Rock" and, citing an article in the Treaty of Fort Laramie regarding surplus federal property, demanded that it be returned to Native people. Although they did not succeed, Alcatraz inspired a series of other occupations and galvanized the Red Power movement.[9] Consider how the core ideas of the Indian of All Tribes manifesto and the language used to convey them compare with the documents in the preceding chapters. Does the document suggest the continuation of a political tradition or the advent of a new one?

MANIFESTO

United Indians of All Tribes call upon our brothers and sisters all across these Americas to hear this, our call and pledge to Indian unity. Hear us, as we open our hearts and minds, and raise our voices! The time has come for all Indians to unite into one brotherhood and to demonstrate, by this unity, the immediate needs of all our people.

The occupation of Alcatraz has seen the beginnings of a concept of unity long dreamed of by all our people. Many Indian organizations have been founded upon this concept of unity, only to fade, or die, or become entangled in bureaucratic manipulations, and red tape. It has become apparent that these many organizations lacked the basic concept of unity; that of dedicating all efforts to the betterment of all. To think within the cage-like confines of a room too often produces box-like results, neatly packaged and labeled in inanities. Many potential leaders have fallen by the wayside because they have allowed themselves, or were forced by others, to become so involved in the intricacies of bureaucracy that their basic goals were forgotten.

New concepts based upon old ideas demand that new leaders emerge. Let yesterday's leaders be a source of wisdom and moral strength, but let youth be the fire of positive action in this new and lasting demand for self-determination. Let us also be sure that this fire is a steady, warming hearth, and never one of destruction.

Youth will not compromise in this struggle for unity. All Indian problems, whether of an individual or tribe, must be shared by all. To separate now, at this great potential time of unity, is to become extinct as a people. Reservation and urban needs, the return of our treaty-guaranteed lands, and other lands illegally taken from us, a new educational process for our children; these are but a few of our goals.

Democracy has never been granted to our people. Genocide yesterday and genocide by sophisticated means today has been and is still the policy of the United States Government. Termination, relocation and assimilation are the current forms of genocide. To break all of our cultural ties with earth and tribe is the means now being used to destroy our people. Divide and conquer is the unwritten law; divide and conquer by any means is the Bureau of Indian Affairs indoctrination and brain-washing-Uncle-Toma-hawkification-technique, as directed by the heads of government.

Our fathers' names are recorded in blood all across America. From sea to shining sea lie the graveyards of military massacres against our people. The surface of America is etched forever with the scars of countless Trails of Tears. The thousands who gave their lives to defend their sacred lands are as numerous as the stars and can never be counted. Their spirits live within our hearts and their deaths must not be forgotten.

We will unite! There will be no compromise! America has a moral obligation before the eyes of all the world to undo the many wrongs inflicted upon our Indian peoples; upon Indians of All Tribes.

We will build a new life and a new philosophy based upon the ancient wisdoms of our fathers. We will unite and in the strength of our unity, our voices will be heard by those whose ears and hearts have been as stone. In unity, the return of portions of our treaty-guaranteed lands will become a reality. We are not a greedy people, but Justice will be ours. The drums of our eternal people will sound once more forever across our lands.

The earth, our mother, awaits our unity. The sacred hoop need only be bound with the sinew of our united courage. The tree of peace will be green and tall forever. Our children will know Freedom and Justice.

34

"We Are an Honorable People—
Can You Say the Same?" (1973)[10]

The Six Nations Iroquois Confederacy

Founded in July 1968, the American Indian Movement (AIM) initially focused on the concerns of urban Indians. In November 1972, however, it spearheaded the Trail of Broken Treaties, a march on Washington that culminated in the takeover of the Bureau of Indian Affairs (BIA). Lost in the clamor was the Twenty Points, a document that encapsulated the Red Power movement's objectives, including the reinstitution of treaty making, the return of 100 million acres of tribal lands, restoration for terminated tribes, the repeal of state jurisdiction, religious freedom, attention to crises in health, housing, and education, and the creation of an office of Federal Indian Relations. Several months later, members of AIM went to the Pine Ridge Reservation to protect traditional Lakotas being persecuted by their own tribal government. To dramatize the situation, they occupied the hamlet of Wounded Knee and triggered a seventy-one-day standoff that saw the Nixon administration respond with Phantom jets, Armored Personnel Carriers, and federal marshals. Consider how representatives of the Iroquois Confederacy, who traveled in and out of Wounded Knee using their own passports, used a looking glass to defend the actions taken by the occupiers.[11]

The Six Nations Iroquois Confederacy stands in support of our brothers at Wounded Knee. We find it deplorable that the Native Americans have to risk their very lives to focus attention on the terrible conditions of our people in this country. We cite the poor health conditions, education, welfare, illegal drafting of our people, and the utter disregard for the treaties that we have paid for with our lives as examples of these conditions.

The issues are national and international—the honor and credibility of the United States is at stake. You should be concerned. All of the people of the United States should be concerned. The President of the United States should be concerned, and further, he should make a statement to that effect. Native Americans should be the top priority of this nation. We number less than 1 per cent of this country's population: now why is it so hard to take care of the obligations to our people that have been promised and promised and promised.

The people at Wounded Knee are making a statement. The question is not what damage or destruction of property has occurred, but why it becomes necessary for our people to have to resort to such extremes to gain some recognition of our desperate situation.

We are a free people. The very dust of our ancestors is steeped in our tradition. This is the greatest gift we gave to you, the concept of freedom. You did not have this. Now that you have taken it and built a constitution and country around it, you deny freedom to us. There must be someone among you who is concerned for us, and if not for us, at least for the honor of your country. In 1976, you are going to have a birthday party proclaiming 200 years of democracy, a hypocritical action. The people of the world would find this laughable.

The solution is simple: be honest, be fair, honor the commitments made by the founding fathers of your country. We are an honorable people—can you say the same? You are concerned for the destruction of property at the BIA building and at Wounded Knee. Where is your concern for the destruction of our people, for human lives? Thousands of Pequots, Narragansetts, Mohicans, thousands of Cherokees on the Trail of Tears, Black Hawk's people, Chief Joseph's people, Captain Jack's people, the Navajos, the Apaches, Sand Creek Massacre (huddled under an American flag seeking the protection of a promise), Big Foot's people at Wounded Knee. When will you cease your violence against our people? Where is your concern for us?

What about the destruction of our properties? The thousands of acres of land, inundated by dams built on our properties, the raping of the Hopi and Navajo territories by the Peabody strip mining operations, timber cutting, power companies, water pollution, and on and on. Where is your concern for these properties?

The balance of the ledger is up to you. Compare the property damage of the BIA and Wounded Knee against the terrible record and tell us that we are wrong for wanting redress. We ask for justice, and not from the muzzle of an M-16 rifle. Now what is to occur?

Remove the marshals and the FBI men. They are hostile, and eager to exercise the sanctions of the United States to subjugate the Indian people.

Do not prosecute the Indians for the methods used to gain your attention, for the fault actually lies with the Government of the United States for ignoring Indians for so long.

Put your energies and money now being expended for the suppression of Indian people at Wounded Knee into a real effort to understand why they are there. And begin here in the capitol through an investigation of the BIA, and of the government policies dealing with our most urgent needs.

Reaffirm and respect the treaties entered into between our two peoples.

Put your house in order with respect to our people, so that we may continue to coexist in peace and friendship as our grandfathers and their grandfathers tried so hard to do.

Show us you are sincere and remember the Creator loves all life and peoples and favors none above the other.

We have not asked you to give up your religions and beliefs for ours.

We have not asked you to give up your language for ours.

We have not asked you to give up your ways of life for ours.

We have not asked you to give up your government for ours.

We have not asked that you give up your territories to us.

Why can you not accord us the same respect? For your children learn from watching their elders, and if you want your children to do what is right, then it is up to you to set the example.

That is all that we have to say at this moment.

Onen.

35

"We Have the Power" (1974)[12]

John Trudell

The American Indian Movement (AIM) struggled to maintain momentum in the wake of Wounded Knee. The organization gained national and international attention, compelled members of Congress and representatives of the Nixon administration to meet with them, and contributed to the declaration of the Independent Oglala Nation. The last of these spoke directly to the inadequacy of the federal government's attempts at promoting self-government through the Indian Reorganization Act (IRA). And yet the controversial IRA government not only remained in place, but tribal chairman Dickie Wilson also launched a campaign of repression known as the "Reign of Terror." Meanwhile, AIM's unity faltered due to internal discord compounded by judicial harassment and FBI infiltration. In the midst of the crisis, AIM national chairman John Trudell (1946–), who rose to prominence during the Alcatraz occupation, called for a renewal of commitment and purpose. Consider how his use of concepts such as colonialism, capitalism, freedom, whiteness, and power compares to the rhetorical and strategic approach taken by Lili'uokalani, the National Congress of American Indians, and the Chicago conference. Did Trudell have anything to say about "honest Americans," American values, and adjustment to the "modern world?"[13]

When we talk about discipline for the American Indian Movement, commitment is just about the number one thing to think about. We've got to have commitment so strong that when we get mad at each other, we overlook it. We've got to have commitment so strong that we don't take no for an answer. We've got to have commitment so strong that we will not accept their rhetoric and lies for an answer. We've got to have commitment so strong we will live and we will die for our people.

We've got to start thinking in terms of love. We get caught up in hating the white man for what he's done to us. And that hate shows; it shows internally in our own organization. We start playing the white man's games. We say we're out for the good of Indian people, but internally if we don't like what someone does, we start backstabbing. We start calling names; we start criticizing. We never come out in the open and talk to the individual or to the people we're displeased with and confront them with how we feel. We go around and agitate and try to build support amongst ourselves. Sometimes I question—does the white man oppress us, or do we oppress ourselves?

I wonder about "respect." We speak of respect, we use the word many times, but then we go and pour alcohol in our bodies—we don't respect our bodies when we do this. We slip ourselves some acid—we don't respect our minds when we do this. We rip off from each other—we don't respect our brothers when we do this. We do not respect our brothers when we talk about them behind their backs.

These are things we have to start thinking about. We have many complaints and many grievances against the white man and against the Bureau of Indian Affairs and against the state. We've got to understand things like colonialism. We've got to understand the processes which the white man uses to exploit and keep us under his thumb.

Colonialism—that means that the white man came to our country and he took our land away from us and put us into the reservations where he continues to exploit our resources and our lives. That's colonialism. It's where we have white bosses and white landlords who come down to our communities and look good while we sit there hungry and sit there without our rights. That's colonialism. Colonialism is when the Bureau of Indian Affairs is run by white people up in the Interior Department. And they get fat and they get rich and they keep us disoriented and they keep us at each other's throats. They keep us from gaining the working knowledge and the working experience we need to control our lives again. That's colonialism.

Our enemy is not the United States. Our enemy is not the individual white man. Our enemy is the collective white man. Our enemy is the American state. The American state is the corporations and the corrupt politicians that are selling us out. These are the enemies. The collective white man sits back and allows this to happen. He is our enemy. You know, when we're going to deal with the truth, the white man is going to have to accept this, because if there is ever going to be peace, love and understanding between the races, he's got to understand that he is in the wrong.

It was white people who created Capitalism. It was white people who created Communism. It was white people who created mission schools.

It was white people who created jails. It was white people who robbed our land and it was white people who sat back in the corner and allowed their government to do it. And then they come to us and talk of love and brotherhood.

They sell us guns and make money off us. They use us. It's something to understand—they've got us set up so they can play on our fears, they can play on our emotions. You know what happened in South Dakota in the courtroom—they planned that. They wanted that to happen.[14] That was not a spontaneous thing. They wanted to teach us a lesson—they think they can still teach us a lesson with their clubs and their guns and their Bibles. But you look at the overall strategy, they are using our spirit and our determination because they want to isolate us. They want to make us like the SLA. They want to make us like the Black Panthers. They want to make us like the Weathermen. They want to make us like the SDS. . . .[15]

They do not want us to talk about freedom. They do not want us getting white people to talk about freedom. They do not want black people to think about freedom. They don't want our own people to think about freedom. So they use violence, they use destruction, they intimidate, they try to tell us that they have power.

They have no power—they have guns, they have bombs, they have their laws, they have methods and tools for destruction. But that is not power.

Power comes from the people.

Power comes from knowledge.

Power comes from love for the people.

Power comes from solidarity.

Power comes from not fighting each other.

Power comes from standing for the issues that we believe in.

Power comes from believing in our right to live.

That is the power. We have the power. All we've got to do is put it together. But we do not have to take this crap from these white people. But we're going to have to continue to put up with it until we can put ourselves together. That's the biggest contradiction that I see in the American Indian Movement—that we don't respect each other. We say we do, but we don't act. . . .

I hear a lot of talk about legal aid, and about laws. I don't see much hope depending on the white man's laws. I don't see much hope in depending on the white man to be understanding. He is not going to change. His technology has changed, but his civilization hasn't. The white man's civilization always has been creating a government, and making the people subservient to that government. That has always been his civilization. . . .

We must not be fooled by them. We must condition our minds and our souls and our spirits to say "No!"—The loud collective voice of "No!" from the people. That is the only way we are going to be able to reason with them. We must tell them "No! No!! NO!!!" . . . Maybe we listen to their lies because we don't want to deal with the truth. If we want to talk about revolution, if we want to talk about freedom, if we want to talk about humanity and people's rights, we're going to have to deal with the truth. . . .

When Europeans first came here, we showed them how to live. We showed them how to survive. We gave them their economy, and they were peaceful to us. They were nice, because they did not know how to live here. Once they found out how to live here, then they started killing us. Then they started stealing our land. Then they brought the black man in to get him to farm and cultivate their land. Then they started their lies and their history of repression and oppression of the native indigenous people of this land.

Now they take us and pump us through their schools to listen to this and they tell us we are free. They say we live in a democracy. They tell us we've got human rights. And they get us to believe it. They create the illusion of freedom because they create a civil rights bill that says you have certain rights. We know we have these rights. But why can't we send our kids to school with long hair? Why can't we put our people in to decide what our education is going to be? We cannot decide what our religion is going to be —we can't get our religion recognized. There is no freedom in this country unless you are extremely rich—or unless you have liberated your own self. That's where freedom comes. . . . Our number one priority must be the brotherhood of the native American sovereign people.

36

"For the Continuing Independence
of Native Nations" (1974)[16]

International Indian Treaty Council

The story of Native activism from Alcatraz to Wounded Knee has become familiar—and, insofar as American Indian Movement (AIM)-centrism flattens and overdefines a complex period—problematically so. But even our understanding of AIM is incomplete. The roles of women and gender within the movement represent vastly neglected areas. Another important but less-well-known aspect of AIM is the International Indian Treaty Council (IITC), established in June 1974 during a meeting of five thousand representatives from more than ninety indigenous nations on the Standing Rock Sioux Reservation. In 1977 the IITC secured consultative status with the United Nations Economic and Social Council and used that to assert the rights of indigenous peoples under international law. The "Declaration of Continuing Independence," issued at the founding meeting in 1974, affords an opportunity to consider the intellectual ground traveled from D'Arcy McNickle's and the National Congress of American Indians' patriotic parallels with modernization and development to the rise of much harsher critiques of colonialism and calls for liberation. Consider, too, whether the way in which the IITC articulated itself is suggestive of uncertain interrogations or clairvoyant revelations.[17]

A long time ago my father told me what his father told him. There was once a Lakota Holy man called Drinks Water, who visioned what was to be; and this was long before the coming of the Wasicus. He visioned that the four-legged were going back into the earth and that a strange race had woven a spider's web all around the Lakotas. And he said, "When this happens, you shall live in barren lands, and there beside those gray houses you shall starve." They say he went back to Mother Earth soon after he saw this vision and it was sorrow that killed him.

Black Elk, Oglala Sioux Holy Man

PREAMBLE

The United States of America has continually violated the independent Native Peoples of this continent by Executive action, Legislative fiat and Judicial decision. By its actions, the U.S. has denied all Native people their International Treaty rights, treaty lands and basic human rights of freedom and sovereignty. This same U.S. Government, which fought to throw off the yoke of oppression and gain its own independence, has now reversed its role and become the oppressor of sovereign Native people.

Might does not make right. Sovereign people of varying cultures have the absolute right to live in harmony with Mother Earth so long as they do not infringe upon this same right of other peoples. The denial of this right to any sovereign people, such as the Native American Indian Nations, must be challenged by *truth* and *action*. World concern must focus on all colonial governments to the end that sovereign people everywhere shall live as they choose: in peace with dignity and freedom.

The International Indian Treaty Conference hereby adopts this Declaration of Continuing Independence of the Sovereign Native American Indian Nations. In the course of these human events, we call upon the people of the world to support this struggle for our sovereign rights and our treaty rights. We pledge our assistance to all other sovereign people who seek their own independence.

DECLARATION

The First International Treaty Council of the Western Hemisphere was formed on the land of the Standing Rock Sioux Tribe on June 8–16, 1974. The delegates, meeting under the guidance of the Great Spirit, represented 97 Indian tribes and Nations from across North and South America.

We, the sovereign Native Peoples recognize that all lands belonging to the various Native Nations [now situated within the boundaries of the U.S.] are clearly defined by the sacred treaties solemnly entered into between the Native Nations and the government of the United States of America.

We, the sovereign Native Peoples, charge the United States of gross violations of our International Treaties. Two of the thousands of violations that can be cited are the "wrongfully taking" of the Black Hills from the Great Sioux Nation [in 1877, this sacred land belonging to the Great Sioux Nation] under the Fort Laramie Treaty of 1868. The second violation was the forced march of the Cherokee people from their ancestral lands in the state of Georgia to the then "Indian Territory" of Oklahoma after the Supreme Court of the United States ruled the Cherokee treaty rights inviolate. The treaty violation, known as the "Trail of Tears," brought death to two-thirds of the Cherokee Nation during the forced march.

The Council further realizes that securing United States recognition of treaties signed with Native Nations requires a committed and unified struggle, using every available legal and political resource. Treaties between sovereign nations explicitly entail agreements with [sic] represent "the supreme law of the land" binding each party to an inviolate international relationship.

We acknowledge the historical fact that [the struggle for] Independence of the Peoples of our sacred Mother Earth have always been over sovereignty of land. These historical freedom efforts have always involved the highest human sacrifice.

We recognize that all Native Nations wish to avoid violence, but we also recognize that the United States government has always used force and violence to deny Native Nations basic human and treaty rights.

We adopt this Declaration of Continuing Independence, recognizing that struggle lies ahead – a struggle certain to be won – and that the human and treaty rights of all Native Nations will be honored. In this understanding the International Indian Treaty Council declares:

The United State[s] Government in its Constitution, Article VI, recognizes treaties as part of the Supreme Law of the United States. We will peacefully pursue all legal and political avenues to demand United States recognition of its own Constitution in this regard, and thus to honor its own treaties with Native Nations.

We will seek the support of all world communities in the struggle for the continuing independence of Native Nations.

We the representatives of sovereign Native Nations united in forming a council to be known at [sic] the International Indian Treaty Council to implement these declarations. The International Indian Treaty Council will establish offices in Washington, D.C. and New York City to approach the international forces necessary to obtain the recognition of our treaties. These offices will establish an initial system of communications among Native nations to disseminate information, getting a general consensus of concerning issues, developments and any legislative attempt affecting Native Nations by the United States of America. The International Indian Treaty Council recognizes the sovereignty of all Native Nations and will stand in unity to support our Native and international brothers and sisters in their respective and collective struggles concerning international treaties and agreements violated by the United States and other governments. All treaties between the Sovereign Native Nations and the United States Government must be interpreted according to the traditional and spiritual ways of the signatory Native Nations.

We declare our recognition of the Provisional Government of the Independent Oglala Nation, established by the Traditional Chiefs and Headmen under the provisions of the 1868 Fort Laramie Treaty with the Great Sioux Nation at Wounded Knee, March 11, 1973.

We condemn the United States of America for its gross violation of the 1868 Fort Laramie Treaty in militarily surrounding, killing and starving the citizens of the Independent Oglala Nation into exile.

We demand the United States of America recognize the sovereignty of the Independent Oglala Nation and immediately stop all present and future criminal prosecutions of sovereign Native Peoples. We call upon the conscionable nations of the world to join us in charging and prosecuting the United States of America for its genocidal practices against the sovereign Native Nations; most recently illustrated by Wounded Knee 1973 and the continued refusal to sign the United Nations 1948 Treaty on Genocide.

We reject all executive orders, legislative acts and judicial decisions of the United States related to Native Nations since 1871, when the United States unilaterally suspended treaty-making relations with the Native Nations. This includes, but is not limited to, the Major Crimes Act, the General Allotment Act, the Citizenship Act of 1924, the Indian Reorganization Act of 1934, the Indian Claims Commission Act, Public Law 280 and the Termination Act. All treaties made between Native Nations and the United States made prior to 1871 shall be recognized without further need of interpretation.

We hereby ally ourselves with the colonized Puerto Rican People in their struggle for Independence from the same United States of America.

We recognize that there is only one color of Mankind in the world who are not represented in the United Nations; that is the indigenous Redman of the Western Hemisphere. We recognize this lack of representation in the United Nations comes from the genocidal policies of the colonial power of the United States.

The International Indian Treaty Council established by this conference is directed to make the application to the United Nations for recognition and membership of the sovereign Native Nations. We pledge our support to any similar application by an aboriginal people.

This conference directs the Treaty Council to open negotiations with the government of the United States through its Department of State. We seek these negotiations in order to establish diplomatic relations with the United States. When these diplomatic relations have been established, the first order of business shall be to deal with U.S. violations of treaties with Native Indian Nations, and violations of the rights of those Native Indian Nations who have refused to sign treaties with the United States.

We, the People of the International Indian Treaty Council, following the guidance of our elders through instructions from the Great Spirit, and out of respect for our sacred Mother Earth, all her children, and those yet unborn, offer our lives for our International Treaty Rights.

37

"For Human Rights and Fundamental Freedoms" (1977)[18]

Geneva Declaration

The horror of the Holocaust spurred the United Nations to issue its Universal Declaration of Human Rights and its Convention on the Prevention and Punishment of the Crime of Genocide in 1948. These initiatives, along with the UN's 1960 Declaration on the Granting of Independence to Colonial Countries and Peoples, served as the backdrop for the reassertion of Native rights in the context of international law. Just as civil rights presented opportunities and challenges, so too did a human rights framework that did not take into account the particular status and concerns of indigenous peoples. Indeed, like the League of Nations before it, the United Nations did not recognize indigenous peoples as nation states.[19] In 1977 indigenous representatives attending the International Non-Governmental Organizations Conference on Discrimination against Indigenous Populations in the Americas held in Geneva, Switzerland, inaugurated the movement for the Declaration on the Rights of Indigenous Peoples by adopting the following statement. Consider to what extent this document echoes the sentiments of Liliʻuokalani, Deskaheh, and the other activists featured in chapter 1.

PREAMBLE

Having considered the problems relating to the activities of the United Nations for the promotion and encouragement of respect for human rights and fundamental freedoms,

Noting that the Universal Declaration of Human Rights and related international covenants have individuals as their primary concern, and

Recognizing that individuals are the foundation of cultures, societies, and nations, and

Whereas, it is a fundamental right of any individual to practice and perpetuate the cultures, societies and nations into which they are born, and

Recognizing that conditions are imposed upon peoples that suppress, deny or destroy the culture, societies or nations in which they believe or of which they are members,

Be it affirmed that,

I. RECOGNITION OF INDIGENOUS NATIONS

Indigenous peoples shall be accorded recognition as nations, and proper subjects of international law, provided the people concerned desire to be recognized as a nation and meet the fundamental requirements of nationhood, namely:

a. Having a permanent population
b. Having a defined territory
c. Having a government
d. Having the ability to enter into relations with other states

2. SUBJECTS OF INTERNATIONAL LAW

Indigenous groups not meeting the requirements of nationhood are hereby declared to be subjects of international law and are entitled to the protection of this Declaration, provided they are identifiable groups having bonds of language, heritage, tradition, or other common identity.

3. GUARANTEE OF RIGHTS

No indigenous nation or group shall be deemed to have fewer rights, or lesser status for the sole reason that the nation or group has not entered into recorded treaties or agreements with any state.

4. ACCORDANCE OF INDEPENDENCE

Indigenous nations or groups shall be accorded such degree of independence as they may desire in accordance with international law.

5. TREATIES AND AGREEMENTS

Treaties and other agreements entered into by indigenous nations or groups with other states, whether denominated as treaties or otherwise, shall be recognized and applied in the same manner and according to the same international laws and principles as the treaties and agreements entered into by other states.

6. ABROGATION OF TREATIES AND OTHER RIGHTS

Treaties and agreements made with indigenous nations or groups shall not be subject to unilateral abrogation. In no event may the municipal laws of any state serve as a defense to the failure to adhere to and perform the terms of treaties and agreements made with indigenous nations or groups. Nor shall any state refuse to recognize and adhere to treaties or other agreements due to changed circumstances where the change in circumstances has been substantially caused by the state asserting that such change has occurred.

7. JURISDICTION

No state shall assert or claim to exercise any right of jurisdiction over any indigenous nation or group or the territory of such indigenous nation or group unless pursuant to a valid treaty or other agreement freely made with the lawful representatives of the indigenous nation or group concerned. All actions on the part of any state which derogate from the indigenous nations' or groups' right to exercise self-determination shall be the proper concern of existing international bodies.

8. CLAIMS TO TERRITORY

No state shall claim or retain, by right of discovery or otherwise, the territories of any indigenous nation or group, except such lands as may have been lawfully acquired by valid treaty or other cessation freely made.

9. SETTLEMENT OF DISPUTES

All states in the Western Hemisphere shall establish through negotiations or other appropriate means a procedure for the binding settlement of disputes, claims, or other matters relating to indigenous nations or groups. Such procedures shall be mutually acceptable to the parties, fundamentally fair, and consistent with international law. All procedures presently in existence which do not have the endorsement of the indigenous nations or groups concerned, shall be ended, and new procedures shall be instituted consistent with this Declaration.

10. NATIONAL AND CULTURAL INTEGRITY

It shall be unlawful for any state to take or permit any action or course of conduct with respect to an indigenous nation or group which will directly or indirectly result in the destruction or disintegration of such indigenous nation or group or otherwise threaten the national or cultural integrity of such nation or group, including, but not limited to, the imposition and support of illegitimate governments and the introduction of non-indigenous religions to indigenous peoples by non-indigenous missionaries.

11. ENVIRONMENTAL PROTECTION
It shall be unlawful for any state to make or permit any action or course of conduct with respect to the territories of an indigenous nation or group which will directly or indirectly result in the destruction or deterioration of an indigenous nation or group through the effects of pollution of earth, air, water, or which in any way depletes, displaces or destroys any natural resource or other resources under the domination of, or vital to the livelihood of an indigenous nation or group.

12. INDIGENOUS MEMBERSHIP
No state, through legislation, regulation, or other means, shall take actions that interfere with the sovereign power of an indigenous nation or group to determine its own membership.

13. CONCLUSION
All of the rights and obligations declared herein shall be in addition to all rights and obligations existing under international law.

38

"Why Have You Not Recognized Us as Sovereign People Before?" (1977)[20]

Marie Sanchez

Women stood at the center of Native activism throughout the late nineteenth and twentieth centuries. And yet the mainstream Native rights movements often did not speak to the particular concerns of women. That changed during the 1970s with the founding of organizations such as the Women of All Red Nations (WARN). Established in Rapid City, South Dakota, in 1974 by an eclectic group of women, many of whom had experience in the American Indian Movement, WARN aspired to create "a national organization in which women can organize to struggle." One of their early campaigns targeted the Indian Health Service's practice of sterilizing Native women without their consent or through coercion. Marie Sanchez (Northern Cheyenne) anticipated this issue in her address at the Conference on Discrimination against Indigenous Peoples in Geneva, Switzerland, in September 1977. Consider how Sanchez, who became a tribal judge on the Northern Cheyenne Reservation, related the issue of women's rights and sterilization abuse to sovereignty, genocide, and global indigeneity.[21]

I come with greetings from the women of the Western Hemisphere. I come here to pose questions to this conference and hopefully to receive positive actions in some of the questions that I present. The Indian women of the Western Hemisphere are the target of the genocide that is still ongoing, that is still the policy of the United States of America. We are undergoing a modern form called sterilization, which has been going on for hundreds of years, to totally exterminate the Red man. Our brothers were the ones who had to undergo murders and other inhumane acts. And you heard this morning from our brothers, the Warriors and protectors of our nations. The Native American woman is the carrier of our nation.

Therefore, I again state, we are the target for a total, final extermination of us as people. The question I would like to put forth to this conference, to the delegates of other countries here present is that why have you not recognized us as sovereign people before? Why did we have to travel this distance to come to you? Had you not thought that the U.S. government in its deliberate and systematic attempt to suppress us, had you not thought that was the reason that they did not want to recognize us as sovereign people? The positive thing that I feel will come out of this conference is if you are going to include us as part of that international family. It is for you to give us that recognition.

Only with that can we continue to live as completely sovereign people. There are other concerns of the Native American women. They do not just stop at the concern of being sterilized. They go beyond that because of our relationship to Mother Earth. The raping, plundering, because of the greed of the United States of America for our natural resources, it is still yet a form of sterilization. Because we depend on Mother Earth for life. And you also, because you are part of the family in this world, should also be very concerned, because the current enemy is your enemy too. And that enemy dictates the policy to your governments also. And I want to warn you not to be so dependent on the country and the government that we are under. We have demonstrated to you how many hundreds of years we have survived, but only because we are still united we can still be together in struggle. And we wish to continue to exist.

I have a message of Panama. "The Indian women of Panama greet our inseparable companions in the struggle, in the Indian movement that are present here today to question and to achieve positive acts for our nations. Our groups are the most exploited and most segregated of all the peoples from the time of invasion and conquest of our land. We, the Indigenous women of Panama have already committed ourselves when it deals with the unity of our people because we have contributed, although in a passive form, to the progress and development in the areas of strengthening our cultural, spiritual and traditional values, hereditary wealth of our ancestors. We are conscious of our historic position and we are sure we will not defraud our future brothers and sisters because we are here constructing little by little the basis together with you all. Let us be brave men and women so that once again for the history of the world the richness of our indigenous society shines.

"Delegates, this is a very great mission and it requires the participation of all its members, because we want and desire the full vindication of all our rights because here, in one form or another, we are united by blood, by a history weighed down by the constant murders and humiliations towards us and because all the Indian nations are raising our voices before the protectors of the state, who at great height pretend to maintain us under a situation of segregation as though they did not recognize the objectives which they want to attain, our own extermination.

"We would like to make it known to the public here that for the women, her defense, her rights and equality are concepts in practice and real life we do not know. The rights of better social conditions, on par with culture, with our education, because the great majority of us are domestic servants and we are not permitted to go to school even at night-time. We are cheap labor. In the houses where we serve they oblige us to renounce our traditional dress, our dances, our language, for a miserable wage. They oblige us and condition us to think and to feel as whites. They teach us and oblige us to look down on the Indian that forms part of our history, who is our brother and our father.

"We are objects of investigation on the part of the so-called scientists, the anthropologists and we are against this because nobody wants to be studied. This is our reality. There has never been a pronouncement made about the exploitation of the indigenous women. We are the objects of jokes and humiliations as if being an Indian woman was a painful shame for the country. We constitute a problem in the social, economic, political and cultural aspects due to the exploitation and alienation to which we are subjected. We are abandoned to our own fate. Our representative on behalf of the government could say it is certain that the indigenous woman of Panama does not carry a tremendous weight upon her shoulders and that the indigenous women present at this conference should say if this is not the sad truth.

"All these situations form part of the politics of integration into a civilized life into which they wish to induce us, and we oppose that. For that reason we wish to make a call to all the Indian brothers present here to struggle together, all united under one flag, under one religion, the religion of the Indian nation. And in that struggle we should all participate together, the men and women together in this struggle, because both strengths are necessary to guarantee the support of our own various ethnic groups. We have many problems and must fight according to the possibilities to achieve our rights in favor of the enrichment of our culture and of our peoples because we have always been and are now women who fight with a sense of our own values.

"On a national level we would like to terminate the politics of paternalism, integration and discrimination which also affects us and enormously and that which they try to impose upon us in our land, in our work and in whatever place, wherever we are. Indigenous brothers, we have confidence in you and we have confidence always that our voices will be heard, all united under one Indian religion only without different borders. We will fight for that one day when the richness of our culture and the greatness of our indigenous people will shine again in all its splendor. This is a challenge to all of us and we will fight to overcome."

So you see our concerns from both the North and the South Americas are the same and that is survival. To keep our nations going and united Native American nations, of course, would like to be a part of the United Nations.

39

"Our Red Nation" (1978)[22]

Diné, Lakota, and Haudenosaunee Traditional Leaders

In 1978 the Longest Walk, a months-long march from San Francisco to Washington, D.C., led by the American Indian Movement, highlighted the survival of tribal nations and brought attention to legislation that threatened tribal sovereignty. While it is frequently referred to as the end of the Red Power movement, such a designation reifies a narrow conception of Native political activism. Perhaps because of this periodization, the Longest Walk rarely receives the attention it deserves or is understood on its own terms. Rather than being an end, it might better be reimagined as a critical turning point in an ongoing effort to assert a global indigenous identity in the context of international law—one rooted in spirituality, sovereignty, and the land. Consider how the following document, authored by Diné, Lakota, and Haudenosaunee traditional leaders, located international concern for human rights and genocide in an indigenous context. How does the language and philosophy compare and contrast with previous documents in this volume and what might account for those differences?[23]

For countless thousands of years our people have lived on this continent in peace and tranquility, coexisting with all Natural Life. In the beginning we were told that the human beings who walk upon the Earth have been provided with all the things necessary for life. We were instructed to carry a love for one another, and to show a great respect for all beings of this Earth. We were shown that our life exists with the tree life, that our well-being depends on the well-being of the vegetable life, that we are close relatives of the four-leggeds. In our way, Spiritual consciousness is the highest form of politics.

Our roots are deep in the lands where we live. We have a great love for our country, for our birthplace is here. The soil is rich from the bones of thousands of our generations. Each of us were created in these lands and it is our duty to take great care of them, because from these lands will spring the future generations of our peoples. We walk about with great respect, for the Earth is a very Sacred Place.

Our traditional governments are truly governments "of the people, by the people, and for the people." All power of authority at all levels comes from the people and can be withdrawn at any time if the power is abused or responsibilities not met.

Our traditional governments cannot be adequately compared to the different forms of government that exist around us today. As with all aspects of Native life, our governments have their roots in the religious systems. Leaders are chosen for, among other things, the way they live their lives according to the four main virtues of bravery, fortitude, generosity, and wisdom. They are men who have proven themselves and show commitment to uphold and enforce the Spiritual and Natural Law, and also the laws of the people.

We are peoples who strongly believe in the cycles of the Universe. Everything is based on concepts of harmony and balance. With the coming of the peoples from the East, this hemisphere has experienced a 486-year conflict between Western Civilization and the Natural World Peoples.

The Western culture has been horribly exploitative and destructive of the Natural World. Over 140 species of birds and animals were utterly destroyed since the European arrival in the Americas, largely because they were unusable in the eyes of the invaders. The forests were leveled, the waters are polluted, our people subjected to genocide. The vast herds of herbivores are reduced to mere handfuls, the buffalo nearly became extinct. Western technology and the people who employ it have been and continue to be the most amazingly destructive forces in all human history. No natural disaster has ever destroyed as much. Not even the Ice Ages counted as many victims.

Many would like to believe that all of these injustices have ended. This couldn't be further from the truth. . . . Our people are the most abused of all peoples in North America. The extreme wrongs which are committed against our people today affect our everyday lives. Under the laws and policies of the United States we do not possess recognition of even the most fundamental rights necessary to our survival. We have no real rights in our lands, no rights to determine our Way of Life, no rights to our economic development. We are not even allowed to protect our communities against unfair actions by any people who choose to invade our homelands. Our lands are [leased?] "for us" by the Bureau of Indian Affairs. Our governments are frequently controlled or hindered by the Interior

Department. Our rights to exist as communities and nations are not protected, and are often denied by the courts. We are a horribly oppressed people in our own land. The most basic justice is denied to our peoples, and only to our peoples!

. . . . Our people are often subjected to such extensive bureaucratic control and manipulation that the process amounts to the denial of even the slightest amount of real self-government. Although there are laws and policies that give the appearance of participation in the processes that affect our land and peoples, the reality is that we have no power over the bureaucracies or laws and policies which affect our lives. Indeed, the practices of the United States have the impact of foreign control over our affairs. The official U.S. position states that there exists on our lands a significant measure of self-determination. This is an illusion created to confuse the people of the U.S. and the world. Our peoples possess the least self-determination of any communities in North America.

. . . Presently the Human Rights, Rights of Nationhood, Right of Self-Determination, and the basic right of existence of our peoples are being actively denied in the United States. . . . The definition of Genocide as stated in Article II of the International Convention on Genocide provides the basis of our peoples' charge of Genocide made at the United Nations in Geneva, Switzerland, in September, 1977.

Article II states: "In the present Convention, genocide means any of the following acts committed with intent to destroy, in whole or in part, a national, ethnical, racial, or religious group, such as:

(a) Killing members of the group;

(b) Causing serious bodily or mental harm to members of the group;

(c) Deliberately inflicting on the group conditions of life calculated to bring about its physical destruction in whole or in part;

(d) Imposing measures intended to prevent births within the group."

. . . United States police and intelligence agencies have directed illegal military operations against our peoples, such as COINTELPRO. These actions have resulted in the violent deaths of a number of our leaders. . . . According to a GAO report issued last year, 24% of our women were forcibly or illegally sterilized during the period 1971–1975. Nearly one out of three of our children are being placed in non-Indian foster homes daily by various county, state and federal agencies. The Indian Reorganization Act of 1934 continues to destroy the traditional government of our people, causing widespread disruption of a tranquil Way of Life, and literally putting brother against brother.

The clear-cut policy of genocide of the last century continues in more sophisticated forms in this century. Our religions have been attacked, and degraded. Our children continue to be processed through various forms of Western educational programs. The Spiritual leaders of our nations are now being subjected to the destructive nature of government program moneys. Taxpayers' moneys are being used to regulate the practice of our natural religions. There are even efforts to certify our medicine peoples and to despiritualize the nature of our healing culture. That practice is a policy that is destroying our natural healing practices. It is a policy which is an outrageous attempt to interfere with, and ultimately destroy our natural religion.

Finally, the bills currently before Congress which call for the abrogation of Indian treaties, and termination of our lands, resources, and water, present a clear signal that the threat of genocide to the existence of our peoples is alive and well. The fact that the present Congress of the United States, in the year 1978, can consider such legislation should alarm the people of the United States. When a government denies the human rights of one people, it is only a matter of time before those rights will be denied to all of its peoples.

. . . We call upon the United States to acknowledge its responsibilities under international law to respect Indian treaties, to insure genuine self-determination for our nations, and to correct past wrongs in an honorable and equitable manner. . . . We call upon all the peoples of the world to join with us in seeking peace, and in seeking to insure survival and justice for all indigenous peoples, for all the Earth's creatures, and all nations of the Earth. . . .

40

"These Are Inherent Rights" (1978)²⁴

The Longest Walk Statement

The Longest Walk began with a pipe ceremony on Alcatraz Island, a symbolic affirmation of its place in the Red Power movement of the 1970s, and it culminated at the Washington Memorial in the heart of Washington, D.C. On their way through the city, the marchers assembled in Malcolm X Park, but they did not linger there or long reflect on previous efforts to forge connections with the black freedom struggle. As this document attests, they turned their attention to building a hemispheric movement on behalf of indigenous peoples. Consider how this statement evaluated past efforts to promote tribal sovereignty, confronted the question of citizenship, drew parallels to the experiences of indigenous peoples in Latin America, and brought to the fore yet another question of belonging—that of national boundaries. Do you hear in the language adopted in the documents from Alcatraz to the Longest Walk a different rhetorical mode?²⁵

We are the sovereign and free children of Mother Earth. Since before human memory, our people have lived on this land. For countless generations, we have lived in harmony with our relatives, the four-leggeds, the winged beings, the beings that swim and the beings that crawl. For all time our home is from coast to coast; from pole to pole. We are the original people of this hemisphere. The remains of our ancestors and of our many relatives are a greater part of this land and any other's remains. The mountains and the trees are a part of us—we are flesh of their flesh. We are the Human Beings of many nations, and we still speak many tongues. We have come from the four directions of this Turtle Island. Our feet have traveled our Mother Earth over many thousands of miles. We are the evidence of the Western Hemisphere, the carriers of the original ways of this area of the world, and the protectors of all Life [on] this Turtle Island.

Today we address you in the language of the oppressor, but the concepts predate the coming of the invaders. The injustice we speak of is centuries old, and has been spoken against in many tongues. We are still the original people of this land. We are the people of The Longest Walk.

For many generations we have been seeking justice and peace from the European refugees and their descendants who have settled on our sacred Turtle Island. It has been an incredibly long struggle. We have entered into many agreements for peace and friendship with the governments of these people, and yet we have received neither peace nor friendship. Most of our original homelands have been illegally taken from us. Our people have been, and continue to be, mercilessly hunted and slaughtered to serve the needs of corporations, governments, and their agents.

Today, the conditions in Central and South America are identical to the conditions in this country during the 19th Century. The process of annihilation and destruction are carried on with money, sophisticated weapons, missionaries, widespread sterilization, so-called developmental programs, CIA and FBI organized training of terrorists and provocateurs that are sponsored and provided by the United States. We can find no other words for the description of these acts other than murder and terrorism. This process is hidden from the peoples of the world by a conscious suppression of information coming from the offending countries.

Our people are often forced to leave their beloved homelands and are sent to lands where they greatly suffer. Our grandfathers and grandmothers were forced to walk many times in front of the guns of the invaders. Today we have been forced to walk again, in front of guns and the threat of destruction that comes from words in legislation. . . .

We know that the present attacks on our lands and sovereignty will, unless halted, ultimately benefit the interest of corporations which seek coal, uranium, water and other parts of our Mother Earth. We understand that the attack on our existence originates with these interests. The land speculators of the last century have been replaced by the oil refineries and the ore processors of this century. The United States government failed to protect our interests against land speculators, who were far less powerful than the transnational corporations we face today. The present-day racism against our people is fueled by these organizations, and the denial of our rights will open up our air, water and lands to a ruthless exploitation unparalleled in history. Uncontrolled Western development will destroy our ways of life, and will threaten all life on this Turtle Island.

The Creator gave to us our original instructions, telling us how to walk about on this Earth as protectors and relatives to all life. As long as the sun rises, the grasses grow, and the cycles continue, we are to carry on this duty. Around us live a people who act in a way that will bring about the total destruction of all life. The transnational corporations destroy life in the waters, air, and land. Huge trawlers attack our relatives in the sea, giant machineries strip our Mother Earth's skin bare, factories and vehicles filled the sky with tons of poison. The recent rush to use nuclear power poses the most potent threat to ending all life in one generation.

. . . How do we explain to the American people that we love our Mother Earth and ways of life? How can we state that we do not need the United States government to tell us how to be indigenous people? What will it take to convince the U.S. government to allow us to live in peace? How do we convince the US government to simply leave us alone to live according to our ways of life?

The federal system has tried many programs for the so-called improvement of our lives. There have been an endless procession of such programs: the BIA, the Dawes Act, the 1924 Citizenship Act, the 1934 Indian Reorganization Act, the Indian Claims Commission, Termination, Relocation, Self-determination, Housing, and on and on. Our conditions have not improved.

There are those of our people who have been destroyed by words and promises of a better way of life through the American system. The American government chooses to see them as leaders of indigenous people. They form corporations and committees. But a corporation is not a nation!

On many of our territories, we are subjected to governments created under the Indian Reorganization Act of 1934, which fosters dissidents who are willing to sell out for an American sanctioned position. . . . From the beginning these puppet governments have brought the wishes of the federal government to the indigenous people. They have never been able to effectively bring the wishes of the indigenous people to Washington. These governments are the clearest manifestation of federal policy in the indigenous communities. They do not, and cannot, effectively represent the people. They represent a policy which, when advocated by indigenous individuals, presents what can best be described as a kind of self-destruction. . . .

In order for our people to be happy, healthy, and productive, we must have access to all of our relatives and the self-esteem, respect, affection, and a sense of belonging we receive from them. There are many policies and regulations that remove our many relatives from us. Our relatives in the waters are being removed by millions of sports fishermen and commercial fishing fleets. Our relatives, the four-legged creatures, are being hunted, trapped, slaughtered, driven away, and forced into extinction. Our relatives in the sky are faced with the same problems and have the same threats upon them. This indiscriminate barbarism is beyond the reason of our people. Our people only took the lives of those other beings when it was necessary for our survival and not the mere "sport" of it. Our Grandmother, the Moon, has been molested and a part of her being has been removed. . . .

Our cultures are structured for Human Beings. They are based on principles of respect and responsibility for everyone and everything. The manner in which the people are to live is described to the people through our religious teachings. These religious teachings were given to the Creation by the Creator in order to insure our existence in this world. To remove our children from our communities, and to deny them access to these original instructions leads to the collapse of our families, societies, and nations. It is our commitment to reverse this process and rebuild our country.

We understand that self-esteem derives from the things that people do every day. Our elder people teach a respect for one another and the respect for all the things of this place, including Mother Earth, the Grasses, the Waters, and the many things which support our lives. We have a high regard for the affection of our people. In our ways, we are taught our relationship to the generations yet unborn, to those who have gone before us, and to our nations of people. We are deeply rooted in the land and our peoples' roots draw sustenance from our Mother Earth. We, the traditional people, are instructed in the old ways and every day we still live these instructions.

. . . The occupiers' borders defining the settler regimes of Mexico, the United States, and Canada, divide our territories and peoples. Each of these regions seeks to impose fake identities of being Mexican, American, or Canadian. Border policies inhibit the free flow of the members of our nations and break up the cultural continuity and integrity of our peoples. The national laws of these regimes function uniformly toward the destruction and exploitation of our peoples. Land laws in Mexico force our people from their lands, and force them northward to seek survival. The immigration laws of the United States deny entrance to the indigenous people coming from Mexico. Yet these same laws are distorted to allow for a legalized kidnapping of our children from the Canadian area. Throughout the hemisphere, immigration laws have historically been used to bring in large groups of immigrants to further the colonization and destruction of our Mother Earth and People. Since those immigrants are coming to this hemisphere to occupy our lands, we are asserting our right to determine who enters our lands and we are asserting our right to deport those people who *we* determine to be illegal aliens.

... Your laws were made to protect not your people, but the greed of the wealthy. So there is no respect in your laws and no justice in your courts. We do not recognize your self-appointed control over our lives and freedom.

As a people we have the right to gather together to give a greeting and a thanksgiving to the Creation. We have the right to live in peace and tranquility. We have the right to the fruits of our own lands and to feed, shelter and clothe our people. We have a right to conceive and to give birth according to our natural ways. We have the right to educate our children to our ways of life. We have the right to protect ourselves and our lands against abuses and to settle disputes that arise within our own territories. We have the right to clean air, clean water, and the peaceful usage of our lands. We have the right to be a people. These are inherent rights. All people possess these rights under the laws of the Universe as well as man-made laws. These are rights that cannot be given to or denied by one group of people over another. As the traditional people, we recognize and understand that these rights came from the Creator and not by actions of humans.

The United States has claimed to confer U.S. citizenship upon our people. Even that act has been used as a weapon against our people. It may be true that the United States has the power to confer citizenship upon whomever seeks it, but it has no right to deny our citizenship to our own nations. Today it comes to our ears that we are "privileged citizens" and that the treaties should be "abrogated" in order that we may be made equal to United States citizens.

We are not United States citizens. We have treaties with the United States, and the U.S. does not make treaties with its own citizens. We protested the 1924 Citizenship Act. We do not claim U.S. citizenship. Nothing the US has done in its relations with us has moved us to want to change that position. ...

We call for the restoration of all lands illegally removed from our protection. We call for the payment of war reparations due to us for the reconstruction of our nations. We call for an end to the confusing situation regarding state and federal jurisdiction, and we direct America's attention to our treaties and agreements which defined the relationship of our countries. We call upon organized religion to become allies in the process of liberation, and to stop their competition for our "souls." We are here to make it clear to the American government and the people of the world that there is only one definition of who we are as a people. That definition arises from our religions, governments, and the ways of life that we follow. No one else on the Mother Earth has the right to attempt to define us or our existence. ...

41

"Get the Record Straight" (1987)[26]

James Hena

Among the most effective engines for economic development in Indian Country has been tribal gaming. During the 1970s, the Florida Seminoles pushed the envelope with high-stakes bingo. The Cabazon Band of Mission Indians followed their lead in California, and soon the number of gaming operations grew, as did state resistance. In February 1987, the Supreme Court decided in favor of the argument advanced by tribes that owning and operating casinos on trust lands was an act of sovereignty and could not, therefore, be regulated by state governments. Congress swiftly moved to impose limitations on this decision with the Indian Gaming Regulatory Act (IGRA). The legislation, which became law in 1988, defined three classes of gaming. Class III included casino-style games and provided state governments a voice in negotiating and a cut of the revenue. Consider the economic and historical context in which James Hena, governor of Tesuque Pueblo, placed the right to engage in gaming during hearings leading to IGRA's passage and what message he intended to convey.[27]

I am here today on behalf of my Pueblo and the other gaming Pueblos in New Mexico. . . . It is quite clear to everyone who is involved in this issue that the real difference between H.R. 964 and H.R. 2507 is in the area of jurisdiction over class III gaming. The Pueblo support Federal legislation to regulate gaming on Indian lands along the lines proposed in H.R. 2507. We do not and will not support any bills which provide State jurisdiction over gaming on Indian lands. Those who favor State jurisdiction over class III gaming have raised a concern about creating enclaves for organized crime resulting from runaway Indian controlled gaming. Some proponents of State jurisdiction also seem to feel that our tribal governments are temporary in nature and that we lack the capacity to handle our own affairs.

Let us get the record straight. The fear of organized crime was raised when the tribes first began bingo games several years ago. To this day, there is not any evidence of organized criminal activity in tribally controlled games. The tribes are not about to let this valuable source of revenues and employment fall into the hands of organized crime, and H.R. 2507 will help us to ensure that this cannot happen in the future.

The real concern about jurisdiction over class III gaming emanates of a fear of economic competition. The so-called organized non-Indian gaming interests simply do not want to have competition with the tribes. H.R. 2507 addresses this concern with the requirement that Indian controlled class III games be conducted in an identical manner to State controlled class III games. This approach to regulating class III gaming by Indian governments is consistent with the decisions of the Federal Courts and longstanding Federal policies to promote tribal self-government.

With respect to the idea that tribal governments are temporary in nature and that we lack the capacity to handle our own affairs, let us also get the record straight. The Pueblos have been self-governing for centuries. Although a few of our Pueblo governments are now organized under the Indian Reorganization Act, most continue operating with a traditional form of government we have used for hundreds of years. Pueblo governments pre-date the U.S. Government, and even most of the governments in the international community. We have withstood attempts by a variety of outside forces to diminish or restrict our governmental authority over these years.

It is ironic to hear that we lack the capacity to govern ourselves effectively, because we have been self-governing for more than 750 years. The State of New Mexico is now celebrating its 75th year of self-government. When New Mexico became a state in 1912, the U.S. Congress required New Mexico to disclaim jurisdiction over Indians and Indian lands. New Mexico agreed to this disclaimer of jurisdiction, and the disclaimer clause is still a part of the New Mexico Constitution today. From our point of view, both the Congress and the State of New Mexico recognized and reaffirmed our inherent rights of self-governance through that disclaimer clause. The U.S. Constitution itself recognizes our inherent sovereignty by placing with the Congress the authority to regulate trade and commerce with Indian tribes.

Tribal governments are a part of the Federal system of the United States. As a result, proposals to place Indian gaming under State jurisdiction are contrary to the Constitutions of both the United States and the State of New Mexico, and inconsistent with 200 years of Federal policy and action to recognize and promote tribal self-governance. We strongly urge this committee to reject any proposals to place Indian gaming under State jurisdiction, but to promote instead legislation that requires cooperation rather than imposition of one government's views over the other. We urge you to uphold the Federal tribal relationship as it is mandated in the Constitution. We pledge to you our fullest cooperation as you work to enact legislation which will promote tribal self-sufficiency and ensure the integrity of Indian controlled gaming.

42

"This Way of Life—The Peyote Way" (1992)[28]

Reuben Snake

Another long-standing issue that resurfaced during the 1990s involved the sacramental use of peyote, a small spineless cactus that contains hallucinogenic qualities when ingested. The United States government considered it a controlled substance; followers of the peyote way, or the Native American Church, considered it medicine. Some practitioners even treated it, as with the bread of communion in the Protestant and Catholic traditions, as the body of Christ. The American Indian Religious Freedom Act of 1978 (AIRFA) purportedly protected free exercise, but a Supreme Court decision in 1990 found that it did not include peyote. In response, advocates of religious freedom pushed for a congressional amendment to AIRFA that explicitly protected its sacramental use. Reuben Snake (1937–93), a Ho-Chunk who had served in the military and held leadership positions in his nation, the National Congress of American Indians, American Indian Movement, and the Native American Church, played an instrumental role in what would be a successful effort. Consider how Snake talked "the language of the larger world" in his response to charges that peyote represented a dangerous drug that fostered corruption, immorality, and licentiousness.[29]

Mr. SNAKE. Mr. Chairman, at this time I want to say thank you for the invitation to be present here at this hearing and to give testimony on behalf of a very important part of the Native American community—that is, those of us that adhere to the ages-old, traditional religion of the peyote way, as we call it amongst ourselves, and known in the larger society as the Native American Church. I want to begin by saying that in every organized social order of man there are institutions which are created to create stability within that social structure and to bring harmony to that social structure. This Nation, the United States of America, professes to be a Godly Nation. The national motto of our country is, "In God we Trust."

Because the vast majority of the citizens of this country originate from the other side of the world, from that part of the world known as Europe, this country has been greatly influenced by the Judeo-Christian philosophy of life. Within the Judeo-Christian philosophy of life, there are ten commandments that were given to humankind so that they could have a harmonious, stabilized social order. In these 10 commandments there are four major concerns about human interaction. These are: Thou shalt not kill, thou shalt not steal, thou shalt not commit adultery, thou shalt not lie, thou shalt not bear false witness. These are the basics upon which the Judeo-Christian way of life has been practiced.

These standards of life are what this country is supposed to be adhering to. When the Supreme Court made its ruling on April 17, 1990, these questions came to my mind when they ruled as they did that somehow or other those of us who use this divine herb, this divine medicine, were somehow not in control of our senses and somehow or other were breaking the law.

These questions came to my mind:

Where in the documentation of the U.S. Drug Enforcement Administration, law enforcement agencies, wherever such records are kept—where is there any documentation that any Native American Church member has ever been convicted of mass murder?[30]

Where in the documentation is there any evidence that any Native American Church member was convicted of any part of the S&L scandals which have brought economic ruin to our country?[31]

Where is there any documentation that any Native American Church leader has been accused of sexual harassment of their subordinate staff?[32]

Where is there any documentation that any Native American Church member was an active player in the CIA/Noriega international drug trafficking activity?[33]

Where is there any documentation that any Native American Church member was a part of the Iran contra scandal where the top leaders of our Nation lied to you, Senator, to other Members of Congress, and to the American public as to what happened in that situation?[34]

There is no such documentation that any Native American Church member was involved in the violation of these very basic standards of life: not to kill, not to steal, not to be sexually promiscuous, not to lie. There is no record, because it never happened.

The Native American Church has standards that they teach to every generation, and when you look at the record that exists here in this land within the Indian Nations, many, many of the tribal leaders throughout the United States and Canada and Old Mexico are practitioners of this way of life—the peyote way.

Many, many of our tribes who have lost so much of their ancient tradition have turned to the Native American Church as a means of spiritual health and spiritual wellbeing, and Native American Church leaders provide guidance and counsel and support to many, many of their tribal members.

As you, yourself, have indicated, Native Americans in every conflict, from the first World War up to Desert Storm, have had the highest per-centage on a per capita basis of people serving in the Armed Forces. When you look at the record, many, many of these Native American warriors have been active members of the Native American Church.

This is my testimony. In 1952 the President of these United States, Dwight D. Eisenhower, said these words, "Whatever America desires for the world must first come to pass in the heart of America." Today our national leaders, our President, and members of his Administration, the Secretary of State—they travel to the four corners of the globe professing support of human rights in all the different nations of the world. They say, "Live up to your teachings and protect the human rights of people." While they are doing that, here within this country the indigenous people of this land continue to suffer these gross injustices and deprivation of our religious freedom.

In closing, I want to say, Senator, quoting Edmund Burke, that the only thing necessary for evil to triumph is for good men to do nothing.

43

"Let Catawba Continue to Be Who They Are" (1992)[35]

E. Fred Sanders

Located primarily in South Carolina, the Catawbas grappled with forms of racism and discrimination similar to those of other southern Indians. Like the Mississippi Band of Choctaw Indians, they successfully gained federal recognition through the Indian Reorganization Act during the 1940s. Less than two decades later, however, Congress terminated them. This set the stage for a movement to secure the restoration of the federal trust relationship—something virtually all of the tribes, bands, and rancherias that experienced termination engaged in during the 1960s through the 1990s. In this document, Catawba Assistant Chief Fred Sanders testified in favor of restoration legislation (H.R. 5562) and set Catawba claims to nationhood against the backdrop of the imminent Columbian Quincentennary. Consider, however, how another conflict involving the taking of reservation lands established by treaty during the early 1760s complicated his efforts, as well as the language the assistant chief used to discredit his opponents and win allies. Although the Catawbas reached a settlement the following year, Sanders did not successfully disentangle the issues. In return for federal acknowledgment and a monetary award, the Catawbas agreed to relinquish the land claim.[36]

The bill 5562 has to do with restoring Catawba to a government-to-government Federal relationship, which we had at one time and was caught in the termination trap by the policies of the Federal Government in the mid-1950s. Catawba has put off seeking restoration because there was a lawsuit involved with the State of South Carolina concerning a treaty land violation, and we were hoping to get that bill, along with doing the same process. Nevertheless, it was not a part of the lawsuit, and we want to make that very clear today.

We have two different issues. The lawsuit pertains to a treaty violation of 1840 with the tribe and the State of South Carolina, which was protected under the 1790 Non-Intercourse and Trade Act. This policy of the Federal Government in 1950 had to do with terminating a number of tribes throughout the United States, which would not continue to provide Federal service to those tribes, which they were receiving as Federally-recognized tribes. So we are dealing with two different issues here.

I would like to say I speak on behalf of my tribe, which consists of approximately 1,400 people, and I represent the executive committee, since I am the assistant chief. I have served on the council in that position since 1975. We have a census, which was taken by the colonists in South Carolina in 1715, and through that census data, they said there were 1,470 Catawbas. Prior to that, there were thousands of Catawbas, but through disease brought to this country by the foreign population, it was depleted. Two hundred and seventy-seven years later, today, there are approximately the same number of Catawbas. Doesn't seem right, does it?

Nevertheless, we have a record indicating historically we were aboriginal people in the same Piedmont area when the colonists arrived that we are presently occupying. Rock Hill, South Carolina, is the town nearest the Catawba Indian Reservation, which is southeast, and we have occupied that territory and the other territories for centuries prior to the coming of the discovery of America. So we have survived 500 years in that territory. Certainly, we need to be looked after and treated as an American Indian population with some dignity.

With the treaty of 1760, what the British call "Pine Tree Hill," which is now known as Camden, South Carolina, the Catawbas at that time agreed to relinquish over 8.5 million acres of property to the colonies in order to be guaranteed a reservation, which would be platted and designated, which gave them a recognized title, and that was the 15 square miles, or 144,000 acres, and that is the thing we are in court about under the Federal—under the lawsuit with the State of South Carolina.

It is not in the court about the restoration for the tribe. Federal restoration will bring the tribe back into the position of where we will be able to receive the services that all Federally-recognized tribes receive. We don't have to elaborate on that. We know it has to do with education opportunities, housing opportunities, and it has to do with an economic growth in the community for the Indian and non-Indians alike.

I would like to say that at this point we do not have the support of the South Carolina delegation from the House or the Senate side. And the reason for that is they would like to be able to say to the public and to the Congress that restoration for Catawba at this time would infringe upon settling the lawsuit.

I would like to tell you that is not the truth. The people who are saying this are people who are actually defendants in the lawsuit or represent defendants in the lawsuit. Our very own Congressman is a defendant in the lawsuit. He owns over 800 acres or is occupying over 400 acres in the lawsuit territory. He has a conflict.

We have people who are negotiating the lawsuit, who were appointed by the governor of South Carolina, who are defendants that occupy the land. They have a conflict of interest. Any time you have someone negotiating a settlement for you that has a direct conflict of interest, normally it is not equitable to the person they are negotiating for.

We need someone to negotiate an equitable settlement for the lawsuit, and we certainly need to be restored and not continue to wait for someone to come out and say we are going to give you something. Congress was the ones that terminated the Catawba Indians: they are the ones that have to restore us, not the State of South Carolina. Restoration can only be a plus for Catawba and let Catawba continue to be who they are.

The American Indian population in the State of South Carolina—they have some theory in the State of South Carolina, if you reach some status in life, you can quit being who you are. I want to tell you that isn't true. I happen to know that in 1840 my grandmother, great grandmother was born, when this treaty with the State of South Carolina went to court about. My grandmother, who was born in the 1860s, my mother, who was born in 1896, are people who have seen the devastation of not being treated as citizens of the State of South Carolina.

We have been attempting to settle the lawsuit since the year of 1886. It is still under the courts—under jurisdictional questions. Talk about the due process of justice. I don't think there is any other tribe in the United States that has ever approached the courts, and it has been in the courts or been at process or negotiated with the tribe for over 100 years.

We don't know when that question will ever be answered and settled, the lawsuit. Restoration cannot depend on that. It depends on the Congress going to the fellow Members of the Congress and the Senate and getting the tribe restored. Catawbas will support settlement of the lawsuit in addition to the restoration because we have always worked with South Carolina, but they must talk to us.

I wrote to the governor of South Carolina, as chairman of the restoration project, and offered to sit down with him and converse with him about the necessity of restoration for the tribe and the tribe's decision to seek restoration through the Congress, and got no reply. The thing that we did get, we got one letter from the Congressman saying, Fred, if you seek restoration for the tribe, the governor is surely going to oppose it. And not only will he oppose it, but he will write letters to all the South Carolina Federal delegation and ask them not to support it.

And when I wrote to the governor, I said, is that really true? He didn't answer. That didn't curb what the Attorney General did. He wrote a letter to every member of the South Carolina Federal delegation and said do not support the Catawba restoration bill. We are talking about the politically powerful against the politically powerless, and I hope this country has enough guts to stand up and say this isn't the way it is supposed to be. We have citizens out there you are elected to represent, and let us get on with the show.

44

"Return the Power of Governing" (1994)[37]

Wilma Mankiller

During the 1970s, Congress responded to demands for more power at the local level with incremental reforms, such as the Indian Self-Determination and Education Assistance Act (1975). Though a welcome departure from the near absolute control of the Bureau of Indian Affairs, critics argued that its emphasis on self-administration did not go far enough. Washington continued to hold the purse strings. By 1990, in response to the Reagan administration's empowering government-to-government rhetoric but debilitating budget slashing actions, Congress enacted legislation that enabled select tribes to enter into compacts with the federal government. These compacts, expanded and made permanent in 1994, provided for tribal control over the administration and management of Indian Bureau programs, functions, and services and the authority to redesign them to fit tribal needs. Wilma Mankiller (1945–2010), the first woman to serve as principal chief of the Cherokee Nation of Oklahoma, supported self-governance and, in the following excerpts from three testimonies, explained why. Consider how her views of the federal government and the Bureau of Indian Affairs compare to those of Arthur Parker, Carlos Montezuma, D'Arcy McNickle, and Bruce Wilkie in previous chapters.[38]

I am convinced by my own work for the last twenty-five years in Indian communities that the best solution to problems in native communities come from within our own communities and our own tribes. . . . I believe very strongly that the BIA is an anachronism. It has barely changed since its inception, yet tribal governments have changed and the capacity of tribes to do things for themselves has changed dramatically. We have a lot of new initiatives that support tribal communities in the revitalization of tribal government and tribal communities, but the present BIA structure and attitude does not support tribal government and tribal revitalization. . . .

Cherokee principal chief Wilma Mankiller and Mississippi Band of Choctaw Indians chief Phillip Martin (Document 23) appear before the Senate Affairs Special Investigations subcommittee hearing in Washington, D.C., on 30 January 1989. AP Photo/Marcy Nighswander.

The Cherokee Nation has a history of treaty-making that began in 1785, and we view this self-governance compact basically as our newest treaty with the United States. It's a very important initiative for us. . . . The self-governance project offers a real opportunity for the federal government to let go without diminishing or abrogating its trust and inter-governmental relations with the Cherokee Nation. . . . This has led the Nation in many endeavors to contract health care, to sponsor self-help community projects, and engage in the promotion of industries for tribal and private sector purposes throughout the northeastern Oklahoma area. . . . It is believed the single most important accomplishment is the assumption of direct administration of federal responsibilities overall. This reflects at least a mature relationship between the two sovereignties involved, the Cherokee Nation and the United States of America. . . . For the Cherokee Nation, the Self-Governance Project is the realization of an ideal to return the power of governing back to the Cherokees. . . .

We are very concerned that the U.S. government will see this as just another demonstration project and will not make this legislation permanent. . . . [The Self-Governance Act] has allowed us to allocate the resources where they are most needed, and respond to local needs, and it has been successful from our standpoint. . . . I also believe that the self-governance project or demonstration project, as it is now known, should include both the Bureau of Indian Affairs and the Indian Health Service. This piecemeal way of dealing with self-governance just through the BIA is not going to work. I think it has to be kind of across-the-board. . . . Always there are these great speeches about supporting tribal governments and that sort of thing in Washington from the leadership, but it needs to permeate every layer of these agencies, people we deal with on a day-to-day basis. . . .

HEALTH CARE IS not the only issue we are concerned about. The BIA funds for operating Indian schools are terribly insufficient. . . . The status of Indian tribes as sovereign governments, especially Self-Governance tribes, places a heavy responsibility on both the tribes and the federal government to assure that health programs for Indians are responsive to needs and lead to improvement of the overall health of persons served by the Indian health care system. . . . Because the purpose of the Self-Governance program is to enhance the inherent sovereignty of tribal governments and strengthen the government-to-government relationship between the United States and Indian tribal governments . . . the Subcommittee should ensure that the tribes themselves are consulted and participate in the planning and implementation of agency restructuring. There is real danger that the agencies will give only lip service to tribal participation.

PART V

TESTING THE LIMITS, 1994–2015

Indigenous peoples secured important symbolic and substantive victories during the late twentieth and early twenty-first centuries. In 1993 the United States Congress issued an Apology Resolution with regard to the overthrow of the Kingdom of Hawai'i. Seven years later, Assistant Secretary of the Interior Kevin Gover (Pawnee) offered a "formal apology to Indian people for the historical conduct" of the Bureau of Indian Affairs. Congress, too, formally apologized to all Native peoples in 2010, though the document, folded into a defense appropriations bill, received virtually no public attention.[1] In 2009 President Barack Obama received accolades for inaugurating an annual White House Tribal Nations Conference that underscored his support for government-to-government relations. And after voting against the United Nations (UN) Declaration on the Rights of Indigenous Peoples in 2007, the United States changed its position in 2010. Practical legislative gains, such as the American Indian Trust Fund Management Reform Act, Native American Housing Assistance and Self-Determination Act, Tribal Law and Order Act, and Violence Against Women Act bolstered these symbolic gestures.[2]

As in preceding decades, legislative pendulum swings and an unsympathetic Supreme Court curtailed the gains. *Seminole Tribe v. Florida* (1996) granted states sovereign immunity, strengthening their hand against tribes when negotiating Class III gaming compacts. Meanwhile, *Nevada v. Hicks* (2001) circumscribed the jurisdictional reach of tribal courts, and a circuit court decision in 2004 allowed scientific research on the nine-thousand-year-old remains of Kennewick Man, whom several tribes in the Pacific Northwest called the Ancient One and claimed as an ancestor through the Native American Graves Protection and Repatriation Act (NAGPRA), to continue.[3] Fearful of giving the Supreme Court an opportunity to set a precedent that might undermine NAGPRA, the tribes involved in the suit chose not to appeal the decision. Two additional cases, *Carcieri v. Salazar* (2009) and *Adoptive Couple v. Baby Girl* (2013), made it more difficult for tribes to have the federal government take land into trust on their behalf and limited the Indian Child Welfare Act. Tribal nations seeking federal recognition, protection from state taxation, defense of natural resources, respect for sacred lands, and the honoring of treaties also faced uncertainty in Congress and in the courts.[4]

In these uncertain times, the global indigenous rights movement continued to evolve. Native people sent petitions and delegations to the United Nations, while individuals built activist networks and collaborative relationships. During the 1990s and early 2000s, Western Shoshone sisters Mary and Carrie Dann, for instance, elicited UN support for their nation's claim that the United States had illegally taken more than 20 million acres of traditional territory guaranteed to their people in the Treaty of Ruby Valley.[5] In November 2012, a series of teach-ins in Saskatchewan swiftly metamorphosed into a vast movement known as Idle No More. This unstructured "movement of movements" emphasized inherent sovereignty, the reinstitution of traditional laws and treaty relationships, defense of tribal lands and resources, and resistance to all forms of colonial oppression.[6]

Idle No More brought increased attention, clarity, and urgency to long-standing concerns over economic and resource development During the 1950s and 1960s, as we have already seen, many Native activists offered modernization and development as an alternative to termination. Since that time, organizations, such as the Alaska Federation of Natives and the Council of Energy Resource Tribes, advanced this movement by lobbying for legislation to promote the economic interests of tribes. At the same time, individual communities brought suit over inequitable long-term leases, environmental destruction, and tribal regulation and taxation of non-Native corporations.[7]

The costs of nation building through resource exploitation grew more salient during the 1970s. And by the 1990s and early 2000s, heightened concerns over sustainability and climate change contributed to a push for different forms of economic development, such as solar, wind, and other renewables. Through organizations such as the Indian Country Renewable Energy Consortium and the Intertribal Council on Utility Policy, and with the support of federal legislation and innovative partnerships with states, tribal governments and organizations have made strides in resource management and the production of clean energy. Indigenous people have also taken to the streets, evidenced by the massive Peoples Climate March held in New York City in advance of the United Nations climate summit in September 2014.[8]

If Native people have pushed back against corporate exploitation of tribal resources, they have also engaged in difficult and often divisive conversations within their communities. "It's easy to say yes to development in Indian Country, but it's hard to say no," Ray Cross, a son of Gros Ventre leader Martin Cross and a key player in securing compensation for the destruction wrought by the Garrison Dam, argued in a November 2014 editorial. "The past tribal administration on Fort Berthold Indian Reservation gave its unqualified yes to the largely unregulated development of its oil and gas resources" in the Bakken Formation. The hundreds of millions of dollars generated by tax revenues and oil royalties contributed to financial wealth but threatened "their most important resource: their sovereignty." Critical conversations like this one, as documents in chapter 5 suggest, continue to take place across indigenous America.[9]

Like the eye of a hurricane, sovereignty advocates offered calm amid the furious storms that raged in and beyond Indian Country during the late twentieth and early twenty-first centuries. And like their forebears, they held fast to the ground on which they stood, uneven and contested though it was. Not content with the gains that had been made during a century that opened with predictions of their disappearance, tribal nations and Native individuals pressed on, intent upon testing the limits of sovereignty. As the documents in this chapter show, these challenges involved everything from the status of a kingdom that never acceded to annexation and the power to define the meaning of citizenship to environmental justice, the protection of sacred lands, the power of tribal courts, and energy sovereignty.

As in the past, indigenous peoples did not merely engage in a dialogue—the contests of the mid-1990s and after, just as the ones a century before, could not be understood solely in terms of "Native peoples" against "whites." Each of the issues explored in the pages that follow were multivalent, simultaneously producing conversations and contestations between and within indigenous communities and individuals. Rather than being straightforward and heroic, testing the limits of sovereignty revealed ambiguity and ambivalence. To "say we are nations" proved no easier a proposition at the dawn of the twenty-first century than it had been in the waning light of the nineteenth.

45

"We Already Know Our History" (1996)[10]

Armand Minthorn

Non-Native people have been looting American Indian graves for more than five hundred years. Not until 1990 did the U.S. Congress respond to demands for purposeful action to stop it. That year, the Native American Graves Protection and Repatriation Act (NAGPRA) mandated that federal agencies and institutions receiving federal assistance inventory the human remains, funerary and sacred objects, and items of cultural patrimony in their vast collections. Tribes could, upon demonstrating cultural affiliation, reclaim them. In moving ceremonies, Native communities returned the remains of ancestors to the earth, provided for the safekeeping of sacred objects, and reintegrated items back into their ritual lives. NAGPRA also set the stage for more conflict. Consider how the tribal nations represented by Armand Minthorn, an Umatilla political and religious leader, asserted and tested the limits of sovereignty in the contest over human remains that archaeologists referred to as "Kennewick Man" and they revered as the "Ancient One." In 2004 a federal district court, citing the tribes' inability to prove cultural affiliation, determined that he would remain above contested ground.[11]

In the summer of 1996 a human burial, believed to be about 9,000 years old, was discovered near Columbia Park in Kennewick, Washington. Scientists and others want to study this individual. They believe that he should be further desecrated for the sake of science, and for their own personal gain. The people of my tribe, and four other affected tribes, strongly believe that the individual must be re-buried as soon as possible. My tribe has ties to this individual because he was uncovered in our traditional homeland –a homeland where we still retain fishing, hunting, gathering, and other rights under our 1855 Treaty with the US Government.

Like any inadvertent discovery of ancestral human remains, this is a very sensitive issue for me and my tribe. Our religious beliefs, culture, and our adopted policies and procedures tell us that this individual must be re-buried as soon as possible. Our elders have taught us that once a body goes into the ground, it is meant to stay there until the end of time.

It is not our practice to publicize these types of discoveries, both for the protection of the individual as well as sensitivity to our tribal members. In this case, however, we must take the opportunity this incident has created to help educate the general public about the laws governing these discoveries and what these discoveries mean to us, as Indians. We also hope to give people a better understanding of why this is such a sensitive issue.

The Native American Graves Protection and Repatriation Act (NAGPRA) and Archaeological Resources Protection Act (ARPA), as well as other federal and state laws, are in place to prevent the destruction of, and to protect, human burials and cultural resources. The laws also say that authorities must notify affected Tribes and consult with tribal officials on how to handle the discovery, as well as protection and preservation. Our Tribe was not properly notified and if we had been, this difficult situation might have been avoided.

Under the Native American Graves Protection and Repatriation Act, tribes are allowed to file a claim to have ancestral human remains reburied. My tribe has filed a claim for this individual and when it is approved, we will rebury him and put him back to rest. In filing this claim, we have the support of the four other tribes who potentially have ties to this individual. These tribes are the Yakama, Nez Perce, Colville, and Wanapum. We share the same religious belief, traditional practices, as well as oral histories that go back 10,000 years.

If this individual is truly over 9,000 years old, that only substantiates our belief that he is Native American. From our oral histories, we know that our people have been part of this land since the beginning of time. We do not believe that our people migrated here from another continent, as the scientists do. We also do not agree with the notion that this individual is Caucasian. Scientists say that because the individual's head measurement does not match ours, he is not Native American. We believe that humans and animals change over time to adapt to their environment. And, our elders have told us that Indian people did not always look the way we look today.

Some scientists say that if this individual is not studied further, we, as Indians, will be destroying evidence of our own history. We already know our history. It is passed on to us through our elders and through our religious practices. Scientists have dug up and studied Native Americans for decades. We view this practice as desecration of the body and a violation of our most deeply-held religious beliefs. Today thousands of native human remains sit on the shelves of museums and institutions, waiting for the day when they can return to the earth, and waiting for the day that scientists and others pay them the respect they are due.

Our tribal policies and procedures and our own religious beliefs, prohibit scientific testing on human remains. Our beliefs and policies also tell us that this individual must be re-buried as soon as possible. Our religion and our elders have taught us that we have an inherent responsibility to care for those who are no longer with us. We have a responsibility to protect all human burials, regardless of race. We are taught to treat them all with the same respect.

Many people are asking if there's any chance for a compromise in this issue. We remind them that not only has this individual already been compromised, but our religious beliefs have once again been compromised. Many non-Indians are looking for a compromise—a compromise that fits their desires. And, many non-Indians are trying to bend the laws to fit their desires. The Native American Graves Protection and Repatriation Act was passed by Congress in 1990 to protect Native American burials and set in place a mechanism to have human remains and artifacts returned to the tribes.

We are trying to ensure that the federal government lives up to its own laws, as well as honoring our policies, procedures, and religious beliefs. We understand that non-Indian cultures have different values and beliefs than us, but I ask the American people to please understand our stance on this issue. We are not trying to be troublemakers, we are doing what our elders have taught us—to respect people, while they're with us and after they've become part of the earth.

46

"We Would Like to Have Answers" (2003)[12]

Russell Jim

Resource exploitation as a means of promoting economic development has long been a contentious issue in Native America. During the 1990s and after, uranium mining brought hardship to the Diné people, the Mescalero Apache debated whether to host a nuclear waste storage site, and the Prairie Island Indian Community pressed the federal government to address problems associated with an aging nuclear power plant and waste storage casks on their ancestral lands. The Confederated Tribes and Bands of the Yakama Indian Nation faced similar challenges. The Manhattan Project led in 1943 to the establishment of the Hanford Nuclear Site along the Columbia River in Washington State. Waste from the reactors, located in an area to which the Yakamas retained reserved hunting, fishing, and gathering rights, contaminated the air, soil, and water. In this document, Yakama elder Russell Jim (1936–), project director for his nation's Environmental Restoration and Waste Management Program, related the environmental crisis to Yakama reverence for the land and treaty rights. Consider what it meant to Jim for the Yakamas to exercise sovereignty.[13]

The Hanford area was our wintering ground, the Palm Springs of the area. And the winters were milder here, and so therefore we moved here and disbursed to all other parts of the country when the spring came. And our usual and accustomed places involve Canada, western Montana, northern Arizona, northern California, and the Pacific coast. So consequently in the Treaty of 1855, we included such language as accepted by the United States of America, in a contract called a treaty. And as a consequence, we thought then we would forever have the right to utilize the natural foods and medicines and to hunt and fish in all usual and accustomed places.

We lived in harmony with the area, with the river, with all of the environment. All the natural foods and medicines were quite abundant here. And as the snows receded, we followed back up clear into the Alpine

Yakama elder Russell Jim, head of the Confederated Tribes and Bands of the Yakama Indian Nation's Environmental Restoration and Waste Management Program, has been actively involved in the movement to clean up the Hanford Nuclear Site for decades. Photo courtesy of Jason E. Kaplan.

areas, into the fall season. And then storing our food that we had gathered all spring and summer, we picked it up on the way back here to Hanford.

With the coming of the Manhattan Project, it was simplified eventually, by them putting in writing, that the area had the abundant water—cold water, clean water—that they needed to cool their reactors. The abundance of electricity was provided by Grand Coulee Dam and Bonneville Dam. The area was an isolated wasteland, and the people were expendable. And that was in writing. And therefore the Manhattan Project was justified here, and everyone was moved out, including the Yakama Nation people. The non-Indian community was compensated for their removal. Of course there were a few that refused, but their land was condemned, and they were paid a dollar.

But the Yakama Nation refused any compensation eventually, because the words in the treaty meant more to them, to be able to utilize the land as it was intended in the beginning. And so as time went on, we participated in the war effort. There were many Yakama people that went to the Second World War; we lost many people there. Matter of fact, statistics on a national basis show that the indigenous people of this country—in comparison to the population status percentage-wise—provided more bodies to war efforts and police actions than any other race.

And so as the consistent, mass public deception continued on until 1986 that, "Don't worry, everything's fine," there was a forced release of 19,000 declassified documents. And in those documents showed that there were tremendous releases of radioisotopes to the environment, primarily iodine-131, and some intentionally, in what they call the "Green Run," an intentional release to test on the people and the environment. And I think as a result of all this the Yakama people and many others are suffering the consequences, health-wise. . . .

And so there is a concerted effort now by the Yakama Nation to influence the cleanup of the site. We know that it will never be returned to pristine status in the next 500 years, but at least there should be an effort to set the stage for cleanup. And there is yet a new and innovative technology that could be utilized. Instead, there is a lot of activity out here, but hardly any cleanup.

And so, what are the consequences of our health issues? We need to have some scientific studies done, some diligent efforts, of course the funding, to determine what has happened to the health of the Yakama. What may happen to the gene pool of the Yakama in the future? And I think my question of fifteen years ago was: when is the time the mutations are going to show up? When are immune deficiencies going to be as a result of some of the effects on the gene pool? The gene damage? The DNA damage? The chromosome damage? I think it's now. There is evidence of a vast amount of cancers and related illnesses now in the Yakama people.

And so we have attempted in our work to be of assistance to the Department of Energy and others to influence this cleanup. We have some good ideas. We have a mandate to preserve and protect our land and resources for the future generations. And we do not look out just for the Yakama people; we look out for all people. The Yakama Nation has taken the stance that—since 1978, our position is that we are neither pro-nuclear nor anti-nuclear. We are pro-safety for all people. And so we are going to continue in our efforts as best as possible until people begin to understand what needs to be done here, not just for the Yakama people, but for all people of the future.

And the treaty is alive and well. There are many people that truly misunderstand what the treaty means to us. To us it is as long as a mountain stands, the river flows, the grass shall grow, the sun shall shine, etc. For good reason is that we do not wish to assimilate to the mainstream of society. We can live side by side. We can utilize modern technology and help preserve and protect the culture of the Yakama.

And that's the efforts that we have influenced some of many of the younger generation to get the education. We have four interns every year in our program. And those interns are very interested in the environmental issues. And we hope that they can eventually replace the PhDs and the Master's degrees people that we depend upon that are non-Indian. But many of the non-Indians that assist us have been a tremendous help. We are in deep debt to these people. Their conscience has allowed them to come work for us and try to influence, under the holistic approach of environmental management, the eventual return of the integrities of the environment here, so that people can again live in harmony with the resources and with the land and the environment.

The Columbia River is the lifeline of the Pacific Northwest. It has been such since the beginning of time. And now, for instance, you have a study by the Environmental Protection Agency [EPA] finished last August and released that says, "The indigenous people have one chance in fifty of getting cancer from the chemicals if we continue to eat the fish from the Columbia, especially around the Hanford area," as we have in the past.

And so it makes you wonder: equity, fairness. When the national statistics and numbers are used, like ten to the minus six is one cancer in one million. Ten to the minus four is one cancer in one hundred thousand. Under the law, if there is one cancer in ten thousand, something must be done.

But after this release, we asked the EPA what they were going to do about this. And they asked, "Well, what do you want us to do?" Well, it's obvious: we would like to have it corrected. They said, "We don't have any money." If this happened in the suburbs of New York or Cincinnati, it would have been cleaned up yesterday.

And so there is this seeming unfairness, along with the attempts in a paranoiac way that many of us have, that, you know, there is this consistency to assimilate us into the mainstream of society.

But we cling to our ways; we will continue to do so. The fish is going to continue to be the leading food among our people, and behind that will be the deer and the elk and the foods out of the ground and the berries. And there are tremendous amounts of food out there—at least 70 different types—and equal amount of medicines that have sustained us for centuries.

And now all this is affected. And I think there should be funds provided by the government to investigate all of this. Instead there are piecemeal efforts and no real concerted effort to involve the Yakama Nation on a true government to government basis on the situation. We are a sovereign nation. We out-rank the state of Washington in sovereignty, and yet we are treated like third-class people. And all this is related to your basic question: "What does the land mean to us?" All of this is tied together to our sovereignty, our government, our culture, our religion—all tied to the foods and medicines, our language, our way of life.

The land, because of the Manhattan Project and the boundary that encircles what is now the Hanford Nuclear Reservation, has provided some protection to the archeological sites and some of the gravesites. But there had been a lot of looting, especially by the workers on weekends, throughout the years past. Much of the graves around here have been disturbed. There were pot-hunters galore—it used to be a weekend past-time.

And so although there has been sort of a protection, because of the creation of the reservation here, there is the other side of the coin, where there is a tremendous amount of releases into the environment. There was twelve million curies of radioisotopes going into the river for years. And there are something to the tune of eleven billion cubic yards of material out there that need to be administered to, enough to fill up 300 Empire State buildings.

And so as the fire of 2000—for instance, an occurrence of that nature—someone said, "There's plutonium in the soil." And we said, "My God, what does that mean? How much?" He says, "Well, it could be at safe levels." But I learned a long time ago that one-millionth of a gram of plutonium that you would ingest into your lung, and you have problems. And there has not yet been a true answer to us, a good answer, as to how much plutonium is in the soil. We know there are contaminants in the soil, in the vegetation. It was admitted by the Department of Energy many years back. And so consequently, the 1980 fire, for instance, carried away much of those radioisotopes, especially to the east, to the down-winders. And so the effects on the land has been horrendous, but to what extent we do not know. And even though some may feel it's not been harmed, there is no proof that it hasn't or has. We would like to have answers.

And there has been studies, but there has been contrasts also. Battelle says they have scientific studies on the river and they say everything's fine. If so, then how come the EPA came out with this study that says there is one chance in fifty of getting cancer from very contaminated salmon and fish? And so what we would like to see in the future would be a true coordinated effort with the Yakama Nation. Now the federal government and each administration in the last few administrations said, "We must work with these indigenous people on a government-to-government basis," but there have been different definitions of that. And we need truly to sit down at the front end of any major project and discuss, so that we don't run into problems after the decisions are made.

And to rectify or to resolve those problems, a lot of times there are court cases, like the one recently where the Department of Energy wanted to reclassify the waste. And the judge says, "No, you must go by what the definition of the Nuclear Waste Policy Act says." Relative to that to us, that means you start to have to characterize some land, some soil, some vegetation, to determine what is clean and what is not clean. And they do ask the question, how clean is clean?

Now we're back to this relativeness of, you know, some people are trying to imply the Yakama Nation wants it pristine. We know that's not a possibility in the near future. But we want it at least to a point where eventually in the near future, as the NRC, the Nuclear Regulatory Commission, has in their rules and regulations after one hundred years, there will be unrestricted use.

47

"The Sovereign Expression of Native Self-Determination" (2003)[14]

J. Kēhaulani Kauanui

Kanaka Maoli (Native Hawaiians) have always considered the overthrow of the Kingdom of Hawai'i and the incorporation of the islands into the United States a gross violation of sovereignty. Whether reconciliation could ever be achieved remained an open question throughout the twentieth century. In 1993 Congress took some responsibility for the past by issuing a formal Apology Resolution. The succeeding years saw Hawai'i's senators champion legislation to recognize Native Hawaiians as "American Indians" and to extend the federal government's trust relationship to them. Each iteration, and there have been several, has proved divisive. Some Kanaka Maoli support recognition, arguing that it serves as a necessary, if not fully satisfactory, first step toward restoring sovereignty. The following document clarifies the position taken by nationalists opposed to incorporative legislation. Consider how Kanaka Maoli scholar J. Kēhaulani Kauanui called upon a history of resistance, distinguished between racial and political identities, and articulated a different vision of citizenship and belonging to test the limits of sovereignty.[15]

The current draft of the bill S. 344 proposes to recognize Hawaiians as an indigenous people who have a "special trust relationship" with the United States and, hence, a right to self-determination under U.S. federal law. The passage of the bill would lay the foundation for a nation-within-a-nation model of self-governance, like that of over three hundred federally recognized American Indian tribal nations—as a domestic dependent nation. But dozens of Hawaiian sovereignty groups have persistently and consistently rejected the application of U.S. federal Indian law that would recognize a Hawaiian domestic dependent nation "as ward to guardian" under the plenary power of Congress.

Senator Akaka[16] has described the proposal as the reconciliation piece of legislation he spearheaded nearly a decade ago which amounted to an apology by the U.S. to the Hawaiian people for its role in the overthrow of the Kingdom of Hawai'i. But there are severe contemporary conditions that serve as forces for the proposal regarding federal recognition of Hawaiians. The U.S. Supreme Court ruling in the case of *Rice v. Cayetano* in February 2000 prompted the legislation. In the case, the court held in favor of Harold F. Rice, a fourth generation white resident of Hawai'i who was denied the right to vote. He was turned away because, identifying as a white American, he is not Hawaiian by any statutory definition. This was a case about Hawaiian-only elections for trustees of the Office of Hawaiian Affairs. Since the Office's inception in 1978, trustee elections were limited to residents of Hawai'i who are of Hawaiian ancestry but without any minimum blood criterion. The U.S. Supreme Court's majority opinion decreed that the state's electoral restriction—limited to Hawaiians—enacted race-based voting qualifications and violated the 15th Amendment's guarantee that the right of citizens to vote shall not be denied or abridged on account of race, color or previous condition of servitude. . . .

Now, while the majority opinion in *Rice v. Cayetano* did not rule on the 14th Amendment (and so did not affect the actual trust that the Office of Hawaiian Affairs is meant to manage), there are now several more lawsuits in motion. These suits threaten the very existence of all Hawaiian-specific funding sources and institutions—based on plaintiffs' charges that they are unconstitutional and racially discriminatory, and so violate the equal protection clause of the U.S. Constitution. These lawsuits call into question the Office of Hawaiian Affairs, all federal funds for Hawaiian health, education, and housing, the state Department of Hawaiian Home Lands, and the lands they manage, based on the 1920 Hawaiian Homes Commission Act (which is also being challenged). Within this context of assault, many Hawaiians and their allies support Akaka's proposal for federal recognition because it is understood as a protective measure against these lawsuits.

Some people think we need this legislation to protect Hawaiian entitlements from future lawsuits like what we saw in *Rice v. Cayetano*. Those same advocates have faith that federal recognition would redefine Hawaiians as a political entity and so challenges of "racial" distinctions would be moot in terms of equal protection under the U.S. Constitution. But it is clear to me that there is no guarantee whatsoever that federal recognition for Hawaiians would guarantee that protection. It seems more likely that this limited model would be more like those of over 200 Alaska Native villages—where the U.S. Supreme Court has already ruled that their lands do not constitute "Indian Country" and the current Administration is attempting to remove the villages from the Department of Interior's list of indigenous self-governing entities. It is not at all clear that the passage of S. 344 bill would protect anything at all for Hawaiians. But it is guaranteed that the federal recognition will not provide for our claims under international law. Supporting S. 344 or any bill akin to it would ultimately severely limit assertions of Hawaiian sovereign self-determination by containing them within a U.S. federal framework. A self-governing model provided by the bill would be no more than a domestic dependent entity under the full and exclusive plenary power of Congress.

Indeed, Section 1(1) of the bill states: "The Constitution vests Congress with the authority to address the conditions of the indigenous, native people of the United States." For any bill Hawaiian federal recognition to pass, it would have to include some claim that Congress has plenary power over Native Hawaiians under the commerce clause of the Constitution, in order for it to pass constitutional muster. But that is precisely the problem: the proposal minimizes the political and legal spheres inherent in the sovereign expression of native self-determination and does not account for the need and application of United Nations and international law in the domestic arena.

Furthermore, S. 344 undercuts what the 1993 Apology Resolution already acknowledges. In the Apology Resolution, Public Law (103–150), S. J. Res. 19, United States government admitted guilt to the Hawaiian people for its role in the illegal and armed overthrow of Queen Lili'uokalani and the Kingdom of Hawai'i in 1893. . . . I say illegally because the United States never upheld U.S. constitutional law or international law when it purportedly annexed Hawai'i. There was no treaty of annexation. . . .

Under President McKinley, pro-annexationists proposed a joint-Senate resolution even though to admit Hawai'i this way as a new territory (and not a state) violated the U.S. Constitution. With a joint-senate resolution, all that was needed was a simple majority in both houses of Congress. And so the Newlands Resolution passed in 1898. One hundred years later, in 1998, the United Nations issued the findings of a nine-year treaty study and called the annexation of Hawai'i into legal question. More specifically, it assessed that the so-called annexation is invalid.[17]

. . . Hawaiians continue to contest to the problematic process by which Hawai'i became a state. Like many other colonial territories, in 1946 Hawai'i was inscribed onto the United Nations list of Non-Self-Governing Territories. And as such, Hawai'i was eligible for decolonization under international law. However, the United States—in clear violation of U.N. policies and international law at the time and existing through the present—predetermined statehood as the status for Hawai'i. . . .

The U.S. Apology does not mention this history of the illegal annexation or the details of so-called statehood. But it does include some very strong language, admissions, and findings of fact. On November 28, 1993, the U.S. Congress issued this apology in a joint-senate resolution, now Public Law 103–150. Specifically, the U.S. government apologized to the Hawaiian people for its role in the illegal, armed overthrow of Queen Lili'uokalani and the Kingdom of Hawai'i in 1893. The Apology maintains, "the indigenous Hawaiian people never directly relinquished their claims to their inherent sovereignty as a people or over their national lands to the United States, either through their monarchy or through a plebiscite or referendum." But the current proposal for federal recognition refuses to acknowledge our inherent sovereignty as a people over our national lands. At the very least, these lands are the Kingdom Crown and Government Lands (now unfortunately better known as the so-called "ceded" lands), amounting to 1.8 million acres of land.

Nonetheless, the Apology Resolution is a finding of fact. Importantly, this resolution defines "native Hawaiian" as "any individual who is a descendant of the aboriginal people who, prior to 1778, occupied and exercised sovereignty in the area that now constitutes the State of Hawai'i." As many of you know, 1778 is the year Captain Cook first arrived in the island archipelago. Hence, that year marks a time when it is assumed that there was no one other than Hawaiians present in these Islands. The way that "native Hawaiian" is defined here is the most inclusive statutory definition of a Hawaiian person; it makes no reference to any blood quantum minimum or state residency requirement. Aside from this all-encompassing definition of indigeneity for Hawaiian people, the apology was not extended to those who are not Hawaiian but who also endured the legacy of the overthrow—namely, those descendants of other citizens of the Kingdom of Hawai'i.

Hawaiian Kingdom sovereignty was not lost via conquest, cession, or adjudication. And, in addition, the Hawaiian people's loss of self-determination at no time amounted to a legal termination of indigenous inherent sovereignty. With regard to these claims under international law, one need only read the current federal proposal to see the fine line being negotiated between indigenous and national claims. Indeed, within S.344, there are internal contradictions and problems. For example, the language reveals how the drafters of the bill need the history of the overthrow to justify the right for Hawaiians to have federal recognition. While the 1893 marker provides a timeline tied to Hawaiian sovereignty, it complicates any definition that is exclusively aboriginal. So then, it should not come as a surprise that the definition specifically references both the overthrow date and the status of aboriginality. But to take the history of the over-throw seriously calls the model of federal recognition itself into question as the solution. And, the specific requirement that one also be the lineal descendant of a Hawaiian also works to limit broader sovereignty claims that could be made not only by Hawaiians but also by any lineal descendant of a Kingdom citizen. This containment of the sovereignty claim staves off demands for Hawai'i's independence and decolonization from the United States, based on international law, for both Hawaiian people and others. Federal protection is now being sold to Hawaiians as a defense against average citizens who challenge the Hawaiian trusts that the United States has never upheld in the first place; a trust that itself is based on the theft of a nation. . . .

In Hawai'i today, the independence claims can be roughly divided into two different categories—decolonization and de-occupation. One centers on the political process of decolonization under U.N. protocols while the other centers on the restoration of the Kingdom of Hawai'i based on the law of nations and The Hague Regulations. These two projects differ from pushing for the rights if indigenous peoples under international law. In the Hawaiian context, activists who support the rights of indigenous peoples at the U.N. tend to also support U.S. federal recognition for a Hawaiian governing entity, and so that work cannot fairly be described as pro-independence.

Hawaiians are being compelled by the state to support federal recognition to protect indigenous-specific funding sources and institutions, but at the expense of the total independence claim. Senator Akaka has claimed, "We must not let this window of opportunity close." But our sovereignty cannot fit through any old window. While some scramble to keep a window open, the federal government could forever close its doors to an independent nation. This is why the voice of Hawaiians-at-large rings a resounding "no consent!" Hawaiian sovereignty and self-determination are inherent—as acknowledged in the U.S. Apology Resolution—and, therefore, cannot be legislated by the United States.

48

"I Will Not Rest Till Justice Is Achieved" (2005)[18]

Elouise Cobell

One of the great ironies of federal-Indian relations became undeniably clear at the beginning of the twenty-first century. The Bureau of Indian Affairs, an agency established to administer programs for peoples perceived as incapable of managing their own affairs, was revealed to be utterly incompetent. Indians had consistently complained about the misappropriation, poor accounting, and outright theft of tribal trust funds and Individual Indian Money Accounts. But these issues exploded into public view in 1996 when Elouise Cobell (1945–2011), a Blackfeet citizen and founder of the first tribally owned national bank, served as lead plaintiff in a suit that called for a full accounting of the trust funds. The government's response was stunning. After failing to comply with court orders, the Interior Department revealed that it did not know how much was owed or to whom. In 2010 Congress passed legislation to carry out a negotiated settlement worth $3.4 billion. In this document, Cobell recounts the history of the suit and what motivated her to take on what must have seemed like an impossible mission.[19]

I am here today on behalf of myself and the more than 500,000 individual Indian trust beneficiaries represented in the lawsuit we filed in the Federal court, *Cobell v. Norton*. I would also like to explain to you that the Blackfeet pray at the Baker massacre on a yearly basis and we pray that the Federal Government will never treat us like they treated us then.[20] I also pray on a daily basis going to work on the Blackfeet Reservation at Ghost Ridge where 500 Blackfeet died of starvation because the Indian agent withheld rations.

So, I apologize to you if I hurt the committee's feelings when I explained what I felt about S. 1439, but that is the only way that I could express myself because I have to tell you that it has been a very difficult task in making the U.S. Government accountable for individual Indian beneficiaries. I did not want to be in a 9-year lawsuit. I think this could have been over very quickly if the U.S. Government would admit that they could not give an accounting to individual Indian beneficiaries. . . . In the 50 principles, the Work Group put forward a reasonable and well-founded aggregate settlement amount of $27.487 billion. This is not reparations. This is not damages, nor is it welfare. It is quite simply a return of a portion of the money that was and is being taken from us. . . .[21]

Let me reiterate what I have said in prior testimony, there is nothing I would like more than a quick and just resolution to this lawsuit. We are in the tenth year of this litigation. Because of obstruction and delay by government counsel—for which they have been repeatedly sanctioned—justice has been delayed for individual trust beneficiaries. Delay and obstruction is not in our interest. Understand though that trust beneficiaries I have spoken with have—to a person—told me that they want a fair resolution, even if it takes a little longer. They do not want to be sacrificed on the altar of political expediency as they have so many times before.

Since 1887, members of the class have been subjected to injustice after injustice. Report after report for generation after generation have cited the rampant mismanagement and malfeasant administration of the Individual Indian Trust. As you know a congressional report from 1915 spoke about this scandal in terms of "fraud, corruption, and institutional incompetence almost beyond the possibility of comprehension." A 1989 Investigative Report of this Committee also found similar fraud and corruption. In 1992, the Misplaced Trust Report from the House Committee on Government Operations made similar findings of malfeasance. The Court of Appeals described the disastrous historic and continuing management of individual Indian property as "malfeasance"—not misfeasance or nonfeasance, but malfeasance—and held further in 2001 that the continuing delay was "unconscionable." Most recently [in 2005], the Federal District Court Judge Royce C. Lamberth—a former Justice Department senior official, appointed to the bench by President Ronald Reagan—who has presided over this case for nearly a decade—appropriately described the utter failure to reform by the Interior Department and continuing abuse of the Indian beneficiaries in this way in a recent opinion:

"For those harboring hope that the stories of murder, dispossession, forced marches, assimilationist policy programs, and other incidents of cultural genocide against the Indians are merely the echoes of a horrible, bigoted government - past that has been sanitized by the good deeds of more recent history, this case serves as an appalling reminder of the evils that result when large numbers of the politically powerless are placed at the mercy of institutions engendered and controlled by a politically powerful few. It reminds us that even today our great democratic enterprise remains unfinished. And it reminds us, finally, that the terrible power of government, and the frailty of the restraints on the exercise of that power, are never fully revealed until government turns against the people.

"The entire record in this case tells the dreary story of Interior's degenerate tenure as Trustee-Delegate for the Indian trust—a story shot through with bureaucratic blunders, flubs, goofs and foul-ups, and peppered with scandals, deception, dirty tricks and outright villainy—the end of which is nowhere in sight."

I could not have said it better. This property was taken from Indians to be held in trust in 1887 because the US government thought it could do a better job of managing it than Indians themselves. By setting up the trust, the government promised to abide by common trust laws—like investing the property profitably and providing an accounting to the beneficiaries. As you and many others have recognized, the government has made a criminal mess of the situation, and it has only gotten worse over the years. It has failed even the most simple of trustee duties. It is shocking to say, but the government cannot even say how much money is in each beneficiary's account.

Imagine the outrage if suddenly a major US financial institution were to announce that it had no idea how much money was in each depositor's account. Imagine the headlines. Imagine the congressional hearings, the class action lawsuits that would be filed as a result. Heads would surely roll on Wall Street.

Yet that's exactly what has happened here. In the nine years that our lawsuit has been proceeding, we've won on virtually every single substantive point. Both Judge Lamberth and the Court of Appeals have agreed with us that the government has done a despicable job—that it has completely failed us—the individual Indians. Understand the extent that we have prevailed. The government argued that they had no duty to account for our money prior to 1994. The District Court and Court of Appeals agreed with us that they did have such a duty and that they would have to account for "all funds." The Courts held that the duty to account "preexisted" the 1994 Trust Fund Reform Act. The Courts have also held that the government is in breach of its trust duties. They have held that interest and imputed yields are owed the beneficiary class. The Courts have rejected the government's position that the Courts have limited remedial powers and that this suit is controlled by the limitations—such as deferential review—of the Administrative Procedures Act. The government's position that the statute of limitations limits the accounting back to 1984 has been repudiated as well. The government has challenged the court's jurisdiction; they lost that one too. Time after time on major issue after major issue, the Courts have made clear that the law and the facts are on our side. These have been hard won victories, nine years of brutal litigation that has taken its toll on those of us involved. But we will not sell out individual Indian beneficiaries—we have worked too hard to get where we are.

One would have thought that our government's response to the wholesale repudiation of its case time and again would have resulted in reforms, acquiescence to the rule of law and obedience to Court orders. Sadly, it hasn't. Instead, government officials have continued what the Court of Appeals has termed their "record of agency recalcitrance and resistance to the fulfillment of its legal duties" and "intransigent" conduct. Further, not satisfied with flouting orders, government officials have attempted to vilify the Court itself. They—along with certain allies in Congress—have tried to paint the District Judge as a rogue. What is the evidence? There is none. No court filing nor even the whispered slander has identified any fact that Judge Lamberth got wrong. The Court has—similar to the Court of Appeals—simply called a spade a spade and cited the government's routine and continuing utter disregard for the law.

To be sure, this case continues to be about mismanagement, breach of trust and the victimized Indian beneficiaries—abused by a century of dishonorable dealings. But this case has become something else as well—it has become about the Judiciary attempting to bring an intransigent executive branch into compliance with its crystal clear fiduciary duties and the things that certain Executive Branch officials will do to keep business as usual.

Because of the government's legendary, obstructionist tactics in this case, it has taken nine years to get to this point, and who knows really how long it will take to get to a judgment. Again, don't take my word for it; listen to the words of the judge: "Despite the breadth and clarity of the record, Interior continues to litigate and relitigate, in excruciating fashion, every minor, technical legal issue. This is yet another factor forestalling the final resolution of the issues in this case and delaying the relief Indians so desperately need."

Because of the government's position in this litigation, we can be assured that we will be litigating for years before we see victory. We are quite willing to do so if necessary, but we would like to find a way to bring the case to a just resolution sooner if possible. We are simply losing too many elders who have waited a lifetime for this debacle to be corrected. Every time one of them dies, my heart breaks. They should see this fixed in their lifetime. . . .

I say these things because I have an obligation—a fiduciary obligation—to represent the many other individual Indians out there who rely on me. Like Mary Johnson, a Navajo grandmother who relies almost exclusively on the few dollars from her allotment she receives to support herself and her family. She receives pennies of what a non-Indian is paid for the gas from her land. Or Mary Fish, a seventy-year old Creek woman, who cannot replace the windows in her small home because she lacks the fund yet there are five oil wells that have been pumping constantly for decades on her land. There are so many more—across every reservation, grandmothers and grandfathers, parents and children all suffering the same indignities of their forebears. And why? Because, in the end, people in Washington have always cared more about their own parochial interest than the Indian beneficiaries. The powerful have always assured that the gravy train for corporations—oil companies, gas companies, timber companies—doesn't stop. Too many have been willing to cut the expedient deal, despite the negative affect of beneficiaries.

I won't do that. I've promised too many that I will not rest till justice is achieved. We have been in this for nine years and I want an end, but I am prepared to fight for as long as it takes to achieve fairness—to make this right. A century of "fraud, corruption and institutional incompetence" is enough. . . . We have vigorously pursued litigation because we want resolution. We do not care if achieving fairness and stopping abuse of individual Indian beneficiaries comes through litigation, mediation or a settlement act, or arbitration for that matter. The means are unimportant. What is important is that we do so quickly and fairly.

I look forward to continuing our work together to finally and conclusively put an end to the criminal administration of our trust property. We have a chance right now to stop this "fraud, corruption, and institutional incompetence" that has pervaded the system for a century. We will not rest until that is completed and we pledge to work with you to get that done. With help from this Committee, we can make sure that the abuse present since 1887 is not still present in 2007.

49

"An Organization, a Club, or Is It a Nation?" (2007)[22]

Osage Constitutional Reform Testimony

During the early 2000s, the Cherokee Nation created an uproar when it disenfranchised Cherokee Freedmen who did not descend from individuals listed as "Cherokee by Blood" on their allotment rolls. While advocates of the Freedmen couched the debate in terms of racism, civil rights, and treaty violations, supporters of exclusion viewed it as acting upon the inherent sovereign power to determine citizenship. Other tribes across Indian Country engaged the same question of what it means to be and belong to an indigenous nation—and who decides. In some communities, revenue from gaming and natural resources intensified the controversy and led to disenrollment. This document provides a window into how the Osages set about drafting a new constitution to replace one built around a select group of shareholders of the Osage Mineral Estate (some of whom were not Osage). Consider how the following series of comments by Osages regarding citizenship criteria in the new constitution reveals ongoing conversations in Native America about indigeneity, being, belonging, and the relationship between race, blood, and nation.[23]

Those Opposed to a Blood-Quantum Requirement for Tribal Membership

"I think that there should be no blood quantum. If we stop now and try to clean up our roll, it is going to bog us down and we'll be bogged down for the next 50 years and never accomplish a thing and not get a membership. . . . If you take another tribe, say across the river, the Poncas. . . . Right now they are dealing with lowering their membership quantum. I think that all the tribes are going to have to do that eventually if they have one set at one quarter because we are living in a time period where people marry other races and other tribes and so the bloodlines are really thinning out."

"It (citizenship) is who you are culturally and socially, I think. To me blood has very little to do with it. We have people that live right here that, or maybe I should say, people that live away from here who are more Osage than some people that live right here in the community because those people are recognized as Osages, culturally."

"It is important to remember that Indian Nationhood is not a racial or ethnic matter, it is a political status. So blood quantum should be irrelevant. Being Osage is more of a state of mind; it is being part of a community. . . ."

"The blood issue that seems to come up in every Indian Nation is a slippery slope for our people. This is a white man's game. We as original human beings never thought of blood; we thought of family and deeds. We adopted others into our tribe and treated them with love and respect as equals. There are no full bloods, so by thinking of degrees of blood then there are no more Osage people either. I feel that blood degree is a form of discrimination. We need to be Indians not white Indians."

Support for a Blood-Quantum Requirement

"By 1906 clearly it was obvious that if you could get on the roll it might pay off, which of course it did. So I would say as a personal thing I would think that the 1901 roll would be more reliable as to who was more likely to be culturally identified as Osage. By 1906 it is pretty demonstrable that a number of people who are on the 1906 role are not of Osage blood."

"Let's face it, you ought to be Osage to be a member of the Osage tribe. But if they can prove that you're not, then why do you want to be part of our tribe. . . . If you want to be a member of the tribe you should be of Osage blood."

"There are some families that go around here and say that they know they are not Osage. But they said they sure will use what we give them. I believe not all are like that, but I just feel that when you have a tribe and membership that it should be by blood. Yes, they did adopt a lot in the Osage Tribe. I just don't think that it is right that they get a vote or anything when our own Osage children don't get much not because of how many of the adopted ones and people that were on by fraud get the same as in Osage by blood. I am not saying people can't feel like they are Osage. It is different to feel than to actually be an Osage by blood. I have several friends that are really not Osage, and I feel that they are taking away from my children. I am not trying to make anyone mad but just telling my feelings on it. . . ."

"Is this an organization, a club or is it a nation and tribe? Is this an organization just out there to make money or out there, or is it a tribe. Blood quantum is encouraging, blood quantum is what it does is encourage, it doesn't. . . . You have a choice, everybody has a choice, but it encourages marrying back into the tribe, if you don't that's what's going to happen. . . ."

Other Views

"I would strongly support a decision to allow 'blood quantum/degree of Osage blood' to determine the amount of vote a tribal member possesses. For example, if a member is 1/4 Osage, this would mean that he/she possesses one 1/4 of a vote, 1/8 Osage blood would equal 1/8 vote and so forth. This would not limit membership to any person and would give voting privilege to all. In addition, as many of you are aware, the original allottee roll contained the names of individuals who were not of Osage descent and who were otherwise frequently listed as tribal members. Therefore, the descendants of the non-Osages should not be allowed to acquire membership. . . ."

"I believe we should only let those who live on Osage Reservation vote on Reform decisions."

"I think we should utilize all the scientific methods that are available to us today. And if we really have a question about blood quantum, why don't we utilize DNA. That might have some very interesting outcomes."

"I think in terms of benefits and such that full bloods, 3/4 bloods, half bloods, and so on should get FIRST PRIORITY. If a full blood and a 1/32 blood both apply for housing the full blood should get it first. I know many people think this is wrong, but facts are facts, people. The full bloods are our last remaining link to our past. These people's blood is not mixed, it is pure Osage. I think that is important."

"My idea of what's an Osage is somebody that goes to the church, helps out at the Inlonshka and wants to learn the language. And we've got a tribe of around 18–20,000 Osages, and we don't have but 180 that want to learn the language. Then you look at all these people that say they're Osage, but they never help out drum keepers, and then you never see them in a church, you hardly ever see them at a hand-game, but yet they're wanting blood quantum, and if they want a blood quantum, they ought to practice what we do. But instead just a few of us are trudging on trying to keep it going. To be an Osage, you have to have 3 things. You have to have land base, then you have to have language, then you also have to have culture."

"I would propose that mixed-bloods (of whatever degree is decided on) would be required to register in person at Inlonshka every 4 years between the ages of 21 and 50 or 55, unless serving in the armed services abroad (or perhaps Osages living out of the country?). . . ."

"I will one day be a shareholder, when it is my turn, because my family held on to their headrights. Those who gave their headrights away have no right to change the existing government or any part of the mineral estate. Only the shareholders should be allowed to vote. Our government should not be changed to suit those who have not maintained their connection to the tribe."

50

"The Gwich'in Are Caribou People" (2011)[24]

Sarah Agnes James

Neither the Anti-Discrimination Act of 1945 nor the advent of statehood in 1959 resolved Alaska Native land claims. Renewed pressure to act attended the discovery of oil on the Arctic coast and proposals for a pipeline to transport it across disputed areas. In 1971 the Alaska Native Claims Settlement Act quieted title to a huge swath of land and divided an additional 90 million acres among twelve regional corporations composed of hundreds of Alaska Native villages. Calls for drilling in the Arctic National Wildlife Refuge, which contained Gwich'in ancestral lands, crescendoed during the early 2000s. In the midst of economic collapse and an energy crisis, advocates argued that drilling would bring jobs and energy independence. Opponents focused on protecting the pristine wilderness area, a position that gained the support of President Barack Obama in early 2015. Consider how Sarah Agnes James, chairperson of the Gwich'in Steering Committee, framed the issue as a matter of identity, sovereignty, human rights, international law, and sacred land in this 2011 testimony.[25]

I am honored to speak on behalf of this Committee for my nation, which is Gwich'in Nation. I feel real honored to be here. English is my second language, so I will address to you and translate it in my language back to English. I will speak Gwich'in. English is my second language. . . .

I say: We came a long ways. We all came a long ways. We still have a long ways to go. On behalf of the elders that cannot be here today, and on behalf of the children that is not yet born, my people have been traveling all over the country trying to tell a story about a special place in the world, which is *Iizhik Gwats'an Gwandaii Goodlit*, "sacred place where life begins." We do that for our future generation. . . .

The Gwich'in are caribou people. Caribou is our main food, it is in our tools and clothes and songs and stories and beadwork. We have lived right here with the caribou for hundreds of generations and will stay right far into the future. There are maybe 7,000 of us, mostly living in 15 small communities and villages scattered across northeast Alaska and the northwest corner of Canada. We are among the most remote and most traditional people in America.

The Gwich'in Steering Committee was created by resolution of our Chiefs in 1988 at the first gathering of all our people in more than 100 years—the Gwich'in Niintsyaa. Our job is to speak with one voice for all our Gwich'in people on the caribou issue. The Chiefs gave us two directions:

- to tell the world about the caribou and the Gwich'in way of life, and what oil development would mean for the Gwich'in; and
- to do it in a good way.

So, Mr. Chairman, I am especially honored to be here today to carry out this important task for my Chiefs and my people.

We respect the difficult job you have. We know about the problems of jobs and energy. In Arctic Village we only have jobs in the summer, and there are not enough to go around, so we know what it is like to be unemployed and to worry about how to pay our bills.

We also know about energy problems. In Arctic Village everything is flown in. If you have a 4-wheeler or snow-machine, you will pay about $15/gallon for gas. Fuel for electric generators is flown in too, so electricity is really expensive. I'm not complaining, I love my life, but we do know what it means to have a "deficit" when life is expensive. But in the winter you can't just turn out the lights. You have to get the money to pay the bills. Go to town to get a job, or raise taxes. You have to keep the lights on at home.

The idea of waiting to pay the bills for 10 or 15 years while you hope to find oil in the Arctic Wildlife Refuge is backwards. People need to go to work now. Our country, our government needs to fix our schools and roads and towns, and find a way to meet new needs like icebreakers - not 10 or 20 years from now, but now. If it costs more money, we will pay our fair share. To go on pretending you can just cut costs without ruining our country is not telling the truth.

But the question of oil development in the Arctic National Wildlife Refuge is not just about money and oil. It is about the most basic human rights of the Gwich'in. For the Gwich'in, this is a simple issue: Oil development in the birthplace and nursery grounds of the Porcupine (River) Caribou Herd would hurt the caribou and threaten the culture and way of life of my people and the viability of our communities.

We know the coastal plain of the Arctic National Wildlife Refuge as *Iizhik Gwats'an Gwandaii Goodlit*, "the Sacred Place Where Life Begins." After migrating 400 miles and giving birth, the mother caribou cannot be disturbed at this time, and our people may not go there then. The cows and their calves will move from place to place to find the cotton-grass and other new green sprouts they need to recover their strength and feed their calves. Depending on weather, the prime area for feeding might change from year to year, especially for the first weeks. Sometimes when snows are deep the caribou are born in Canada, but studies of radio-collared caribou show that as soon as she can, the mother caribou will lead her calf onto the Arctic Refuge's coastal plain. From what we know, every Porcupine caribou gets their start in life right there, at *Iizhik Gwats'an Gwandaii Goodlit*.

When oil development around Prudhoe Bay came close to the calving grounds of the Central Arctic Caribou Herd, the cows and their calves were pushed away onto new calving- and nursery grounds. Because there was lots of good ground, this did not hurt them and those caribou prospered.

The problem for Porcupine caribou is, in the Arctic Refuge the mountains come close to the Arctic Ocean—and the coastal plain is only a few miles wide. There are already more caribou per square mile on the Porcupine caribou calving and nursery grounds than almost any other caribou herd. If the caribou are disturbed they have nowhere to go. Caribou biologists believe oil development, or any large-scale disturbance and noise, risks displacement of cow and calve caribou from essential habitats, would likely hurt productivity, leading to declines, and possibly alter migration patterns.

These are the expected and unavoidable effects of oil development even if it is done right. This is not the risk we face if there is a spill or other large industrial accident.

As indigenous people, we have the right to continue our way of life, and that right is guaranteed by the International Covenant on Civil and Political Rights, signed by the President and Ratified by the Senate. Article 1 of that Covenant reads in part: "In no case may a people be deprived of their own means of subsistence."

The U.S. and Canadian governments signed an international agreement for management and long-term protection of the Porcupine Caribou Herd (Ottawa, July 17, 1987), forming the International Porcupine Caribou Commission (IPCC). The objectives of the agreement were: "To conserve the Porcupine Caribou Herd and its habitat through international cooperation and coordination so that the risk of irreversible damage or long-term adverse effects as a result of use of caribou or their habitat is minimized; To ensure opportunities for customary and traditional uses of the Porcupine Caribou Herd ; To enable users of Porcupine Caribou to participate in the international coordination of the conservation of the Porcupine Caribou Herd and its habitat; To encourage cooperation [and] communication among governments, users of Porcupine Caribou and others to achieve these objectives."

Much of the language used in this international (governments-to-governments) agreement admits and supports the Gwich'in human and cultural rights regarding caribou habitat. . . . There are other documents that support our claim, but it is the very simple human right to continue to live our lives on our traditional lands that I hope you will remember.

51

"I Want to Work for Economic and Social Justice" (2012)[26]

Susan Allen

Colonization and decolonization take many forms, including the ways in which a person imagines one's self and oneself in relation to others. Indeed, questions of being and belonging, so central to Native politics since 1887, revolved around these issues. And they, in turn, were informed by ideas regarding gender and sexuality. The ideal type "citizen" in the late nineteenth century, for instance, was not just racialized (white), gendered (male), and faithed (Christian), but also sexed (straight). Accordingly, Native conceptions of gender and sexuality were assaulted along with other aspects of indigenous identity. For some American Indians, then, decolonization involves not just a reckoning with blood, race, and national identity, but also the reclaiming of indigenous conceptions regarding gender and sexuality. Among the people making this argument is Susan Allen (1963–), a citizen of the Rosebud Sioux Tribe who in 2012 became the first lesbian American Indian to be elected to any state legislature. Consider, however, how Allen described her self and herself in relation to others as an American Indian, a lesbian, a lawyer, a progressive, and a representative of the people.[27]

I am a political newcomer. I am, however, a lifelong Democratic voter. I believe my progressive values are aligned with the DFL [Democratic-Farm-Labor] party's values of equality, opportunity and fairness. The DFL values are also consistent with my cultural values of generosity and inclusiveness. . . . I want to work for economic and social justice. In our community and in my district there are unmet needs. Half of the children live in poverty. There are disparities in wages, there is an educational achievement gap, and this is something I initially wanted to work on for tribes when I became an attorney.

I am a progressive candidate from a district in which I do not have to hide. I can be outspoken on a number of issues. I will be using my professional experience as an attorney who has designed tribal tax systems. When I entered this campaign, I was concerned about becoming part of an institution that is predominantly male and white, but there are many legislators committed to working for social and economic justice. I will be able to use my skills and my professional and life experiences to benefit my constituents, and the American Indian community in general. . . .

Going back [to the Rosebud and Pine Ridge Reservations] often and seeing that extreme poverty has had a huge impact on me. The conditions that American Indian people were living in [during] the 1960s and 1970s just seemed to me to be a struggle for political existence. Indian people were basically starving. It was a very, very dire situation. I saw this at a young age. My parents were very involved in organizing people to pay attention to American Indian people living in urban areas and reservations throughout the country. They fought discrimination, which they faced every day—in social settings like restaurants or in getting access to health care. . . .

I don't think we have come very far in alleviating the extreme poverty, high unemployment, low graduation rates, or high rates of alcoholism and drug abuse and crime on most reservations. I do believe that there are many positive aspects of reservation life, including strong kinship and community systems and the opportunity to live a more traditional way of life. There is also evidence that tribal governments have made some improvements regarding access to health care on reservations and that the quality of housing, water and sanitation has also improved. Nonetheless, I believe that economic development is extremely difficult due to the isolation of most reservations. We need to find new ways to finance infrastructure investments to support economic growth and improve the quality of life on reservations. . . .

I recall being bullied in school because of my race—mostly derogatory remarks about being Indian. I remember feeling angry, but I learned to not react. I credit my parents for instilling confidence in me, and teaching me that my self-worth was not tied to what others thought of me.

Once I made the decision [to come out as a lesbian at age thirty], it was very freeing. The response was wonderful. It was a turning point in my life. I was a young attorney, so there were some professional considerations as far as being out. The big difference now with all of this publicity is that not all of my clients knew. Your private life is not something you talk about with your clients, but I don't know if I could be any more out now. . . .

My family has been supportive from the very beginning, and my son handled it very well. I think each generation gets better. However, as a young girl, I was very aware of gender issues. And I recognized very early on the inequality based on gender. My parents were not traditional in terms of gender. I was never taught that I had limitations based on my gender. Those were barriers I could overcome. There were educational disadvantages and economic disadvantages that I could see and I could overcome those. I had the support of my family and the abilities to do that. . . .

Because I believe that all families deserve to be treated with respect, I intend to join the fight to defeat the proposed constitutional amendment in Minnesota to deny marriage equality to LGBT community members and families.[28] I also want to use my 2012 reelection campaign as a vehicle to bring out new voters who oppose writing discrimination into our state constitution. . . .

Something else to add to all of this is that I have been in recovery for the past twenty-three years, and alcohol is a problem in Indian communities. I have worked very hard to maintain my sobriety for twenty-three years. I would not be here today if it wasn't for that. I got sober when I was 25 years old, because I understood that I could have a better life. Essentially, I had an awakening that time was running out and I could no longer tolerate the physical, emotional and mental damage caused by my drug and alcohol abuse. I was fortunate to have people in my life who cared about me and helped me completely change the way I lived.

Being American Indian wasn't really an issue [in her campaign to get elected]; nor was being a lesbian. . . . I think it would have been difficult in any other district for me to get elected. This really does say a lot about our district. But as far as what this means for Indian women, an American Indian friend of mine, Daniel Yang, went to the state capitol and looked at the pictures and said, "I want to be a state representative," his African American friend told him, "You can't—look, they're all white."

He was devastated; and he volunteered for my campaign. He told me that when his daughter grows up, she will go to the state capitol to be able to see someone that looks like her—that is when I knew that what I'm doing is really important.

52

"I Could Not Allow Another Day of
Silence to Continue" (2012)[29]

Deborah Parker

Civil and criminal jurisdiction has served as one of the most important tests of the limits of sovereignty. Congress and the courts have attempted to discern where federal, state, and tribal laws begin and end in the context of everything from taxation to murder. Making matters more complex, jurisdiction shifts if the situation involves only Indians, only non-Indians, or both; whether it occurs on trust land matters, too. Among the most important debates is that on violence against women. According to national statistics, rates of rape, physical assault, and stalking of Native women exceed those for whites, African Americans, Hispanics, and Asians. Non-Native perpetrators of these crimes often elude justice because of the restrictions placed on tribal courts and a federal government that often seems unable or unwilling to prosecute. In 2012 Deborah Parker, vice chairperson of the Tulalip Tribes in Washington, provided testimony in support of reauthorizing the Violence Against Women Act and, in so doing, offered a window into the personal politics of sovereignty. A year later, Congress enacted compromise legislation. It limits tribal judicial power to pursue non-Indian perpetrators of sexual and domestic violence against Native women.[30]

I am here today to support the Violence Against Women Act. I was here on an environmental protection issue on Monday and did not plan on providing my story while at the nation's capital. However, I could not allow another day of silence to continue.

Yesterday I shared with Senator Murray the reasons why the Violence Against Women Act is so important to our Native American women. I did not expect that I would be sharing my own personal story.[31]

I am a Native American statistic. I am a survivor of sexual and physical violence. My story starts in the '70s as a toddler. You may wonder, how do I remember when this occurred? I was the size of a couch cushion—a red velvet approximately two-and-a-half feet couch cushion. One of the many girls violated and attacked by a man who had no boundaries or regards for a little child's life. My life.

The man responsible was never convicted. In the early '80s at a young age, I was asked to babysit my auntie's children. During the late hours of the evening, she arrived but was not alone. Instead of packing my things to go home, my sense was to quickly grab the children. . . . The four or five men who followed my auntie home raped her. I had to protect the children and hide. I could not save my auntie. I only heard her cries. Today is the first time that I have ever shared this story. She died at a young age. The perpetrators were never prosecuted.

During this time on our reservation, there was no real law enforcement. And because I know the life for a Native woman was short, I fought hard to attend college in the early '90s, and study criminal justice so I could be one to protect our women. However, I am only one. And we still have no real protection for women on our reservations.

In the late '90s I returned from college and began a program to help young female survivors. We have saved many lives during the creation of this program. However one of my girls, Sophia, was murdered on my reservation. By her partner. I still remember this day very strongly. And yet another one of our young girls took her life. A majority of our girls have struggled with sexual and domestic violence—not once, but repeatedly.

My question for Congress was, and has always been, why did you not protect me or my family? Why is my life, and the lives of so many other Native American women less important?

It is now 2012. I am urging Congress to uphold the US Constitution and honor US treaty agreements to provide protection, education, health, and safety of our indigenous men and women of this country. Please support the Violence Against Women Act, and send a strong message across the country that violence against Native American women is unlawful and is not acceptable in any of our lands.

Our tribal courts will work with you to ensure that violators are accountable and victims are made whole and well. . . . Thank you for listening to my story. I am blessed to be alive today. I send my love and prayers to all of the other victims and survivors of sexual and domestic violence.

53

"Indian Enough" (2013)[32]

Alex Pearl

Identity has always been a core issue in Native America. No less pressing, as the preceding documents attest, is the question of who decides. These issues matter because whose definition of being and belonging prevails carries real consequences for people's everyday lives. This can be seen clearly in the context of the Indian Child Welfare Act. Adopted in 1978, the legislation addressed the removal of American Indian children from Native families by investing tribal governments with the power to determine cases involving child custody. Advocates argued that this was necessary to address one of the most wrenching legacies of colonialism and to guarantee the future health of tribal nations. The limits of tribal jurisdiction, however, remained unclear. The act defined areas of exclusive jurisdiction according to residence and wardship status. But in cases involving concurrent jurisdiction, state governments earned a reputation for either ignoring tribal sovereignty or investing in its own courts the right to define whether a child had been born into an "existing Indian family." Consider how Chickasaw scholar Alex Pearl questioned the blood logic involved in a 2013 Supreme Court decision that prevented a Cherokee father from gaining custody of his child, "Baby Veronica."[33]

There are a lot of very good assessments of the *Adoptive Couple v. Baby Girl* decision, and I will not attempt to add to that thoughtful analysis of the holding. Instead, I'd like to focus on a different aspect of the Court's opinion, which is its misplaced and worrisome obsession with whether Veronica is Indian enough. While not the stated basis for the Court's decision, the repeated references to Veronica's percentage of Cherokee ancestry display a misunderstanding of tribal citizenship laws and (ironically, given the Court's color-blind bent) reinforce an inchoate racialization of Native people. The Court's message seems to be: if children like Veronica lack sufficient "Indian blood," they do not warrant the legal protections that their *political status* as American Indian tribal members otherwise affords.

What's in a number? More than you would think. Justice Alito began his majority opinion with this statement: "This case is about a little girl (Baby Girl) who is classified as an Indian because she is 1.2% (3/256) Cherokee." Thankfully, the Court references Baby Veronica's blood quantum by BOTH fraction and percentile for those math challenged readers. This has the effect of attempting to reiterate that Baby Veronica really isn't *that much of an Indian*, so this isn't really that big of a deal. Under Cherokee membership requirements, Veronica's so-called blood quantum is irrelevant, however. The *only* thing that matters is whether she descends from an ancestor on the Cherokee Nation's Dawes Roles. Justice Alito later acknowledges this, referencing Baby Veronica's "remote ancestor" which, again, attempts to delegitimize her Indian-ness.

However, Baby Veronica's actual quantum of blood is simply irrelevant, which Justice Sotomayor points out in her vigorous dissent. (slip op. at 23–24). The plain fact, which the Majority gets wrong, is that Baby Veronica is a Cherokee Indian—no matter the extent to which this fact challenges their own personal notions of who an Indian is and what an Indian looks like. She is a citizen of the Cherokee Nation. Her citizenship in the Cherokee Nation is not up for debate, diminution, or question. Indeed, this is one of the many purposes of the Indian Child Welfare Act, to prevent non-Indians from making these types of judgments about who is/isn't/might be/looks like an Indian.

The Majority's statement about the "low" percentage of blood attempts to make more palatable the idea of this Cherokee girl facing a likely increased difficulty in connecting with her tribal culture and tribal family. I say "likely" because my sincere hope is that wherever Baby Veronica is, she be given the opportunity to connect with her Cherokee community and engage with Cherokee culture. But, this is difficult because engaging with one's tribal community culture, I'll generalize briefly here, entails interaction with family. The presumptive adoptive parents may not be inclined to encourage Baby Veronica's connection to her biological father's family. This, I might add, was a fundamental purpose of the Indian Child Welfare Act—to protect tribal culture. This is perhaps another benefit of the Majority's use of "3/256," to try and differentiate the statute's purpose—protecting Indian children and tribal culture—from the facts of the current case, *i.e.* Baby Veronica isn't *really* an Indian.

Baby Veronica is, or is eligible for, enrollment as a citizen of the Chero-kee Nation of Oklahoma. By the way, the Cherokee Nation isn't like your local public library—not just anyone can join. It's like the United States. Not everyone can join us here—the U.S. has citizenship requirements. It would be unintelligible to say that someone is 3/256 American, right? You either are or are not a citizen of a nation. The usage of blood quantum in this way by the Majority conflates Indian identity and tribal citizenship. Scholars of all types (legal, humanities, and social sciences) continue to grapple with these concepts and recognize the entanglement of the racial and political. An example might help.

Some individuals may have a parent enrolled as a tribal citizen but the Tribe's citizenship criteria may be such that the child is not eligible for citizenship. Nonetheless, the non-citizen child lives in the tribal commu-nity, participates in cultural activity, and is by all accounts a member of the tribal community. The child identifies as an Indian, but is not a tribal citizen. This is not that radical of an idea. There are thousands of people in this country that recognize their underlying national heritage (speak the language, celebrate the national holidays, etc.) but are not eligible for citizenship in that country. I fully concede that this is an easy error to make. Furthermore, Indian identity politics, tribal enrollment (and disen-rollment) issues, and indigenous citizenship are extraordinarily complex and extremely sensitive. Professor Sarah Krakoff has an excellent article out that gives these concepts far better treatment than I have done here. These complexities, however, provide all the more reason for the Court to avoid becoming (needlessly) embroiled in them while perpetuating mis-conceptions about Indians. I make these observations to point out that there remains a fundamental and likely widespread misunderstanding, or innocent ignorance, of Indian-ness. . . .

I'll end on this brief personal note. I'm an enrolled member of the Chick-asaw Nation of Oklahoma, and grew up in Oklahoma. I have two young children and my hope is that they encounter the statement, "you don't look Indian," less than I did. That statement questions a person's Indian-ness in the exact same way the Majority utilizes Baby Veronica's blood quantum to delegitimize her status as an Indian. If they hear that less, it means we are moving in the right direction. The continuing misconceptions about Indian-ness are not going to go away anytime soon. But, I think that open discussions about the issues are essential to reform—even if we don't have the right answers yet. Such a process yields benefits to everyone, Indians and non-Indians alike.

54

"We Will Be There to Meet You" (2013)[34]

Armando Iron Elk and Faith Spotted Eagle

The Keystone Pipeline, a vast system that carries oil from Alberta, Canada, through the Dakotas and Nebraska and then branches into Illinois and Texas, traverses nearly 3,000 miles. Keystone XL, a proposed fourth phase, would add another 2,100 miles to the system and cut diagonally from Alberta, through the Bakken region in Montana, and end in Steele City, Nebraska. In getting there, the pipeline would cut through environmentally sensitive areas, including the vital Ogallala Aquifer. First Nations and American Indian activists allied to protest Keystone XL on a number of grounds including carbon dioxide emissions, the disruption of sacred and ancestral sites, and the potential for water contamination. In March 2012, the Black Hills Sioux Nation Treaty Council took direct action by establishing a blockade to prevent trucks carrying equipment for the pipeline from crossing through the Pine Ridge Reservation. Consider how, in this hearing before officials from the State Department in 2013, Lakota activists Armando Iron Elk Sr. and Faith Spotted Eagle called upon the sacredness of creation and treaties as living documents to condemn Keystone XL.[35]

Armando Iron Elk Sr. I am an elected Treaty Council official of the Ihanktonwan [*Iháŋkthuŋwaŋ*—Yankton, "(those) dwelling at the end"]. I present the Department of State with a copy of our new 2013 international treaty to protect the sacred against the tar sands and our resolve to stop this destruction of our land. I leave this message for you. We affirm that our laws define our solemn duty and responsibility to our ancestors, to ourselves, to our future generations. We will stand to protect the lands and waters of our homelands and collectively oppose tar sands projects of any land. We ask you to respect and leave our territories.

My great, great grandfather Smutty Bear, *Matȟó Sab'íč'iya* ["Smutty Bear"], signed two international treaties with the United States on behalf of the Ihanktonwan Oyate [*Iháŋkthuŋwaŋ Oyáte* "Yankton people, nation, tribe"]. These treaties are known as the 1851 and 1868 Fort Laramie Treaties. These treaties are legally binding on the United States, and they establish boundaries of the lands for the exclusive use of the Great Sioux Nation, Oceti Sakowin [*Očhéthi Šakówiŋ* "Seven Council Fires"]. The proposed Keystone XL Pipeline threatens to trespass through our treaty territory without our consent. This is illegal and some would say it's an act of war. I honor my grandfather today by saying no Keystone XL . . .

FAITH SPOTTED EAGLE. *Tȟuŋkáŋ Inážiŋ Wíŋ hé miyé kštó* ["I am Standing Stone (Woman)"]. My name is Standing Stone. I'm an elected official of the Treaty Council of the Ihanktonwan Oyate along the Missouri River in southeastern South Dakota.

Good morning, relatives. I bring you strong words and actions from the Ihanktonwan Treaty Council and the General Council and other elected officials that we reject this intrusion of any threats to our land, water and children and aboriginal and treaty lands of the Oceti Sakowin or Seven Council Fires. The Ihanktonwan people on April 4 formally informed the Department of State that the consultation process is flawed and that any consults must occur on Ihanktonwan homelands. The SEIS states that they have consulted the Yankton 159 times, which is a gross misrepresentation because consultation has not occurred once and the Department of State has broken their own federal laws regarding this process.

Eight thousand acres remain unsurveyed, which puts thousands and thousands of indigenous, cultural and sacred sites at risk. The Department of State imposed a fragmented, divisive process where tribes were forced to survey and compile documents that could not be shared, although all of these territories overlap. This is an egregious event to our people.

Documented linguistic evidence points out that our Siouan dialect survives in five provinces in Canada, we see no border, and 24 states in the US, thus firmly establishing our aboriginal rights to protect NAGPRA sites and ceremonial sites on the cultural landscape which also includes genesis sites within the XL corridor and beyond.

We stand with the Oglala [*Oglála* "Oglala"] Nation in forbidding Trans-Canada or XL, KXL from crossing 1851 and 1868 treaty territory, and we will be there to meet you.

The SEIS [Supplemental Environmental Impact] seeks to destroy our relationship with our seven animal species that are endangered or threatened. In our culture they are deemed significant to our belief system, one of which is the whooping crane. Our singers are called cranes. They are

Citing the role of women as the backbone of tribal nations, Faith Spotted Eagle has been integral to the movement to prevent construction of the Keystone XL pipeline. This has included grassroots activism among tribal nations but also the building of coalitions with non-Indians, such as the Cowboy and Indian Alliance. Here she testifies at the State Department's public hearing on Keystone XL on 18 April 2013. AP Photo/Nati Harnik.

called *ȟ'okȟá* ["singers"]. This is adjacent to the KXL pipeline. Their existence has been minimized and marginalized and they are certainly at risk.

Another item is that we have been given an inferior status in the programmatic agreement that was drawn up. We are not signatories. The states, the federal agencies were deemed much more important than us and were given signatory status. We are only concurring parties. That is totally socially unjust, and it is not acceptable to us.

We do believe that Mother Nature, *Iná Makȟá* ["Mother Earth"], is speaking. On the 11th of April, the Department of State scheduled a consultation at the Ramkota [Hotel] in Rapid City, South Dakota, and you were greeted with another blizzard. And I think, true to what my grandmother said, *nuŋȟčháŋ* means wooden ears. And I would urge the Department of State to listen.

55

"Call Me Human" (2015)[36]

Lyla June Johnston

In January 2015, Diné young people began the first of four marches to their people's sacred mountains in remembrance of the Long Walk and to raise awareness of resource colonization.[37] Dinétah, the Navajo homeland, had been exploited for its oil, gas, uranium, and coal throughout the twentieth century, enriching corporations while impoverishing the land and its people.[38] The nation's leaders pushed back, renegotiating exploitative leases, closing uranium mines, and exercising greater regulatory and taxation authority. But controversies continued as the government allowed fracking and considered allowing an oil pipeline to be constructed across the nation to promote economic development. "Protesting through prayer," Diné men and women sent the message that real energy sovereignty would not countenance "desecration by resource extraction."[39] In the following poem, Lyla June Johnston, a Diné activist, founder of the Taos Regeneration Festival, and 2013 graduate of Stanford University, reflects on history, memory, and the land.[40] Consider the meanings she assigned to citizenship, incorporation, and belonging.

from birth we etch these lines
engrave them inside your mind
by the rockets red glare
the bombs bursting in the air
the war it begins
to make the imaginary country
as real as your skin.

America doesn't exist
it's an idea men have obsessed over since 1776.

an excuse we use to manifest a reality that
destroyed the destiny of Native civilization.

they always told me I was an American
and so I said to them,
"can you show me America?"
can you tell me where it is?
I've been looking for it all my life!
looking for the reason why my people had to die.
but the only place I can find America is inside of your mind.

they said, no don't worry . . . just
stand up
put your hand right there on your heart
now turn just a little bit towards the flag.
there it is. Right there. Don't you see it?
there you go.
okay ready?
Go
I pledge allegiance to an illusion
called the United States of America
and to the non-existent boundaries
for which it stands
one deception
under a Christian god
with which we legitimize the genocide
of its indigenous peoples

America doesn't exist
but is a psychological sickness we catch with years
of exposure to our public schools to baseball games

and once we believe that America is real we believe that we have a
reason to steal a reason to kill.

the Long Walk 1865
9,000 Navajo are marched with barrels at their backs
herded like sheep for over 400 miles
to their own special concentration camp.
in the name of America

Wounded Knee Massacre 1890
U.S. Cavalry descend on a Lakota camp
with 530 women and children

and with "America" in their minds
and red and white stripes blinding their sight
they sunk bullets into the chests of children
that could have been their own
in the name of America

look on the twenty dollar bill my friends, see the man who
marched 15,000 Cherokee—
pregnant women, their children, the elderly—
marched from Georgia to Oklahoma
in the name of America.

do we remember what has been done in the name of an abstract nation
or has it all been buried along with our hearts and our tongues.

and I should not hate fireworks on warm summer nights
and I should not hate a combination of colors
and I should not hate dead men on paper money
and I should not hate.

so let me tell you that I love you
dear soldiers
dear president of the imaginary states of America
dear school teachers
dear man behind the curtain
let me tell you that I love you
and that I am leaving it in the past
let me tell you that I too am in love with my motherland
but know that this Earth is the foremother of your forefathers
she existed before Hancock and before Nixon
before money before America
and that she will exist long after America is forgotten.

raising hands to our hearts for a fairytale
that America is anything more than a word
we've drawn so many maps, we've put so many flags in the ground
we've labeled all the land
we've drawn imaginary lines all around the sand
but people hear me and separate your fact from fabrication
this is the projection of our imagination onto
the holy earth.

and today we unite to remember what is real
to remember that humanity is real
a beating heart is real
the earth beneath us is real
but America is a thought that
has turned us against ourselves
history into myth
entire cultures into forgotten languages
and the free mind into a society, deceived
so please do not call me an American
please do not even call me a Native American
please, I beg you, call me human

and do not call this land America
if you listen hard she will tell you her true name
as the nighthawks dive at twilight
as the wolves howl at moonlight
as the waterfalls rage cascading
when the avalanches fracture breaking
she WILL tell us her true name with earthquakes
that split states and break fences to
remind us she does not
belong to us.
but that we belong to her.

Conclusion

Forgotten/Remembered

The words Faith Spotted Eagle used to conclude her testimony at the public meeting on the Keystone XL pipeline bear repeating. "We do believe that Mother Nature, *Iná Makȟá* ['Mother Earth'], is speaking," she told the panel of government officials. "And I think, true to what my grandmother said, *nuŋȟčháŋ* means wooden ears. And I would urge the Department of State to listen." The symbol of ears has a central place in Lakota diplomacy. "References to ears abound in the written proceedings of treaty councils," anthropologist Raymond DeMallie explains. "Semantically, it appears that the piercing, opening, or mere acknowledgment of possessing ears expressed a willingness to listen to and accept a significant message." To have "no ears" meant the inverse—to be hard of hearing or deaf, to be unwilling to listen or not to understand. When Spotted Eagle used the phrase "wooden ears," just as when she asserted sovereignty by talking the language of the larger world, she participated in a Lakota political tradition. She conveyed the same message her ancestors had in 1851 and again in 1868—and in much the same way. The only thing that changed was the context in which she took politically purposeful action.[1]

All of the documents in this volume, like the one featuring Faith Spotted Eagle, underscore how crucial it is to understand politics and protest in Native America since 1887 as part of the continuing encounters between Natives and newcomers. An awareness of this tradition's history calls into question the old (and all too tenacious) narrative of declension, defeat, and disappearance fashioned by the memory makers of colonies and settler states. It reminds us that, in creating national narratives to substantiate the dispossession of indigenous peoples, they "emplotted" history "in particular ways." Political scientist Benedict Anderson refers to the end result of writing one people into history while simultaneously writing others out as "the remembered/forgotten."[2]

I would like to think of *Say We Are Nations*, like so much of the exciting scholarship being produced in American Indian and indigenous studies, as its antithesis—as the "forgotten/remembered."[3] Taken as a whole, the documents respond to the presumption of indigenous incorporation and disappearance with a collective "not so fast." They, like Vine Deloria Jr. in 1970, seize control of the authorial voice by saying, "We talk, you listen." That is not to suggest, however, that saying we are nations and talking the language of the larger world are simple propositions. They are not. The fifty-five examples I have offered provide a sense of breadth, depth, complexity, contingency, continuity, and even contradiction—but they are not by any means quintessential or exhaustive. In fact, they barely scratch the surface. So, I offer this collection as a beginning again, rather than an end, to an intellectual journey—as an invitation to take part in the excavation of the ideas that make Native politics and protest since 1887 so fascinating. I can't tell you what you'll find, but I am confident that it will be worth the effort.[4]

Notes

ACKNOWLEDGMENTS

1. Cobb, "Asserting a Global Indigenous Identity."
2. C. Warrior, "How Should an Indian Act?," 2.

INTRODUCTION

1. Clifford and Marcus, *Writing Culture*; Behar and Gordon, *Women Writing Culture*; Rosaldo, *Culture and Truth*. Both of Turner's essays can be found in Turner, *Rereading Frederick Jackson Turner*, quote at 21. For Philip Deloria's take on the importance of reflexivity in American Indian Studies, see Deloria, "Historiography," 21.

2. P. Deloria, "Historiography"; P. C. Smith and McMullen, "Making History."

3. P. C. Smith, "Narration."

4. For a review of the literature, see Axtell, "Columbian Encounters." Among those leading the way into the twentieth century were Iverson, *"We Are Still Here"*; V. Deloria and Lytle, *Nations Within*; Hoxie, "Exploring"; Fixico, *Termination*; Philp, *Termination Revisited*; and Bernstein, *American Indians*.

5. On historiography, see Edmunds, "Native Americans." On innovative methods, see Fogelson, "Ethnohistory"; DeMallie, "'These have no ears.'" Emblematic works include Hudson, *Knights of Spain*; Merrell, *Indians' New World*; Richter, *Ordeal*; Calloway, *American Revolution*; White, *Middle Ground*; Green, *Politics*; G. C. Anderson, *Kinsmen*; Hoxie, *Parading*; Hosmer, *American Indians*.

6. Axtell, "Columbian Encounters," 336; Cobb, "Continuing Encounters," 57–69.

7. Comaroff and Comaroff, *Of Revelation and Revolution*, vol. 1; Scott, *Weapons of the Weak*; Fowler, *Shared Symbols, Contested Meanings*; Cobb, "'Us Indians'"; Cobb and Fowler, *Beyond Red Power*.

8. P. C. Smith and Warrior, *Like a Hurricane*. For quote, see P. C. Smith, *Everything You Know*, 32. In their preface to *Like a Hurricane*, viii, Smith and Warrior did express their hope for a broader perspective on the era.

9. Vine Deloria Jr., interview by author, 18 October 2001.

10. Cobb, *Native Activism*. Paul Rosier has also made critical interventions in his important essay "'They are ancestral homelands.'" Sleeper-Smith et al., *Why You Can't Teach*.

11. Vine Deloria Jr., interview by author, 18 October 2001.

12. Hoxie, *Talking Back*; Hoxie, "'Thinking like an Indian'"; Rosier, *Serving Their Country*; Martinez, *The American Indian Intellectual Tradition*. Cobb, "Asserting a Global Indigenous Identity," 443–72.

13. I took the liberty of making silent corrections to some of the transcriptions. This included, for the most part, matters of grammar and spelling. I very selectively inserted into the text additional information in brackets and, on a few occasions, adjusted paragraphing when it allowed for more fluid reading and efficient presentation.

CHAPTER 1

1. On allotment as a multifaceted form of what Michel Foucault terms "subjection," see Biolsi, "Birth of the Reservation." Theodore Roosevelt alluded to some of the larger implications when he noted that it "acts directly upon *the family* and the individual." Roosevelt, "First Annual Message," 3 December 1901.

2. Hoxie, *Final Promise*. On allotment and citizenship as a form of incorporation, see Bruyneel, *Third Space*.

3. Silva, *Aloha Betrayed*; Kauanui, *Hawaiian Blood*; Kaplan and Pease, *Cultures of United States Imperialism*; Goldstein, *Formations*.

4. Britten, *American Indians in World War I*, 51–72.

5. Hagan, *American Indians*, 120–25; Holm, *Great Confusion*, 182–98; Hoxie, *Talking Back*, 139–174; Ellis, "'We don't want your rations.'"

6. Kennedy, *Over Here*, 332, 354, 358–63; Hoxie, *Talking Back*, 129–33.

7. Bruyneel, *Third Space*, 1–25; Hoxie, *Talking Back*, viii; Comaroff and Comaroff, *Of Revelation and Revolution*, vol. 1, 26.

8. Lili'uokalani, *Hawaii's Story by Hawaii's Queen*, 366, 233–34, 237–38, 323–25, 368–70, 372–74.

9. Kualapai, "The Queen Writes Back"; Proto, *Rights of My People*.

10. Lili'uokalani used the now obsolete term "Sandwich Islands" because it would have been familiar to non-Hawaiian or *haole* readers.

11. Here Lili'uokalani referred to men's and women's antiannexation organizations, *Hui Hawaii Aloha Aina* and *Hui Hawaii Aloha Aina o Na Wahine*, respectively.

12. William McKinley was inaugurated as president of the United States in March 1897.

13. After McKinley signed a treaty of annexation in June 1897, a grassroots action on the part of Native Hawaiians resulted in a "Petition against Annexation" signed by more than 21,000 Kanaka Maoli—over half the population according to the most recent census. Excerpts of the 556-page document, which served a pivotal role in delaying annexation, can be found at http://www.archives.gov/education/lessons/hawaii-petition/ (accessed 24 January 2015).

14. John L. Stevens was the United States Minister to the Kingdom of Hawai'i and an ally of the "Committee of Safety," which orchestrated the overthrow of the monarchy and founding of the Republic of Hawai'i.

15. In his 1823 annual message to Congress, President James Monroe expressed United States opposition to further European colonization efforts in the Western Hemisphere.

16. Lili'uokalani invoked the Old Testament story of Naboth, a man whose land was coveted by King Ahab. After Naboth refused to sell or exchange it, Ahab's wife,

Jezebel, had him falsely accused of a crime and put to death. For killing Naboth and taking possession of his land, the prophet Elijah then warned, the house of Ahab would be punished. I Kings 21:1–29, http://biblia.com/books/nrsv/1Ki21.17 (accessed 21 January 2015).

17. U.S. Congress, Senate, *Report of the Select Committee*, 1245–55.

18. C. B. Clark, *Lone Wolf*; Chang, *Color of the Land*, 97–100.

19. Harjo referred to the attack on Creek sovereignty by the state of Alabama that culminated in the Treaty of Cusseta in 1832, which provided for the cession of all the Creeks' lands east of the Mississippi River, their removal, and the reestablishment of their nation in the Indian Territory. Green, *Politics of Indian Removal*, 170–86.

20. In 1861 the Creek Nation signed a treaty of "friendship and alliance" with the Confederate States of America. Chitto Harjo, however, was among a faction of Creeks who remained loyal to the United States, relocated to Kansas, and served in the Union army.

21. The Curtis Act extended the General Allotment Act to the Choctaws, Chickasaws, and Creeks in 1898. Harjo was among a significant number of Creeks opposed to allotment in general and to the Curtis Act in particular.

22. In taking this position, Harjo abandoned an interracial alliance during the early period of the allotment struggle and that would be renewed in later years. See Chang, *Color of the Land*, 97–100, 102, 141–42.

23. U.S. Congress, Senate, *The Cherokee Freedmen*, 3–5.

24. Sturm, *Blood Politics*; Yarbrough, *Race and the Cherokee Nation*.

25. The Cherokees, among others nations in Indian Territory, argued that the federal courts did not have the right to make determinations of tribal citizenship by creating the 1896 rolls. They were abandoned in 1898 with passage of the Curtis Act and the generation of the Dawes Rolls proceeded between 1898 and 1914. Saunt, "Paradox of Freedom."

26. This census included the designations "colored citizens," "colored intruders," and "colored claimants, not decided." Reese, "Cherokee Freedwomen."

27. A. C. Parker, "Making Democracy Safe for the Indians."

28. Hoxie, *Talking Back*; D. A. T. Clark, "At the Headwaters," 70–90; Colwell-Chanthaphonh, *Inheriting the Past*; Porter, *To Be Indian*; Britten, *American Indians*. For more on his complicated approach to identity and change, see A. C. Parker, "Problems of Race Assimilation."

29. During the half century following its founding in 1824, the Bureau of Indian Affairs, the agency that was intended to symbolize the nation-to-nation relationship between the federal government and tribes and to carry out the former's obligations to the latter, had become bloated, corrupt, and paternalistic. Rather than protecting tribal sovereignty, it was generally seen as a colonial institution antagonistic to it. And yet its importance as a symbol of the recognition of treaty rights and American Indian sovereignty remained. This tension created the foundation for the debate within Native America over whether it should be abolished.

30. Montezuma, "United States, Now Free the Indians!," 2–3.

31. Hoxie, *Talking Back*; Iverson, *Carlos Montezuma*; Maddox, *Citizen Indians*; Lomawaima, "The Mutuality of Citizenship and Sovereignty."

32. Armistice Day was 11 November 1918.

33. Wassaja, which translates as "to signal or beckon," was both Carlos Montezuma's Yavapai name and the title of his journal, which he began publishing in 1916. Iverson, *Carlos Montezuma*.

34. The Paris Peace Conference was held at Versailles, near Paris, France, in the wake of World War I. Some thirty nations attended, but it was dominated by the United Kingdom, France, the United States, and Italy.

35. No Heart et al., to Cato Sells, 7 June 1919, file 109123-17-063, Standing Rock Agency, Central Classified Files, Records of the Bureau of Indian Affairs, Record Group 75, National Archives and Records Administration, Washington, D.C.

36. Stremlau, *Sustaining the Cherokee Family*; Hagan, *Quanah Parker*; Adams, *Education for Extinction*; Lomawaima, *They Called It Prairie Light*; Archuleta, Child, and Lomawaima, *Away from Home*; Holm, *Great Confusion*; Troutman, *Indian Blues*. On dance and songs during World War I, see Troutman, "Citizenship of Dance"; Meadows, *Kiowa, Apache, and Comanche*; Powers, *Lakota Warrior Tradition*.

37. The Treaty of Fort Laramie of 1868 established the boundaries of the Great Sioux Reservation and peace on the Northern Plains, both of which proved temporary.

38. Agency Superintendent James McLaughlin.

39. The Grass Dance, also known as the Omaha Dance or Hethu'shka, originated with the Omahas and spread across the Plains through the late eighteenth and nineteenth centuries. First associated with warrior societies, it came to include social dances as well. Ridington, Hastings, and Attachie, "Songs of Our Elders," 112–17.

40. U.S. Congress, House Committee on Indian Affairs, *Indians of the United States*, 599–605.

41. Rosen, *American Indians and State Law*; Sando, *Pueblo Nations*.

42. Lorenzo Martinez served as a leader of the peyote way and the governor of Taos Pueblo. For a photo see http://solo505.tumblr.com/post/8577519305/lorenzo-martinez-govenor-of-taos-pueblo-new (accessed 6 September 2014).

43. In 1848 the United States and Mexico signed the Treaty of Guadalupe Hidalgo and, in so doing, the former agreed to continue to recognize the land grants issued to Pueblos by the Spanish crown.

44. Republican representative Homer Snyder of New York.

45. This is, in fact, an accurate rendering of a long-standing competition over land claims. See Reséndez, *Changing National Identities*, 116.

46. Carlisle Indian Industrial School, an off-reservation boarding school founded in 1879 to promote assimilation.

47. Democratic representative Carl Hayden of Arizona.

48. Republican representative Benigno Hernandez of New Mexico.

49. It would appear Hernandez is referring to the 1876 *Joseph* decision, which upheld the right of Pueblo people to sell their lands, citing their being "civilized Indians" for whom federal trusteeship did not apply. It was reversed in 1913 by the

Sandoval decision which affirmed the federal trust relationship. Court cases soon followed and would culminate in 1922 with an attempt on the part of Congress to settle the controversy through legislative action. Pueblos united with non-Indian allies to defeat the so-called Bursum Bill because it favored non-Indian settlers. Wenger, "Land, Culture, and Sovereignty," 382.

50. Republican representative Charles D. Carter of Oklahoma.

51. "Chief Deskaheh Tells Why He Is Over Here Again" (London, August 1923), George P. Decker Collection, Special Collections, Lavery Library, St. John Fisher College, Rochester, New York.

52. Hauptman, *Seven Generations*, 124–42; Rostkowski, "The Redman's Appeal."

53. In 1867 Canada adopted its own constitution, gaining greater autonomy from the British crown. It was initially referred to as the Dominion of Canada, although the name later fell into disuse.

54. The Covenant Chain refers to an alliance the Iroquois Confederacy first forged with the Dutch and then extended to the British. It is, as Deskaheh reminded his readers, a living relationship that continues to reside at the heart of Iroquois conceptions of sovereignty. R. A. Williams, *Linking Arms*.

55. Council of All New Mexico Pueblos, "Declaration to All Indians and the People of the United States, 5 May 1924, Indian Rights Association Papers, reel 40, Pennsylvania Historical Society, Philadelphia.

56. Sando, *Pueblo Nations*; Sando, *Pueblo Profiles*; Wenger, *We Have a Religion*.

CHAPTER 2

1. The classic exposé is Debo, *And Still the Waters Run*.

2. Prucha, *Great Father*, chaps. 15–23. For a case study featuring these coercive practices and resistance to them, see Ellis, "'We don't want your rations.'" For another perspective, see Treglia, "The Consistency and Inconsistency of Cultural Oppression," 145–65.

3. V. Deloria and Lytle, *Nations Within*.

4. Philp, *John Collier's Crusade*; McMillen, *Making Indian Law*; McLerran, *A New Deal*; Kehoe, *A Passion*.

5. In clear testimony to its marginalization, the Bureau of Indian Affairs moved wholesale from Washington, D.C., to Chicago for the duration of the war. Philp, *Termination Revisited*.

6. Bernstein, *American Indians*; Ellis, *Dancing People*; Rosenthal, *Reimagining*; LaGrand, *Indian Metropolis*; Thrush, *Native Seattle*.

7. Kohlhoff, *When the Wind*.

8. Fixico, *Termination and Relocation*; Metcalf, *Termination's Legacy*; Arnold, *Bartering*; Beck, *Seeking Recognition*; Beck, *Struggle for Self-Determination*.

9. *Meeting of the Commissioner of Indian Affairs*.

10. V. Deloria, *Indian Reorganization Act*; Cohen, *On the Drafting*; Ramirez, "Henry Roe Cloud."

11. *Minutes of the Plains Congress, March 2–5, 1934*. U.S. Department of the Interior Library, Washington, D.C.

12. V. Deloria, *Indian Reorganization Act*, vii–viii, quote at viii.

13. George White Bull volunteered to serve in World War I and returned home to become involved in cattle ranching. He later served in World War II as well. Iverson, *When Indians*, 71.

14. The reference here is to the illegal taking of the Black Hills in 1877. The Lakotas fought to have this case heard in the Court of Claims through the late nineteenth and early twentieth centuries. They finally won a monetary settlement, upheld by the Supreme Court in 1980, which they refused. The Lakotas continue to demand the return of the Black Hills.

15. Ralph H. Case served as an attorney for the Lakotas on the Black Hills land claims but would later fall out of favor with them. Lazarus, *Black Hills/White Justice*.

16. *Proceedings of the Conference at Chemawa, Oregon, April 8 and 9.*

17. Mourning Dove, *Mourning Dove*; Mourning Dove, *Cogewea*.

18. Language had long contributed to difficulties in diplomatic engagements, and few knew this better than citizens of tribal nations in the Pacific Northwest. Chinook, a pidgin trade language used during the treaty-making sessions of the 1850s, contained only five hundred words and, according to lawyer Charles Wilkinson, could not "possibly speak to sovereignty, land ownership, fishing rights, assimilation, freedom, or the futures of societies." Wilkinson, *Messages*, 11.

19. An off-reservation boarding school in Salem, Oregon, established during the 1880s.

20. Emma Goldman (1869–1940) was a well-known anarchist, labor organizer, women's liberationist, and opponent of U.S. involvement in World War I. She was deported to Russia in 1920. In the February 1934, she returned to the United States on a speaking tour.

21. *Minutes of the Special Session of Navajo Tribal Council.*

22. Iverson, *Diné.*

23. This is a reference to two boundary bills that were to extend Navajo lands in Arizona and New Mexico. In exchange, the Navajo tribal council was to agree to further stock reductions—including 150,000 goats.

24. Part of the legislative flurry of President Franklin Roosevelt's first "Hundred Days," the Emergency Conservation Work (ECW) Act established the Civilian Conservation Corps. Between 1933 and 1942, it put thousands of young men to work across the country in forests, national parks, and rural areas and included an Indian Division.

25. This tells only part of the story. On the central role played by Diné women's opposition, see Weisiger, "Gendered Injustice," and Roessel, *Navajo Livestock Reduction.*

26. Joe Chitto to Commissioner of Indian Affairs, 20 August 1934, file 150-54948-1933, Choctaw, Records of the Bureau of Indian Affairs, Record Group 75, Central Classified Files, National Archives and Records Administration, Washington, D.C.

27. Lowery, *Lumbee Indians*; Osburn, "'In a name'"; Biolsi, *Organizing.*

28. Elizabeth and Roy Peratrovich to Ernest Gruening, 30 December 1941, National Archives Microfilm Publication (MF Pub M939), General Correspondence

of the Alaska Territorial Governor, 1909–58 (Washington, D.C., 1973), microfilm reel 273, file 40–4b.

29. Their efforts were bolstered by an Inupiat teenager named Alberta Schenck (1928–2009), who was arrested for refusing to leave the "whites only" section of a movie theater in Nome in March 1944. Cole, "Jim Crow."

30. Ibid.

31. U.S. Congress, Senate Committee on Indian Affairs, *Protesting the Construction of Garrison Dam, North Dakota*, 4–8.

32. The Mandan, Hidatsa/Gros Ventre, and Arikara/Sahnish.

33. Lawson, *Dammed Indians Revisited*. On the gendered dimension of the violence done by the Garrison Dam, see A. K. Parker, "Taken Lands."

34. Democratic senator Joseph O'Mahoney of Wyoming.

35. Republican senator Edward H. Moore of Oklahoma.

36. Republican senator William Langer of North Dakota.

37. Between April 1946 and 1953, the Garrison Dam was constructed, with all of the attendant dislocation, hardship, and destruction anticipated by Cross and others. The Three Affiliated Tribes lost more than 150,000 acres of land, which included home sites, agricultural lands, burial grounds, and places of historical and spiritual significance. An effort spearheaded by Martin Cross's youngest son, Raymond Cross, culminated in additional reparations in 1992. VanDevelder, *Coyote Warrior*.

38. To the President, 28 March 1949, attached to "The Hopi Stand," folder 2, box 1, Hopi Traditionalist Movement Papers, Department of Special Collections, University of Arizona, Tucson, Arizona.

39. Bernstein, *American Indians*; Hauptman, *Iroquois Struggle*; Cobb, "Politics in Cold War Native America"; Clemmer, "Hopi Traditionalist."

40. The North Atlantic Treaty Organization, established on 4 April 1949.

41. U.S. Congress, House Subcommittee on Indian Affairs, *Payment of More Adequate Compensation*, 17–22.

42. Hoxie, *Talking Back*, 148–55; Baird, "Indian Rodeo Cowboys," 222; U.S. Congress, House Subcommittee on Indian Affairs, *Payment of More Adequate Compensation*, 31.

43. It may be for this reason that Oglala Sioux Tribe president Bryan Brewer indicated that nine hundred families had to move. Brewer, "Time for the Tribal National Park," http://indiancountrytodaymedianetwork.com/2014/10/20/time-tribal-national-park-properly-honor-native-culture (accessed 25 January 2015).

44. The United States was engaged in the Korean Conflict (1950–53) at the time of Herman's testimony.

45. Among those evicted were survivors of the 1890 Wounded Knee Massacre and families of soldiers serving in World War II. http://www.oglalalakotanation.org/oln/History.html (accessed 24 January 2015).

46. The Badlands Bombing Range was in use for thirty years. Portions were returned beginning in 1960, and more than 100,000 acres of it were set aside as the Badlands National Monument in 1968. The Air Force and Oglala Sioux Tribe

oversaw the removal of the last unexploded munitions in late 2014. http://www
.oglalalakotanation.org/oln/History.html (accessed 24 January 2015); "Cleanup Is
Wrapping up at Pine Ridge Range," http://www.argusleader.com/story/news/2014/
11/05/cleanup-wrapping-pine-ridge-range/18520545/ (accessed 25 January 2015).

47. National Congress of American Indians, Point Four Program for American
Indians, 21 November 1954, folder 106, box 10, James E. Officer Papers, Arizona
Historical Society, Tucson, Arizona. D'Arcy McNickle originally presented these
ideas in 1951. The statistics were updated and the text was adopted by the Executive Council of the NCAI in 1954.

48. Cobb, *Native Activism*, 8–29; Cobb, Fields, and Cheatle, "'born in the opposition'; Hoxie, *This Indian Country*, 277–335; D. R. Parker, *Singing an Indian Song*.

CHAPTER 3

1. V. Deloria, *Custer Died*, 169–95, especially 179.

2. Hagan, *American Indians*, 137–39, 144–45.

3. Cobb, *Native Activism*; Shreve, *Red Power*; P. C. Smith and Warrior, *Like a
Hurricane*.

4. Hagan, *American Indians*, 143–44, quote at 144.

5. McNickle, *Native American Tribalism*, 122; Cobb, *Native Activism*.

6. Joseph Garry, "A Declaration of Indian Rights," "Emergency Conference Bul-
letin," 1954 folder, box 257, Records of the National Congress of American Indians, (NMAI.AC.010), National Museum of the American Indian, Archive Center,
Smithsonian Institution, Suitland, Maryland.

7. Rosier, "'They are ancestral'"; Cowger, *National Congress*; Fahey, *Saving*.

8. Senate Committee on the Judiciary, *Stenographic Transcript of Hearings*,
10–24.

9. Hauptman, "Alice Lee Jemison"; Cowger, *National Congress*; Wilkinson,
Blood Struggle.

10. U.S. Congress, House Committee on Interior and Insular Affairs, *Relating to
the Lumbee Indians of North Carolina*, 10–19.

11. Metcalf, *Termination's Legacy*; Peroff, *Menominee DRUMS*; Arnold, *Bartering*.

12. Lowery, *Lumbee Indians*; Kidwell, "Terminating the Choctaws."

13. Democratic representative Frank Ertel Carlyle of North Carolina.

14. Democratic representative Wayne Aspinall of Colorado.

15. Democratic representative James Haley of Florida.

16. Philip Martin to Fred A. Seaton, 27 September 1960, folder 11, box 249,
Records (MC147); 1851–2013 (mostly 1922–1995), Public Policy Papers, Department
of Rare Books and Special Collections, Princeton University Library, Princeton.

17. Osburn, *Choctaw Resurgence*; Cobb, "The War on Poverty."

18. During the 1950s, the Bureau of Indian Affairs initiated a voluntary relocation program to encourage Native people to move from their reservation homes
to urban centers. On one level it offered the promise of a better standard of living;
on another it promoted assimilation and depleted the population of reservations,
making it easier to justify termination. Fixico, *Termination*.

19. Like many African Americans in the Deep South, Choctaws struggled to make ends meet, often as migratory laborers and sharecroppers.

20. The Association on American Indian Affairs was a non-Indian directed Native rights organization based in New York City. LaVerne Madigan served as its executive director during the 1950s and early 1960s.

21. Edward P. Dozier, Keynote Address, American Indian Chicago Conference, n.d. folder 7, box 59, Records (MC147); 1851–2013 (mostly 1922–1995), Public Policy Papers, Department of Rare Books and Special Collections, Princeton University Library, Princeton.

22. Cobb, *Native Activism*; Lurie, "Voice"; Lurie, "Sol Tax"; Norcini, *Edward P. Dozier*.

23. American Indian Chicago Conference, *The Declaration of Indian Purpose*, 5, 15–16, 19–20.

24. Cobb, *Native Activism*.

25. This document is drawn from three separate sources, each with their own footnote.

26. It was held on the campus of Colorado College from 1956 to 1958 and at the University of Colorado from 1959 to 1968. In 1968, former students offered workshops of their own on multiple university campuses.

27. Cobb, *Native Activism*, 23–27, 52–58, 62–79, quotes at 27 and 63; Shreve, *Red Power*, 65–93; McKenzie-Jones, "Evolving Voices." For Thomas's thoughts on colonialism, see Thomas, "Colonialism." For perspectives on his life and work, see Pavlik, *A Good Cherokee*.

28. Jeri Cross (Caddo) was a senior mathematics major at Wayland Baptist College in Texas at the time of this writing. While the question to which she was responding is not extant, consider how in this reflection on identity she responds to the supposed binary between "Indianness" and "whiteness" and the assumed "inevitability" of assimilation. She would go on to become an eminent potter in the Caddoan tradition. Her work can be found in the National Museum of the American Indian and has also had a place in the Oval Office of President Barack Obama. She later married Osage author Charles Redcorn. Jeri Cross, "A Thought," 25 June 1962, "Topical Files-Education-Summer Workhsop-1962 Student Papers" folder, Native American Educational Services, Robert Rietz Papers, Special Collections Research Center, University of Chicago Library, Chicago.

29. Sandra Johnson, a Makah from Neah Bay on the Olympic Peninsula in Washington, attended Lewis and Clark College, where she majored in English. Consider how the question pushed her to imagine a different future for her home community and to think about what she might do to realize that vision. Rather than taking twenty years to realize the vision, it took only two. As director of the War on Poverty's Neighborhood Youth Corps and Head Start programs—and then the entire Community Action Program—at Neah Bay, she inaugurated what amounted to revolutionary changes. This included providing incentives for K-12 students to learn Makah language and culture in the context of summer programs and to pay elders to serve as teachers in the Head Start preschool program. She later trained in media studies, founded Upstream Productions with her husband,

Yasu Osawa, and became an acclaimed documentary filmmaker. The full question read: "What do you hope your home community will be like twenty years from now, and why? Answer this question with reference to the terms and concepts of this Workshop. Be realistic, suggesting only what you believe could be possible, and explaining what would have to happen to make it possible." Sandra Johnson, "Final Examination," "Topical Files-Education-Summer Workshop-1962 Student Papers" folder, Native American Educational Services, Robert Rietz Papers, Special Collections Research Center, University of Chicago Library, Chicago.

30. Like Sandra Johnson, Bruce Wilkie (1938–78) was a Makah from Neah Bay. A central figure in NIYC, he became (as Sandra Johnson hoped) the Makah's general manager just a couple of years after writing this essay and later served as the executive director of the NCAI. Hertzberg, "Indian Rights Movement," 316. These excerpts respond to two final exam questions: "Describe the consequences for the world and social relations of a folk people under a colonial administration, and explain your reasoning for expecting these consequences to occur in as much detail as you can, using the terms and concepts of this Workshop"; and "What do you hope your home community will be like twenty years from now, and why? Answer this question with reference to the terms and concepts of this Workshop. Be realistic, suggesting only what you believe could be possible, and explaining what would have to happen to make it possible." Bruce Wilkie, "Final Exam," n.d., "Topical Files-Education-Summer Workhsop-1962 Student Papers" folder, Native American Educational Services, Robert Rietz Papers, Special Collections Research Center, University of Chicago Library, Chicago.

31. C. Warrior, "On Current Indian Affairs."

32. Cobb, *Native Activism*; 52–61, 94–99, 154–172; Shreve, *Red Power*, 94–138; McKenzie-Jones, "'We are among the poor.'"

33. C. Warrior, "Which One Are You?" He addressed the question of identity again in C. Warrior, "How Should an Indian Act?"

34. Bruyneel, *Third Space*.

35. U.S. Congress, Senate Committee on the Judiciary, *Constitutional Rights of the American Indian*, 194–201.

36. Cobb, *Native Activism*, 117–46.

37. A Democrat, LeRoy Collins served as governor of Florida from 1955 to 1961, was considered a moderate on civil rights, and became the first director of the Community Relations Service under the Civil Rights Act of 1964.

38. William A. Creech, Chief Counsel and Staff Director, Subcommittee on Constitutional Rights, United States Judiciary Committee.

39. John L. Baker, Minority Counsel, Subcommittee on Constitutional Rights, United States Judiciary Committee.

40. Glazer and Moynihan, *Beyond the Melting Pot*.

41. Russell, "Reflections on Montgomery."

42. This is a reference to Wilkie, "Look for Results and Action."

43. Nisqually Nation, "Proclamation or Declaration of Facts," 1 January 1965, folder 11, box 20, Virgil J. Vogel Research and Personal Papers, Newberry Library, Chicago.

44. Wilkinson, *Messages*; Harmon, *Indians in the Making*; S. L. Smith, "Indians, the Counterculture, and the New Left." For quote, see http://frankslanding.org/franks-landing/ (accessed 30 January 2015).

45. Mad Bear Anderson, a Tuscarora activist.

46. Tillie Walker Statement, Press Briefing, United States of America, Department of Interior, 1 May 1968, Della and Clyde Merton Warrior Papers, in author's possession.

47. Cobb, *Native Activism*, 147–92; VanDevelder, *Coyote Warrior*.

48. Again, Tuscarora activist Mad Bear Anderson.

49. "Statement of Demands for Rights of the Poor Presented to Agencies of the U.S. Government by the Southern Christian Leadership Conference and Its Committee of 100, 29–30 April and 1 May 1968," attached to Ralph Abernathy to Congressman Harris, n.d., folder 30 [1 of 3], box 48, Carl Albert General Collection, Carl Albert Center for Congressional Research and Studies, University of Oklahoma, Norman.

50. Cobb, *Native Activism*, 147–192; Mantler, *Power to the Poor*.

CHAPTER 4

1. V. Deloria, quoted in Cobb, "Asserting a Global Indigenous Identity," 457.

2. The periodic publications *Akwesasne Notes* and *Americans before Columbus* demonstrate the bridge-building efforts of this period.

3. Anaya, *International Human Rights*; Anaya, *Indigenous Peoples*.

4. Echo-Hawk, *In the Light*.

5. The Twenty Points are summarized in the introduction to Document 34. Given how often the document has been reprinted, I decided not to include it in this volume. It is, however, essential reading. The full text can be read at http://www.aimovement.org/ggc/trailofbrokentreaties.html (accessed 28 January 2015). See also Josephy, Nagel, and Johnson, *Red Power*.

6. Hagan, *American Indians*, 147–56; Wilkinson, *Blood Struggle*, 229–40.

7. R. A. Williams, *Like a Loaded Weapon*, 97–114.

8. "Manifesto," *Indians of All Tribes Newsletter* 1, no. 3 (1970): 2, folder 2, box 20, Virgil J. Vogel Research and Personal Papers, Ayer Modern Manuscript Collection, Newberry Library, Chicago.

9. Clarkin, *Federal Indian Policy*; Castile, *To Show Heart*; Johnson, *American Indian Occupation*; P. C. Smith and Warrior, *Like a Hurricane*, 60–83.

10. "We Support Our Brothers at Wounded Knee."

11. V. Deloria, *Behind the Trail*; P. C. Smith and Warrior, *Like a Hurricane*, 218–44.

12. John Trudell, "We've Got to Have Commitment So Strong . . ."

13. P. C. Smith and Warrior, *Like a Hurricane*, 245–79.

14. This is a reference to a riot that erupted at the Minnehaha County Courthouse in Sioux Falls, South Dakota, in the spring of 1974. AIM members were being tried for their involvement in an earlier riot in Custer, South Dakota.

15. The Symbionese Liberation Army, Black Panthers, Weathermen, and Students for a Democratic Society were radical organizations targeted by the federal

government for subversive activities. They were, of course, very different in character from one another, but all cast themselves as revolutionary. Trudell's point was that they were all portrayed as equally "dangerous" by the federal government.

16. International Indian Treaty Council, "Declaration of Continuing Independence."

17. Cobb, "Asserting a Global Indigenous Identity."

18. "Declaration of Principles for the Defense of the Indigenous Nations and Peoples of the Western Hemisphere."

19. Coulter, "Commentary"; Anaya, "Indigenous Peoples in International Law."

20. "Marie Sanchez: For the Women."

21. O'Sullivan, "'We worry about survival'"; Washinawatok, "International Emergence."

22. "Human Rights from a Native Perspective."

23. Johnson, Nagel, and Champagne, *American Indian Activism*.

24. "Affirmation of Sovereignty of the Indigenous Peoples of the Western Hemisphere."

25. The information on the march is from *Akwesasne Notes* 10, no. 3 (Summer 1978): 9. It should be noted, however, that Dick Gregory did speak at the event in front of the Washington Monument.

26. U.S. Congress, House Committee on Interior and Insular Affairs, Indian Gaming Regulatory Act, 373–75.

27. Sando, *Pueblo Profile*; Light and Rand, *Indian Gaming and Tribal Sovereignty*; Cattelino, *High Stakes*.

28. U.S. Congress, Senate Committee on Indian Affairs, Religious Freedom Act, 24–26.

29. Fikes, *Reuben Snake*; Long, *Religious Freedom*; Calabrese, *A Different Medicine*; Maroukis, *The Peyote Road*.

30. In February 1992, Jeffrey Dahmer was sentenced to fifteen terms of life in prison for raping, murdering, and dismembering seventeen men and boys between the late 1970s and early 1990s.

31. The savings and loan crisis, brought on by lax federal regulation of and corruption on Wall Street, precipitated an economic collapse during the 1980s and early 1990s.

32. During public hearings on Clarence Thomas's nomination to serve on the Supreme Court in October 1991, one of his former employees, Anita Hill, accused him of sexual harassment.

33. Manuel Noriega, a Panamanian military dictator, had received covert support from the United States Central Intelligence Agency for decades. He was ultimately deposed from power in 1989 and found guilty of drug trafficking, murder, and money laundering. His trial had been set to open in April of 1992.

34. The Iran-Contra scandal proved deeply divisive during the late 1980s. Despite an arms embargo, officials within President Ronald Reagan's administration orchestrated sales to Iran. This money, in turn, was used to support U.S.-allied Contras in a war against the communist Sandinista government in Nicaragua, despite a congressional amendment explicitly prohibiting it.

Several high officials in the Reagan administration were convicted for perjury and obstruction of justice.

35. U.S. Congress, House Committee on Interior Affairs, *Federal Acknowledgment of Various Indian Groups*, 406–8.

36. Perdue, "American Indian Survival"; Ulmer, "Tribal Property"; Loftis, "The Catawba's Final Battle"; Ulrich, *American Indian Nations*; Den Ouden and O'Brien, *Recognition, Sovereignty Struggles, and Indigenous Rights in the United States*; Klopotek, *Recognition Odysseys*.

37. U.S. Congress, Senate Select Committee on Indian Affairs, *Federal Government's Relationship with American Indians*, 11–15; U.S. Congress, Senate Select Committee on Indian Affairs, Tribal Self-Governance Demonstration Project Act, 19–20; U. S. Congress, House Committee on Natural Resources, *Oklahoma Tribal Concerns*, 8–9.

38. Janda, *Beloved Women*; Mankiller and Wallis, *Mankiller*.

CHAPTER 5

1. Tsosie, "BIA's Apology"; King, "A Tree."

2. Hagan, *American Indians*, 147–88.

3. After initially being dated at 9,600 years old, the age was revised down to 8,400 to 9,000 years old. http://www.burkemuseum.org/kennewickman/ (accessed 28 January 2015).

4. Hagan, *American Indians*, 147–88.

5. The tribe has repeatedly rejected attempts on the part of the U.S. Congress to force it to accept a monetary settlement. In addition to fighting for their grazing rights, the Western Shoshones resisted below-ground nuclear weapons testing and the consolidation of nuclear waste in a facility located on unceded land. Rusco, "Historic Change"; Luebben and Nelson, "The Indian Wars."

6. Idle No More, "Living History"; Idle No More, "The Story."

7. M. S. T. Williams, *Alaska Native Reader*; Fixico, *Invasion*; Wilkinson, *Blood Struggle*, 304–28.

8. "Indian Country Renewable"; Castillo and McLean, "Energy Innovation"; Hagan, *American Indians*, 162–64, 178–80; Idle No More, "Idle No More at the Peoples Climate March."

9. Cross, "A Tribe."

10. Minthorn, "Human Remains Should Be Reburied."

11. McKeown, *In the Smaller*; Fine-Dare, *Grave Injustice*; Mihesuah, *Repatriation Reader*.

12. Russell Jim Interview, "Voices of the Manhattan Project," Atomic Heritage Foundation, http://www.manhattanprojectvoices.org/oral-histories/russell-jims-interview, accessed 10 April 2014.

13. Bush, "Yakama Nation"; Jacob, *Yakama Rising*.

14. Testimony Submitted by J. Kēhaulani Kauanui, Ph.D., Regarding S. 344, for the Hearing Record, personal communication with author. The hearing before the Senate Committee on Indian Affairs took place on 25 February 2003. This

testimony does not appear to have been included in the print version of the hearings. U.S. Congress, Senate Committee on Indian Affairs, *Policy of the United States Regarding Relationship with Native Hawaiians.*

15. Kauanui, *Hawaiian Blood*; H.-K. Trask, *From a Native Daughter*; Goodyear-Kaopua, Hussey, and Wright, *Nation Rising*; Goldstein, *Formations.*

16. Democratic senator Daniel Akaka of Hawai'i.

17. The United Nations Study on Treaties, Agreements and Other Constructive Arrangements between Indigenous Peoples and Nation States recommended that Hawai'i be relisted as a non-self-governing territory—that is, a territory "whose people have not yet attained a full measure of self-government"—and that decolonization procedures follow. M. B. Trask, "Hawaiian Sovereignty."

18. U.S. Congress, Senate Committee on Indian Affairs, Indian Trust Reform Act, 93, 95, 218–37.

19. Wilkins, *Hollow Justice.*

20. Also known as the Marias Massacre, in which 173 Piegan Blackfeet men, women, and children at peace with the United States were murdered on 23 January 1870. Calloway, *Our Hearts*, 106.

21. The Trust Reform and Cobell Settlement Workgroup established fifty principles to guide legislation.

22. Dennison, "The Will of the People: Citizenship in the Osage Nation," 5–10.

23. Dennison, *Colonial Entanglement.*

24. U.S. Congress House Committee on Natural Resources, *ANWR: Jobs, Energy, and Deficit Reduction*, 76–79.

25. Banerjee, *Arctic Voices*; Bass, *Caribou Rising.*

26. Schilling, "Susan Allen."

27. Driskill et at., *Queer Indigenous Studies*; Rifkin, *When Did Indians Become Straight?*

28. The proposed amendment would have modified the state constitution to recognize marriage only between one man and one woman. It failed to pass, making it the first constitutional amendment against gay marriage to be defeated by voters.

29. Transcribed from "Women Senators, Tribal Leader Discuss Importance of VAWA Improvements."

30. Weaver, "Colonial Context"; Hart and Lowther, "Honoring Sovereignty"; Petillo, "Domestic Violence."

31. Democratic senator Patty Murray of Washington.

32. Pearl, "3/256."

33. Fletcher, Singel, and Fort, *Facing the Future.*

34. The transcription is based on both the print document and the video of the meeting. Many thanks to Dave Posthumus for providing the Lakota words and translations. For text, see U.S. Department of State, *Proposed Keystone XL Project Public Meeting*, 1:8–13.

35. For historical context on the Lakotas, see Ostler, *Plains Sioux*; Ostler, *Lakotas and the Black Hills.*

36. Lyla June Johnston, "Call Me Human," courtesy of the author.

37. The sacred mountains are Tsoodził (Mount Taylor), Doo'o'k'osliid (San Francisco Peak), Dibé Ntsáá (Hesperus, Colo.), and Sisnajiní (Blanca Peak). The Long Walk refers to a four-hundred-mile forced march more than nine thousand Diné and Apaches had to endure. They were relocated from their homelands to the Bosque Redondo Reservation, where they lived in dire circumstances for four years. Iverson notes that it was not a single event but a series traumatic episodes from August 1863 to the end of 1866. "Nihígaal béé Íina"; Iverson, *Diné*, 51–66.

38. Brugge, Benally, and Yazzie-Lewis, *Navajo People*; Pasternak, *Yellow Dirt*.

39. Energy sovereignty is defined as "the right of conscious individuals, communities, and peoples to make their own decisions on energy generation, distribution, and consumption in a way that is appropriate within their ecological, social, economic, and cultural circumstances, provided that these do not affect others negatively." Cotarelo et al., "Defining." The first quote is from Blackhorse, "Fracking." For second quote, see "Nihígaal béé Íina."

40. Dadigan, "Stanford."

CONCLUSION

1. DeMallie, "'These have no ears,'" quotes at 520, 521.

2. B. Anderson, *Imagined*, 198–99.

3. Consider just a few, such as Buss and Genetin-Pilawa, *Beyond Two Worlds*; Child, *My Grandfather's*; V. Deloria, *Indians*; Denetdale, *Reclaiming*; Dennison, *Colonial Entanglement*; Hosmer and Nesper, *Tribal Worlds*; Kelman, *Misplaced*; Lowery, *Lumbee Indians*; McMillen, *Making*; O'Brien, *Firsting*; Simpson, *Mohawk*; Cobb, "Asserting a Global Indigenous Identity"; Snyder, *Slavery*; R. Warrior, *World of Indigenous*.

4. V. Deloria, *We Talk*.

Bibliography

ARCHIVAL AND MANUSCRIPT SOURCES

Albuquerque, New Mexico
    National Indian Youth Council Papers, Center for Southwest Research,
        University of New Mexico
Author's possession
    Della and Clyde Merton Warrior Papers
Chicago, Illinois
    Native American Educational Services, Robert Rietz Papers, Special
        Collections Research Center, University of Chicago Library
    Virgil J. Vogel Research and Personal Papers, Newberry Library
Norman, Oklahoma
    Carl Albert General Collection, Carl Albert Center for Congressional Research
        and Studies, University of Oklahoma
Philadelphia, Pennsylvania
    Indian Rights Association Papers, reel 40, Pennsylvania Historical Society
Princeton, New Jersey
    Association on American Indian Affairs Records (MC147); 1851–2013 (mostly
        1922–1995), Public Policy Papers, Department of Rare Books and Special
        Collections, Princeton University Library
Rochester, New York
    George P. Decker Collection. Special Collections, Lavery Library, St. John
        Fisher College
Suitland, Maryland
    Records of the National Congress of American Indians (NMAI.AC.010),
        National Museum of the American Indian, Archive Center, Smithsonian
        Institution
Tucson, Arizona
    Hopi Traditionalist Movement Papers, Department of Special Collections,
        University of Arizona Library
    James E. Officer Papers, Arizona Historical Society
Washington, D.C.
    Central Classified Files, Records of the Bureau of Indian Affairs, Record Group
        75, National Archives and Records Administration
    National Archives Microfilm Publication (MF Pub M939), General
        Correspondence of the Alaska Territorial Governor, 1909–58
        (Washington, D.C., 1973), microfilm reel 273, file 40–4b
    United States Department of the Interior Library
    "Voices of the Manhattan Project," Atomic Heritage Foundation

Adams, David Wallace. *Education for Extinction: American Indians and the Boarding School Experience*. Lawrence: University Press of Kansas, 1995.

"Affirmation of Sovereignty of the Indigenous Peoples of the Western Hemisphere." *Akwesasne Notes* 10, no. 3 (Summer 1978): 14–16.

American Indian Chicago Conference. *The Declaration of Indian Purpose: The Voice of the American Indian*. N.p., June 26, 1961.

Anaya, S. James. *Indigenous Peoples in International Law*. 2nd ed. New York: Oxford University Press, 2004.

———. "Indigenous Peoples in International Law." Originally published in *Cultural Survival Quarterly* 21, no. 2 (Summer 1997). https://www.culturalsurvival .org/ourpublications/csq/article/indigenous-peoples-international-law. 2 September 2014.

———. *International Human Rights and Indigenous Peoples*. New York: Aspen Publishers, 2009.

Anderson, Benedict. *Imagined Communities: Reflections on the Origins and Spread of Nationalism*. Rev. ed. New York: Verso, 1991.

Anderson, Gary Clayton. *Kinsmen of Another Kind: Dakota-White Relations in the Upper Mississippi Valley, 1650–1862*. St. Paul: Minnesota Historical Society Press, 1997.

Archuleta, Margaret, Brenda Child, and K. Tsianina Lomawaima, eds. *Away from Home: American Indian Boarding School Experiences, 1879–2000*. Phoenix: Heard Museum, 2000.

Arnold, Laurie. *Bartering with the Bones of Their Dead: The Colville Confederated Tribes and Termination*. Seattle: University of Washington Press, 2012.

Axtell, James. "Columbian Encounters: Beyond 1992." *William and Mary Quarterly* 49, no. 2 (April 1992): 335–60.

Baird, Phil. "Indian Rodeo Cowboys of the Dakotas." In *Legends of Our Times: Native Cowboy Life*, edited by Morgan Baillargeon and Leslie Tepper, 221–42. Vancouver: University of British Columbia Press, 1998.

Banerjee, Subhankar, ed. *Arctic Voices: Resistance at the Tipping Point*. New York: Seven Stories Press, 2012.

Bass, Rick. *Caribou Rising: Defending the Porcupine Herd, Gwich'in Culture, and the Arctic National Wildlife Refuge*. San Francisco: Sierra Club Books, 2004.

Beck, David R. M. *Seeking Recognition: The Termination and Restoration of the Coos, Lower Umpqua, and Siuslaw Indians, 1855–1984*. Lincoln: University of Nebraska Press, 2009.

———. *The Struggle for Self-Determination: History of the Menominee Indians since 1854*. Lincoln: University of Nebraska Press, 2005.

Behar, Ruth, and Deborah A. Gordon, eds. *Women Writing Culture*. Berkeley: University of California Press, 1996.

Bernstein, Alison. *American Indians and World War II: Toward a New Era in Indian Affairs*. Norman: University of Oklahoma Press, 1991.

Biolsi, Thomas. "The Birth of the Reservation: Making the Modern Individual among the Lakota." *American Ethnologist* 22, no. 1 (February 1995): 28–53.

———. *Organizing the Lakota: The Political Economy of the New Deal on the Pine Ridge Reservation*. Tucson: University of Arizona Press, 1992.

Blackhorse, Amanda. "Fracking and a Diné Revolution on the Verge." *Indian Country Today*. 14 January 2015. http://indiancountrytodaymedianetwork .com/2015/01/14/blackhorse-fracking-and-dine-revolution-verge-158700. 1 February 2015.

Brewer, Bryan. "Time for the Tribal National Park." *Indian Country Today*. 20 October 2014. http://indiancountrytodaymedianetwork.com/2014/10/20/ time-tribal-national-park-properly-honor-native-culture. 25 January 2015.

Britten, Thomas A. *American Indians in World War I: At Home and at War*. Albuquerque: University of New Mexico Press, 1997.

Brugge, Doug, Timothy Benally, and Esther Yazzie-Lewis, eds. *The Navajo People and Uranium Mining*. Albuquerque: University of New Mexico Press, 2006.

Bruyneel, Kevin. *The Third Space of Sovereignty: The Postcolonial Politics of U.S.-Indigenous Relations*. Minneapolis: University of Minnesota Press, 2007.

Bush, Daniel A. "The Yakama Nation and the Cleanup of Hanford: Contested Meanings of Environmental Remediation." http://nativecases.evergreen.edu/ collection/cases/the-yakama-nation-and-the-cleanup-of-hanford-contested-meanings-of-environmental-remediation.html. 8 September 2014.

Buss, James Joseph, and C. Joseph Genetin-Pilawa, eds. *Beyond Two Worlds: Critical Conversations on Language and Power in Native North America*. Albany: SUNY Press, 2014.

Calabrese, Joseph D. *A Different Medicine: Postcolonial Healing in the Native American Church*. New York: Oxford University Press, 2013.

Calloway, Colin. *The American Revolution in Indian Country: Crisis and Diversity in Native American Communities*. New York: Cambridge University Press, 1995.

———. ed. *Our Hearts Fell to the Ground: Plains Indian Views of How the West Was Lost*. Boston: Bedford Books, 1996.

Castile, George Pierre. *To Show Heart: Native American Self-Determination and Federal Indian Policy, 1960–1975*. Tucson: University of Arizona Press, 1998.

Castillo, Ameyali Ramos, and Kristy Galloway McLean. "Energy Innovation and Traditional Knowledge." *Our World*. http://ourworld.unu.edu/en/energy-innovation-and-traditional-knowledge. 1 February 2015.

Cattelino, Jessica R. *High Stakes: Florida Seminole Gaming and Sovereignty*. Durham: Duke University Press, 2008.

Chang, David A. *The Color of the Land: Race, Nation, and the Politics of Landownership in Oklahoma, 1832–1929*. Chapel Hill: University of North Carolina Press, 2010.

Child, Brenda J. *My Grandfather's Knocking Sticks: Ojibwe Family Life and Labor on the Reservation*. St. Paul: Minnesota Historical Society, 2014.

Clark, C. Blue. *Lone Wolf v. Hitchcock: Treaty Rights and Indian Law at the End of the Nineteenth Century*. Lincoln: University of Nebraska Press, 1994.

Clark, D. Anthony Tyeeme. "At the Headwaters of the Twentieth-Century 'Indian' Political Agenda: Rethinking the Origins of the Society of American Indians." In *Beyond Red Power: American Indian Politics and Activism since 1900*, edited by Daniel M. Cobb and Loretta Fowler, 70–90. Santa Fe: SAR Press, 2007.

Clarkin, Thomas. *Federal Indian Policy in the Kennedy and Johnson Administrations, 1961–1969*. Albuquerque: University of New Mexico Press, 2001.

"Cleanup Is Wrapping up at Pine Ridge Range." 5 December 2014. http://www .argusleader.com/story/news/2014/11/05/cleanup-wrapping-pine-ridge-range/18520545/. 25 January 2015.

Clemmer, Robert O. "The Hopi Traditionalist Movement." *American Indian Culture and Research Journal* 18, no. 3 (1994): 125–66.

Clifford, James, and George E. Marcus, eds. *Writing Culture: The Poetics and Politics of Ethnography*. 1986. Berkeley: University of California Press, 2010.

Cobb, Daniel M. "Asserting a Global Indigenous Identity: Native Activism Before and After the Cold War." In *Native Diasporas: Indigenous Identities and Settler Colonialism in the Americas*, edited by Gregory D. Smithers and Brooke N. Newman, 443–72. Lincoln: University of Nebraska Press, 2014.

———. "Continuing Encounters: Historical Perspectives." In *Beyond Red Power: American Indian Politics and Activism since 1900*, edited by Daniel M. Cobb and Loretta Fowler, 57–69. Santa Fe: SAR Press, 2007.

———. *Native Activism in Cold War America*. Lawrence: University Press of Kansas, 2008.

———. "Politics in Cold War Native America: Parallel and Contradiction." *Princeton University Library Chronicle* 67 (Winter 2006): 392–416.

———. "Talking the Language of the Larger World: Politics in Cold War (Native) America." In *Beyond Red Power: American Indian Politics and Activism since 1900*, edited by Daniel M. Cobb and Loretta Fowler, 161–77. Santa Fe: SAR Press, 2007.

———. "'Us Indians understand the basics': Oklahoma Indians and the Politics of Community Action, 1964–1970." *Western Historical Quarterly* 33, no. 1 (Spring 2002): 41–66.

———. "The War on Poverty in Oklahoma and Mississippi: Beyond Black and White." In *The War on Poverty and Grassroots Struggles for Racial and Economic Justice*, edited by Annelise Orleck and Lisa Hazirjian, 387–410. Athens: University of Georgia Press, 2011.

Cobb, Daniel M., Kyle Fields, and Joseph Cheatle. "'born in the opposition': D'Arcy McNickle, Ethnobiographically." In *Beyond Two Worlds*, edited by C. Joseph Genetin-Pilawa and Jim J. Buss, 253–68. Ithaca: SUNY Press, 2014.

Cobb, Daniel M., and Loretta Fowler, eds. *Beyond Red Power: American Indian Politics and Activism since 1900*. Santa Fe: SAR Press, 2007.

Cohen, Felix. *On the Drafting of Tribal Constitutions*. Edited by David E. Wilkins. Norman: University of Oklahoma Press, 2007.

Cole, Terrence. "Jim Crow in Alaska: The Passage of the Alaska Equal Rights Act of 1945." *Western Historical Quarterly* 23, no. 4 (November 1992): 429–49.

Colwell-Chanthaphonh, Chip. *Inheriting the Past: The Making of Arthur C. Parker and Indigenous Archaeology*. Tucson: University of Arizona Press, 2009.

Comaroff, Jean, and John Comaroff. *Of Revelation and Revolution*. Vol. 1, *Christianity, Colonialism, and Consciousness in South Africa*. Chicago: University of Chicago Press, 1991.

Cotarelo, Pablo, et al. "Defining Energy Sovereignty." *El Ecologista* 81 (Summer 2014). www.odg.cat/sites/default/files/energy_sovereignty_0.pdf. 1 February 2015.

Coulter, Robert T. "Commentary on the UN Draft Declaration on the Rights of Indigenous Peoples." Originally published in *Cultural Survival Quarterly* 18, no. 1 (1994). https://www.culturalsurvival.org/publications/cultural-survival-quarterly/united-states/commentary-un-draft-declaration-rights-indige. 2 September 2014.

Cowger, Thomas W. *The National Congress of American Indians: The Founding Years*. Lincoln: University of Nebraska Press, 1999.

Cross, Ray. "A Tribe Strong Enough to Say No to Oil." *Bismarck Tribune*. 5 November 2014. http://bismarcktribune.com/news/columnists/a-tribe-strong-enough-to-say-no-to-oil/article_614e140a-646a-11e4-91ec-e3eaa0a79292.html. 1 February 2015.

Dadigan, Marc. "Stanford Student Driven to Revive Culture and Prevent Youth Suicide." *Indian Country Today*. 25 August 2012. http://indiancountrytoday-medianetwork.com/2012/08/25/stanford-student-driven-revive-culture-and-prevent-youth-suicide-130471. 1 February 2015.

Davies, Wade. *Healing Ways: Navajo Health Care in the Twentieth Century*. Albuquerque: University of New Mexico Press, 2001.

Debo, Angie. *And Still the Waters Run: The Betrayal of the Five Civilized Tribes*. Princeton: Princeton University Press, 1972.

"Declaration of Principles for the Defense of the Indigenous Nations and Peoples of the Western Hemisphere." *Akwesasne Notes* 10, no. 3 (Summer 1978): 16–17.

Deloria, Philip J. "Historiography." In *A Companion to American Indian History*, edited by Philip J. Deloria and Neal Salisbury, 6–24. Malden, Mass.: Blackwell, 2004.

———. *Indians in Unexpected Places*. Lawrence: University Press of Kansas, 2004.

Deloria, Vine, Jr. Interview by author. 18 October 2001.

Deloria, Vine, Jr. *Behind the Trail of Broken Treaties: An Indian Declaration of Independence*. 1974. Austin: University of Texas Press, 1985.

———. *Custer Died for Your Sins: An Indian Manifesto*. New York: Avon, 1970.

———. ed. *The Indian Reorganization Act: Congresses and Bills*. Norman: University of Oklahoma Press, 2002.

———. *We Talk, You Listen: New Tribes, New Turf*. 1970. Lincoln: Bison Books, 2007.

Deloria, Vine, Jr., and Clifford M. Lytle. *The Nations Within: The Past and Future of American Indian Sovereignty*. 1984. Austin: University of Texas Press, 1998.

DeMallie, Raymond J. "'These have no ears': Narrative and the Ethnohistorical Method." *Ethnohistory* 40, no. 4 (Autumn 1993): 515–38.

Denetdale, Jennifer Nez. *Reclaiming Diné History: The Legacies of Navajo Chief Manuelito and Juanita*. Tucson: University of Arizona Press, 2007.

Dennison, Jean. *Colonial Entanglement: Constituting a Twenty-First-Century Osage Nation*. Chapel Hill: University of North Carolina Press, 2012.

———. "The Will of the People: Citizenship in the Osage Nation." Olympia: Evergreen State College, 2007. http://nativecases.evergreen.edu/collection/cases/will-of-the-people.html. 8 September 2014.

Den Ouden, Amy E., and Jean M. O'Brien, eds. *Recognition, Sovereignty, and Indigenous Rights in the United States*. Chapel Hill: University of North Carolina Press, 2013.

Driskill, Qwo-Li, Chris Finley, Brian Joseph Gilley, and Scott Lauria Morgensen, eds. *Queer Indigenous Studies: Critical Interventions in Theory, Politics, and Literature*. Tucson: University of Arizona Press, 2011.

Echo-Hawk, Walter R. *In the Light of Justice: The Rise of Human Rights in Native America and the UN Declaration on the Rights of Indigenous Peoples*. Golden, Colo.: Fulcrum, 2013.

Edmunds, R. David. "Native Americans, New Voices: American Indian History, 1895–1995." *American Historical Review* 100, no. 3 (June 1995): 717–40.

Ellis, Clyde. *A Dancing People: Powwow Culture on the Southern Plains*. Lawrence: University Press of Kansas, 2003.

———. "'We don't want your rations, we want this dance': The Changing Use of Song and Dance on the Southern Plains." *Western Historical Quarterly* 44, no. 2 (Summer 1999): 133–54.

Fahey, John. *Saving the Reservation: Joe Garry and the Battle to Be Indian*. Seattle: University of Washington Press, 2001.

Fikes, Jay C. *Reuben Snake: Your Humble Serpent; Indian Visionary and Activist*. Santa Fe: Clear Light, 1995.

Fine-Dare, Kathleen S. *Grave Injustice: The American Indian Repatriation Movement and NAGPRA*. Lincoln: University of Nebraska Press, 2002.

Fixico, Donald L. *The Invasion of Indian Country in the Twentieth Century*. Niwot, Colo.: University of Colorado Press, 1998.

———. *Termination and Relocation: Federal Indian Policy, 1945–1960*. Albuquerque: University of New Mexico Press, 1986.

Fletcher, Matthew L. M., Wenona T. Singel, and Kathryn E. Fort, eds. *Facing the Future: The Indian Child Welfare Act at 30*. East Lansing: Michigan State University Press, 2009.

Fogelson, Raymond D. "The Ethnohistory of Events and Nonevents." *Ethnohistory* 36, no. 2 (Spring 1989): 133–47.

Fowler, Loretta. *Shared Symbols, Contested Meanings: Gros Ventre Culture and History, 1778–1984*. Ithaca: Cornell University Press, 1987.

Glazer, Nathan, and Daniel Patrick Moynihan. *Beyond the Melting Pot: The Negroes, Puerto Ricans, Jews, Italians, and Irish of New York City*. Cambridge, Mass.: MIT Press and Harvard University Press, 1963.

Goldstein, Alyosha, ed. *Formations of United States Colonialism*. Durham: Duke University Press, 2014.

Goodyear-Kaopua, Noelani, Ikaika Hussey, and Kahunawaika'ala Wright, eds. *A Nation Rising: Hawaiian Movements for Life, Land, and Sovereignty*. Durham: Duke University Press, 2014.

Green, Michael D. *The Politics of Indian Removal: Creek Government and Society in Crisis*. Lincoln: University of Nebraska Press, 1982.

Hagan, William T. *American Indians*. 4th ed. Revised and expanded by Daniel M. Cobb. 1961. Chicago: University of Chicago Press, 2013.

———. *Quanah Parker: Comanche Chief*. Norman: University of Oklahoma Press, 1993.

Harmon, Alexandra. *Indians in the Making: Ethnic Relations and Indian Identities around Puget Sound*. Berkeley: University of California Press, 1999.

Hart, Rebecca A., and M. Alexander Lowther. "Honoring Sovereignty: Aiding Tribal Efforts to Protect Native American Women from Domestic Violence." *California Law Review* 96, no. 1 (February 2008): 185–234.

Hauptman, Laurence M. *The Iroquois Struggle for Survival: World War II to Red Power*. Syracuse: Syracuse University Press, 1986.

———. *Seven Generations of Iroquois Leadership: The Six Nations since 1800*. Syracuse: Syracuse University Press, 2008.

Hertzberg, Hazel. "Indian Rights Movement, 1887–1973." In *Handbook of North American Indians*, vol. 4, *History of Indian-White Relations*, edited by Wilcomb E. Washburn, 305–23. Washington, D.C.: Smithsonian Institution, 1988.

Holm, Tom. *The Great Confusion in Indian Affairs: Native Americans and Whites in the Progressive Era*. Austin: University of Texas Press, 2005.

Hosmer, Brian C. *American Indians in the Marketplace: Persistence and Innovation among the Menominees and Metlakatlans, 1870–1920*. Lawrence: University Press of Kansas, 1999.

Hosmer, Brian C., and Larry Nesper, eds. *Tribal Worlds: Critical Studies in American Indian Nation Building*. Albany: SUNY Press, 2013.

Hoxie, Frederick E. "Exploring a Cultural Borderland: Native American Journeys of Discovery in the Early Twentieth Century." *Journal of American History* 79, no. 3 (December 1992): 969–95.

———. *A Final Promise: The Campaign to Assimilate the Indians, 1880–1920*. 1984. Lincoln: University of Nebraska Press, 2001.

———. *Parading through History: The Making of the Crow Nation in America, 1805–1935*. New York: Cambridge University Press, 1995.

———. ed. *Talking Back to Civilization: Indian Voices from the Progressive Era*. Boston: Bedford/St. Martins, 2001.

———. "'Thinking like an Indian': Exploring American Indian Views of American History." *Reviews in American History* 29, no. 1 (2001): 1–14.

———. *This Indian Country: American Indian Activists and the Place They Made*. New York: Penguin, 2012.

Hudson, Charles. *Knights of Spain, Warrior's of the Sun: Hernando de Soto and the South's Ancient Chiefdoms*. Athens: University of Georgia Press, 1997.

"Human Rights from a Native Perspective." *Akwesasne Notes* 10, no. 3 (Summer 1978): 13–14.

Idle No More. "Idle No More at the Peoples Climate March." Originally published 22 September 2014. http://ourworld.unu.edu/en/energy-innovation-and-traditional-knowledge. 1 February 2015.

———. "Living History." http://www.idlenomore.ca/living_history. 1 February 2015.

———. "The Story." http://www.idlenomore.ca/story. 1 February 2015.

"Indian Country Renewable Energy Consortium Launched." *Indian Country Today.* 18 August 2009. http://indiancountrytodaymedianetwork .com/2009/08/18/indian-country-renewable-energy-consortium-launched-84023. 1 February 2015.

International Indian Treaty Council. "Declaration of Continuing Independence." http://www.iitc.org/about-iitc/the-declaration-of-continuing-independence-june-1974/. 7 September 2014.

Iverson, Peter. *Carlos Montezuma and the Changing World of American Indians.* Albuquerque: University of New Mexico Press, 1982.

———. *Diné: A History of the Navajos.* Albuquerque: University of New Mexico Press, 2002.

———. *"We Are Still Here": American Indians in the Twentieth Century.* Wheeling, Ill.: Harlan Davidson, 1998.

———. *When Indians Became Cowboys: Native Peoples and Cattle Ranching in the American West.* Norman: University of Oklahoma Press, 1994.

Jacob, Michelle M. *Yakama Rising: Indigenous Cultural Revitalization, Activism, and Healing.* Tucson: University of Arizona Press, 2013.

Janda, Sarah Epler. *Beloved Women: The Political Lives of LaDonna Harris and Wilma Mankiller.* DeKalb: Northern Illinois University Press, 2007.

Jim, Russell. Interview. http://www.manhattanprojectvoices.org/oral-histories/russell-jims-interview. 10 April 2014.

Johnson, Troy R. *The American Indian Occupation of Alcatraz Island: Red Power and Self-Determination.* Lincoln: University of Nebraska Press, 2008.

Johnson, Troy R., Joane Nagel, and Duane Champagne, eds. *American Indian Activism: Alcatraz to the Longest Walk.* Urbana: University of Illinois Press, 1997.

Josephy, Alvin M., Joane Nagel, and Troy R. Johnson, eds. *Red Power: The Indians' Fight for Freedom.* 2nd ed. 1971. Lincoln: University of Nebraska Press, 1999.

Kaplan, Amy, and Donald E. Pease, eds. *Cultures of United States Imperialism.* Durham: Duke University Press, 1993.

Kauanui, J. Kēhaulani. *Hawaiian Blood: Colonialism and the Politics of Sovereignty and Indigeneity.* Durham: Duke University Press, 2008.

———. Testimony Submitted Regarding S. 344 for the Hearing Record. Senate Committee on Indian Affairs. 25 February 25 2003, in author's possession.

Kehoe, Alice Beck. *A Passion for the True and Just: Felix and Lucy Kramer and the Indian New Deal.* Tucson: University of Arizona Press, 2014.

Kelman, Ari. *A Misplaced Massacre: Struggling Over the Memory of Sand Creek.* Cambridge, Mass.: Harvard University Press, 2013.

Kennedy, David M. *Over Here: The First World War and American Society.* 1980. New York: Oxford University Press, 2004.

Kersey, Harry, Jr. *An Assumption of Sovereignty: Social and Political Transformation among the Florida Seminoles, 1953–1979*. Lincoln: University of Nebraska Press, 1996.

Kidwell, Clara Sue. "Terminating the Choctaws." In *Beyond Red Power: American Indian Politics since 1900*, edited by Daniel M. Cobb and Loretta Fowler, 126–41. Santa Fe: SAR Press, 2007.

King, C. Richard, ed. *The Native American Mascot Controversy: A Handbook*. Lanham, Md.: Scarecrow Press, 2010.

King, C. Richard, and Charles Fruehling Springwood, eds. *Team Spirits: The Native American Mascots Controversy*. Lincoln: University of Nebraska Press, 2001.

King, Lise Balk. "A Tree Fell in the Forest: The U.S. Apologized to Native Americans and No One Heard a Sound." 3 December 2011. http://indiancountrytodaymedianetwork.com/2011/12/03/tree-fell-forest-us-apologized-native-americans-and-no-one-heard-sound. 27 April 2015.

Klopotek, Brian. *Recognition Odysseys: Indigeneity, Race, and Federal Tribal Recognition Policy in Three Louisiana Indian Communities*. Durham: Duke University Press, 2011.

Kohlof, Dean. *When the Wind Was a River: Aleut Evacuation in World War II*. Seattle: University of Washington Press, 1995.

Kualapai, Lydia. "The Queen Writes Back: Lili'uokalani's *Hawaii's Story by Hawaii's Queen*." *Studies in American Indian Literature* 17, no. 2 (2005): 32–62.

LaGrand, James B. *Indian Metropolis: Native Americans in Chicago, 1945–1975*. Urbana: University of Illinois Press, 2002.

Lawson, Michael L. *Dammed Indians Revisited: The Continuing History of the Pick-Sloan Plan and the Missouri River Sioux*. Pierre: South Dakota State Historical Society Press, 2009.

Lazarus, Edward. *Black Hills/White Justice: The Sioux Nations versus the United States, 1775 to the Present*. New York: HarperCollins, 1991.

Light, Steven, and Kathryn R. L. Rand. *Indian Gaming and Tribal Sovereignty: The Casino Compromise*. Lawrence: University Press of Kansas, 2005.

Lili'uokalani. *Hawaii's Story by Hawaii's Queen*. Boston: Lee and Shepard Publishers, 1899.

Loftis, Lynn. "The Catawba's Final Battle: A Bittersweet Victory." *American Indian Law Review* 19, no. 1 (1994): 183–215.

Lomawaima, Tsianina. "The Mutuality of Citizenship and Sovereignty: The Society of American Indians and the Battle to Inherit America." *American Indian Quarterly* 37, no. 3 (Summer 2013): 333–51.

———. *They Called It Prairie Light: The Story of the Chilocco Indian School*. Lincoln: University of Nebraska Press, 1994.

Long, Carolyn N. *Religious Freedom and Indian Rights: The Case of Oregon v. Smith*. Lawrence: University Press of Kansas, 2000.

Lowery, Malinda Maynor. *Lumbee Indians in the Jim Crow South: Race, Identity, and the Making of a Nation*. Chapel Hill: University of North Carolina Press, 2010.

Luebben, Thomas E., and Cathy Nelson. "The Indian Wars: Efforts to Resolve Western Shoshone Land and Treaty Issues and to Distribute the Indian Claims Commission Judgment Fund." *Natural Resources Journal* 42 (Fall 2002): 801–33.

Lurie, Nancy Oestreich. "Sol Tax and Tribal Sovereignty." *Human Organization* 58, no. 1 (1999): 108–17.

———. "The Voice of the American Indian: Report of the American Indian Chicago Conference." *Current Anthropology* 2, no. 5 (December 1961): 478–500.

Maddox, Lucy. *Citizen Indians: Native American Intellectuals, Race, and Reform.* Ithaca: Cornell University Press, 2005.

Mankiller, Wilma, and Michael Wallis. *Mankiller: A Chief and Her People.* New York: St. Martin's Press, 1993.

Mantler, Gordon K. *Power to the Poor: Black-Brown Coalition and the Fight for Economic Justice, 1960–1974.* Chapel Hill: University of North Carolina Press, 2013.

"Marie Sanchez: For the Women." *Akwesasne Notes* 9, no. 5 (December 1977): 14–15.

Maroukis, Thomas C. *The Peyote Road: Religious Freedom and the Native American Church.* Norman: University of Oklahoma Press, 2010.

Martinez, David, ed. *The American Indian Intellectual Tradition: An Anthology of Writings from 1772–1972.* Ithaca: Carnell University Press, 2011.

McKenzie-Jones, Paul. "Evolving Voices of Dissent: The Workshops on American Indian Affairs, 1956- 1972." *American Indian Quarterly* 38, no. 3 (Spring 2014): 207–36.

———. "'We are among the poor, the powerless, the inexperienced and the inarticulate': Clyde Warrior's Campaign for a 'Greater Indian America.'" *American Indian Quarterly* 34, no. 2 (Spring 2010): 224–57.

McKeown, Timothy. *In the Smaller Scope of Conscience: The Struggle for National Repatriation Legislation, 1986–1990.* Tucson: University of Arizona Press, 2012.

McLerran, Jennifer. *A New Deal for Indian Art: Indian Arts and Federal Policy, 1933–1943.* Tucson: University of Arizona Press, 2009.

McMillan, Christian. *Making Indian Law: The Hualapai Land Case and the Birth of Ethnohistory.* New Haven: Yale University Press, 2007.

McNickle, D'Arcy. *Native American Tribalism: Indian Survivals and Renewals.* New introduction by Peter Iverson. 1973. New York: Oxford University Press, 1993.

Meadows, William. *Kiowa, Apache, and Comanche Military Societies: Enduring Veterans, 1800 to the Present.* Austin: University of Texas Press, 1999.

Meeting of the Commissioner of Indian Affairs, Hon. John Collier, with the Indians of Western Oklahoma at Anadarko, Oklahoma, March 20, 1934, For the Purpose of Discussing and Explaining the Wheeler-Howard Bill. Washington, D.C.: BIA, 1934. U.S. Department of the Interior Library, Washington, D.C.

Merrell, James H. *The Indians' New World: Catawbas and Their Neighbors from European Contact through the Era of Removal.* Chapel Hill: University of North Carolina Press, 1989.

Metcalf, R. Warren. *Termination's Legacy: The Discarded Indians of Utah*. Lincoln: University of Nebraska Press, 2002.

Mihesuah, Devon, ed. *Repatriation Reader: Who Owns American Indian Remains?* Lincoln: University of Nebraska Press, 2000.

Minthorn, Armand Minthorn. "Human Remains Should Be Reburied." September 1996. http://ctuir.org/kman1.html. 7 September 2014.

Minutes of the Plains Congress, March 2–5, 1934, Rapid City Indian School, South Dakota. Lawrence, Kan.: Haskell Institute, 1934. Edward E. Ayer Collection. Newberry Library.

Minutes of the Special Session of the Navajo Tribal Council, Held at Fort Defiance, Arizona, March 12 and 13, 1934. Washington, D.C.: BIA, 1934. U.S. Department of the Interior Library, Washington, D.C.

Montezuma, Carlos. "United States, Now Free the Indians!" *Wassaja* 3, no. 8 (November 1918): 2–3.

Mourning Dove. *Cogewea: The Half-Blood*. Lincoln: University of Nebraska Press, 1981.

———. *Mourning Dove: A Salishan Autobiography*. Edited by Jay Miller. Lincoln: University of Nebraska Press, 1990.

Murphree, Daniel S., ed. *Native America: A State-by-State Historical Encyclopedia*. Vol. 1. Santa Barbara: Greenwood, 2012.

"Nihígaal béé íina: Our Journey for Existence." https://www.indiegogo.com/projects/nihigaal-bee-iina-our-journey-for-existence. 1 February 2015.

Norcini, Marilyn. *Edward P. Dozier: The Paradox of the American Indian Anthropologist*. Tucson: University of Arizona Press, 2007.

O'Brien, Jean M. *Firsting and Lasting: Writing Indians Out of Existence in New England*. Minneapolis: University of Minnesota Press, 2010.

Osburn, Katherine M. B. *Choctaw Resurgence in Mississippi: Race, Class, and Nation Building in the Jim Crow South, 1830–1977*. Lincoln: University of Nebraska Press, 2014.

———. "'In a name of justice and fairness': The Mississippi Choctaw Indian Federation versus the BIA, 1934." In *Beyond Red Power: American Indian Politics and Activism since 1900*, edited by Daniel M. Cobb and Loretta Fowler, 109–25. Santa Fe: SAR Press, 2007.

Ostler, Jeffrey. *The Lakotas and the Black Hills: The Struggle for Sacred Ground*. New York: Viking, 2010.

———. *The Plains Sioux and U.S. Colonialism from Lewis and Clark to Wounded Knee*. New York: Cambridge University Press, 2004.

O'Sullivan, Meg. "'We worry about survival': American Indian Women, Sovereignty, and the Right to Bear and Raise Children in the 1970s." Ph.D. diss., University of North Carolina at Chapel Hill, 2007.

Parker, Angela K. "Taken Lands: Territory and Sovereignty on the Fort Berthold Indian Reservation, 1934–1960." Ph.D. diss., University of Michigan, 2011.

Parker, Arthur C. "Making Democracy Safe for the Indians." *American Indian Magazine* 6, no. 1 (Spring 1918): 25–29.

———. "Problems of Race Assimilation." *Society of American Indians Quarterly – Journal* 4 (October–December 1916): 285–304.

Parker, Dorothy R. *Singing an Indian Song: A Biography of D'Arcy McNickle.* Lincoln: University of Nebraska Press, 1992.

Pasternak, Judy. *Yellow Dirt: An American Story of a Poisoned Land and a People Betrayed.* New York: Free Press, 2010.

Pavlik, Steve, ed. *A Good Cherokee, a Good Anthropologist: Papers in Honor of Robert K. Thomas.* Contemporary American Indian Issues Series 8. Los Angeles: UCLA American Indian Studies Center, 1998.

Pearl, Alexander. "3/256." Originally published 26 June 2013. http://prawfsblawg .blogs.com/prawfsblawg/2013/06/3256.html. 10 April 2014.

Perdue, Theda. "American Indian Survival in South Carolina." *South Carolina Historical Magazine* 108, no. 3 (July 2007): 215–34.

Peroff, Nicholas. *Menominee DRUMS: Tribal Termination and Restoration, 1954–1974.* 1982. Norman: University of Oklahoma Press, 2006.

Petillo, Jeana. "Domestic Violence in Indian Country: Improving the Federal Government's Response to This Grave Epidemic." *Connecticut Law Review* 45, no. 5 (July 2013): 1841–74.

Philp, Kenneth R. *John Collier's Crusade for Indian Reform, 1920–1954.* Tucson: University of Arizona Press, 1977.

———. *Termination Revisited: American Indians on the Trail to Self-Determination, 1933–1953.* Lincoln: University of Nebraska Press, 1999.

Porter, Joy. *To Be Indian: The Life of Iroquois-Seneca Caswell Parker.* Norman: University of Oklahoma Press, 2001.

Powers, William K. *The Lakota Warrior Tradition: Three Essays on Lakotas at War.* Kendall Park, N.J.: Lakota Books, 2001.

Proceedings of the Conference at Chemawa, Oregon, April 8 and 9, to Discuss with the Indians the Howard-Wheeler Bill. Washington, D.C.: BIA, 1934. U.S. Department of the Interior Library, Washington, D.C.

Proto, Neil Thomas. *The Rights of My People: Lili'uokalani's Enduring Battle with the United States, 1893–1917.* New York: Algora, 2009.

Prucha, Francis Paul. *The Great Father: The United States and the American Indians.* 1984. Lincoln: University of Nebraska Press, 1995.

Ramirez, Renya K. "Henry Roe Cloud: A Granddaughter's Native Feminist Biographical Account." *Wicazo Sa* 24, no. 2 (Fall 2009): 77–103.

Reese, Linda W. "Cherokee Freedwomen in Indian Territory, 1863–1890." *Western Historical Quarterly* 33, no. 3 (Autumn 2002): 273–96.

Reséndez, Andrés. *Changing National Identities at the Frontier: Texas and New Mexico, 1800–1850.* New York: Cambridge University Press, 2005.

Richter, Daniel K. *The Ordeal of the Longhouse: The Peoples of the Iroquois League in the Era of European Colonization.* Chapel Hill: University of North Carolina Press, 1992.

Ridington, Robin, Dennis Hastings, and Tommy Attachie. "The Songs of Our Elders: Performance and Cultural Survival in Omaha and Dane-zaa

Traditions." In *Powwow*, edited by Clyde Ellis, Luke Eric Lassiter, and Gary H. Dunham, 110–29. Lincoln: University of Nebraska Press, 2005.

Rifkin, Mark. *When Did Indians Become Straight? Kinship, the History of Sexuality, and Native Sovereignty*. New York: Oxford University Press, 2011.

Roessel, Ruth, and Broderick H. Johnson. *Navajo Livestock Reduction: A National Disgrace*. Tsaile, Ariz.: Navajo Community College Press, 1974.

Roosevelt, Theodore. "First Annual Message." 3 December 1901. http://www.presidency.ucsb.edu/ws/?pid=29542. 6 September 2014.

Rosaldo, Renato. *Culture and Truth: The Remaking of Social Analysis*. Boston: Beacon, 1989.

Rosen, Deborah A. *American Indians and State Law: Sovereignty, Race, and Citizenship, 1790–1880*. Lincoln: University of Nebraska, 2007.

Rosenthal, Nicolas. *Reimagining Indian Country: Native American Migration and Identity in Twentieth-Century Los Angeles*. Chapel Hill: University of North Carolina Press, 2012.

Rosier, Paul C. *Serving Their Country: American Indian Politics and Patriotism in the Twentieth Century*. Cambridge, Mass.: Harvard University Press, 2009.

———. "'They are ancestral homelands': Race, Place, and Politics in Cold War Native America." *Journal of American History* 92, no. 4 (March 2006): 1300–1326.

Rostkowski, Joelle. "The Redman's Appeal for Justice: Deskaheh and the League of Nations." In *Indians and Europeans: An Interdisciplinary Collection of Essays*, edited by Christian Feest, 435–54. Lincoln: University of Nebraska Press, 1999.

Rusco, Elmer R. "Historic Change in Western Shoshone Country: The Establishment of the Western Shoshone National Council and Traditionalist Land Claims." *American Indian Quarterly* 16, no. 3 (Summer 1992): 337–60.

Russell, Angela. "Reflections on Montgomery." *Americans Before Columbus* 2, no. 6 (November 1965): 3.

Sanchez, Marie. "For the Women." *Akwesasne Notes* 9, no. 5 (December 1977): 14–15.

Sando, Joe S. *Pueblo Nations: Eight Centuries of Pueblo Indian History*. Santa Fe: Clear Light, 1992.

———. *Pueblo Profiles: Cultural Identity through Centuries of Change*. Santa Fe: Clear Light, 1998.

Saunt, Claudio. "The Paradox of Freedom: Tribal Sovereignty and Emancipation during the Reconstruction of Indian Territory." *Journal of Southern History* 70, no. 1 (February 2004): 63–94.

Scott, James C. *Weapons of the Weak: Everyday Forms of Peasant Resistance*. New Haven: Yale University Press, 1986.

Schilling, Vincent. "Susan Allen, First American Indian Lesbian in State Legislature, Fights for Social Equality." 6 February 2012. http://indiancountrytodaymedianetwork.com/2012/02/06/susan-allen-first-american-indian-lesbian-state-legislature-fights-social-equality-95479. 8 September 2014.

Shreve, Bradley. *Red Power Rising: The National Indian Youth Council and the Origins of Native Activism*. Norman: University of Oklahoma Press, 2011.

Silva, Noenoe. *Aloha Betrayed: Native Hawaiian Resistance to American Colonialism*. Durham: Duke University Press, 2004.

Simpson, Audra. *Mohawk Interruptus: Political Life across the Borders of Settler States*. Durham: Duke University Press, 2014.

Sleeper-Smith, Susan, Juliana Barr, Jean M. O'Brien, Nancy Shoemaker, and Scott Manning Stevens, eds. *Why You Can't Teach United States History without American Indians*. Chapel Hill: University of North Carolina Press, 2015.

Smith, Paul Chaat. *Everything You Know about Indians Is Wrong*. Minneapolis: University of Minnesota Press, 2009.

——. "Narration." *Our Peoples* exhibition catalog. National Museum of the American Indian. Washington, D.C.

Smith, Paul Chaat, and Ann McMullen. "Making History." *Our Peoples* exhibition catalog. National Museum of the American Indian. Washington, D.C.

Smith, Paul Chaat, and Robert Allen Warrior. *Like a Hurricane: The Indian Movement from Alcatraz to Wounded Knee*. New York: New Press, 1996.

Smith, Sherry L. "Indians, the Counterculture, and the New Left." In *Beyond Red Power: American Indian Politics and Activism since 1900*, edited by Daniel M. Cobb and Loretta Fowler, 142–60. Santa Fe: SAR Press, 2007.

Snyder, Christina. *Slavery in Indian Country: The Changing Face of Captivity in Early America*. Cambridge, Mass.: Harvard University Press, 2010.

Stremlau, Rose. *Sustaining the Cherokee Family: Kinship and the Allotment of an Indigenous Nation*. Chapel Hill: University of North Carolina, 2011.

Sturm, Circe. *Blood Politics: Race, Culture, and Identity in the Cherokee Nation of Oklahoma*. Berkeley: University of California Press, 2002.

Thomas, Robert K. "Colonialism: Classic and Internal." *New University Thought* 4, no. 4 (1966–67): 37–44.

Thrush, Coll. *Native Seattle: Histories from the Crossing-Over Place*. Seattle: University of Washington Press, 2007.

Trask, Haunana-Kay. *From a Native Daughter: Colonialism and Sovereignty in Hawaii*. Honolulu: University of Hawaii Press, 1999.

Trask, Miliani B. "Hawaiian Sovereignty." *Cultural Survival* 24, no. 1 (Spring 2000). http://www.culturalsurvival.org/ourpublications/csq/article/hawaiian-sovereignty. 1 February 2015.

Treglia, Gabriella. "The Consistency and Inconsistency of Cultural Oppression: American Indian Dance Bans, 1900–1933." *Western Historical Quarterly* 44, no. 2 (Summer 2013): 145–65.

Troutman, John. "The Citizenship of Dance: Politics and Music among the Lakota, 1900- 1924." In *Beyond Red Power: American Indian Politics and Activism since 1900*, edited by Daniel M. Cobb and Loretta Fowler, 91–108. Santa Fe: SAR Press, 2007.

——. *Indian Blues: American Indians and the Politics of Music, 1879–1934*. Norman: University of Oklahoma Press, 2009.

Trudell, John. "We've Got to Have Commitment So Strong . . ." *Akwesasne Notes* 6, no. 3 (Early Summer 1974): 10–11.

Tsosie, Rebecca. "The BIA's Apology to Native Americans: An Essay on Collective Memory and Collective Conscience." In *Taking Wrongs Seriously: Apologies and Reconciliations*, edited by Elazar Barkan and Alexander Karn, 185–212. Stanford: Stanford University Press, 2006.

Turner, Frederick Jackson. *Rereading Frederick Jackson Turner: "The Significance of the Frontier" in American History and Other Essay.* Commentary by John Mack Faragher. New Haven: Yale University Press, 1999.

Ulmer, Mark. "Tribal Property: Defining the Parameters of the Federal Trust Relationship under the Non-intercourse Act: Catawba Indian Tribe v. South Carolina." *American Indian Law Review* 12, no. 1 (1984): 101–45.

Ulrich, Roberta. *American Indian Nations from Termination to Restoration, 1953–2006.* Lincoln: University of Nebraska Press, 2010.

U.S. Congress. House Committee on Indian Affairs. *Federal Acknowledgment of Various Indian Groups.* 102nd Cong., 2nd sess., 8 July 1992. Washington, D.C.: Government Printing Office, 1993.

————. *Indians of the United States: Investigation of the Field Service.* Vol. 3. Washington, D.C.: Government Printing Office, 1920.

U.S. Congress. House Committee on Interior and Insular Affairs. Indian Gaming Regulatory Act.100th Cong., 1st sess., 25 June 1987. Washington, D.C.: Government Printing Office, 1989.

————. *Relating to the Lumbee Indians of North Carolina.* 84 Cong. 1st sess., 22 July 1955. Washington, D.C.: Government Printing Office, 1955.

U.S. Congress. House Committee on Natural Resources. *ANWR: Jobs, Energy, and Deficit Reduction, Parts 1 and 2.* 112th Cong., 1st sess., 21 September 2011 and 18 November 2011. Washington, D.C.: Government Printing Office, 2012.

————. *Oklahoma Tribal Concerns: Oversight Hearings before the Subcommittee on Native American Affairs.* 103rd Cong., 2nd sess., 20 January 1994. Washington, D.C.: Government Printing Office, 1995.

U.S. Congress. House Subcommittee on Indian Affairs. *Payment of More Adequate Compensation to the Indians of the Pine Ridge Reservation for Land Taken from Them by the U.S. in 1942 for Military Purposes.* 83rd Cong., 1st sess., 6 May 1953. Washington, D.C.: Government Printing Office, 1953.

U.S. Congress. Senate. *The Cherokee Freedmen: Memorial of the Cherokee Freedmen to the Congress of the United States.* 63rd Cong., 1st sess., 22 November 1913. Washington, D.C.: Government Printing Office, 1913.

————. *Report of the Select Committee to Investigate Matters Connected with Affairs in the Indian Territory, with Hearings.* Vol. 2. 59th Cong., 2nd sess., 11 November 1906–9 January 1907. Washington, D.C.: Government Printing Office, 1907.

U.S. Congress. Senate Committee on Indian Affairs. Indian Trust Reform Act.109th Cong., 1st sess., 26 July 2005. Washington, D.C.: Government Printing Office, 2005.

————. *Policy of the United States Regarding Relationship with Native Hawaiians and to Provide a Process for the Recognition by the United States of the Native*

Hawaiian Governing Entity. 108th Cong., 1st sess., 25 February 2003
Washington, D.C.: Government Printing Office, 2003.

——. *Protesting the Construction of Garrison Dam, North Dakota, by the Fort Berthold Indians*. 79th Cong., 1st sess., 9 October 1945. Washington, D.C.: Government Printing Office, 1945.

——. *Religious Freedom Act*.102nd Cong., 2nd sess., 7 March 1992. Washington, D.C.: Government Printing Office, 1992.

U.S. Congress. Senate Committee on the Judiciary. *Constitutional Rights of the American Indian: Hearings before the Subcommittee on Constitutional Rights*. 89th Cong., 1st sess., 22–24 and 29 June 1965. Washington, D.C.: Government Printing Office, 1965.

——. *Stenographic Transcript of Hearings, S.J. Res. 4*. 11 May 1954. Washington, D.C.: Alderson Reporting Company, 1954.

U.S. Congress. Senate Select Committee on Indian Affairs. *Federal Government's Relationship with American Indians*. 100th Cong., 1st sess., part 1, 20–31 January 1989 and 1 February 1989. Washington, D.C.: Government Printing Office, 1989.

——. *Tribal Self-Governance Demonstration Project Act*.102nd Cong., 1st sess., 18 July 1991. Washington, D.C.: Government Printing Office, 1992.

U.S. Department of State. *Proposed Keystone XL Project Public Meeting*. Vol. 1 of 2. April 18, 2013. Heartland Events Center, 700 East Stolley Park Road, Grand Island, Nebraska. http://www.scribd.com/doc/173378782/Transcript-U-S-State-Dept-Public-Hearing-on-Keystone-XL-Pipeline-1-of-2. 8 September 2014.

VanDevelder, Paul. *Coyote Warrior: One Man, Three Tribes, and the Trial That Forged a Nation*. New York: Little, Brown, 2004.

Warrior, Clyde. "How Should an Indian Act?" *Americans Before Columbus* 2, no. 5 (June 1965): 2.

——. "On Current Indian Affairs." *Americans Before Columbus* 1, no. 1 (5 May 1964): 2.

——. "Which One Are You?" *Americans Before Columbus* 2, no. 4 (December 1964): 1, 7.

Warrior, Robert, ed. *The World of Indigenous North America*. New York: Routledge, 2015.

Washinawatok, Ingrid. "International Emergence: Twenty-One Years at the United Nations." *New York City Law Review* 3, no. 4 (1998): 41–57.

Weaver, Hillary N. "The Colonial Context of Violence: Reflections on Violence in the Lives of Native American Women." *Journal of Interpersonal Violence* 24, no. 9 (September 2009): 1552–63.

Weisiger, Marsha. "Gendered Injustice: Navajo Livestock Reduction in the New Deal Era." *Western Historical Quarterly* 38, no. 4 (Winter 2007): 437–55.

Wenger, Tisa. "Land, Culture, and Sovereignty in the Pueblo Dance Controversy." *Journal of the Southwest* 46, no. 2 (Summer 2004): 381–412.

——. *We Have a Religion: The 1920s Pueblo Indian Dance Controversy and American Indian Religious Freedom*. Chapel Hill: University of North Carolina, 2009.

"We Support Our Brothers at Wounded Knee." *Akwesasne Notes* 5, no. 2 (Early Spring 1973): 30.

White, Richard. *The Middle Ground: Indians, Empires, and Republics in the Great Lakes Region, 1650–1815*. New York: Cambridge University Press, 1991.

Wilkie, Bruce. "Look for Results and Action." *Americans Before Columbus* 2, no. 3 (July 27, 1964): 3.

Wilkins, David E. *Hollow Justice: A History of Indigenous Claims in the United States*. New Haven: Yale University Press, 2013.

Wilkinson, Charles F. *Blood Struggle: The Rise of Modern Indian Nations*. New York: W. W. Norton, 2005.

———. *Messages from Frank's Landing: A Story of Salmon, Treaties, and the Indian Way*. Seattle: University of Washington Press, 2000.

Williams, Maria Shaa Tláa, ed. *The Alaska Native Reader: History, Culture, Politics*. Durham: Duke University Press, 2009.

Williams, Robert A., Jr. *Like a Loaded Weapon: The Rehnquist Court, Indian Rights, and the Legal Theory of Racism in America*. Minneapolis: University of Minnesota Press, 2005.

———. *Linking Arms Together: American Indian Treaty Visions of Law and Peace, 1600–1800*. New York: Oxford University Press, 1997.

"Women Senators, Tribal Leader Discuss Importance of VAWA Improvements." Originally published 25 April 2012. http://www.youtube.com/watch?v=ylV7-XASQy8. 8 September 2014.

Yarbrough, Fay A. *Race and the Cherokee Nation: Sovereignty in the Nineteenth Century*. Philadelphia: University of Pennsylvania Press, 2008.

Index

Page numbers in *italics* refer to illustrations.

H. EUGENE AND LILLIAN YOUNGS LEHMAN SERIES

Lamar Cecil, *Wilhelm II: Prince and Emperor, 1859–1900* (1989).

Carolyn Merchant, *Ecological Revolutions: Nature, Gender, and Science in New England* (1989).

Gladys Engel Lang and Kurt Lang, *Etched in Memory: The Building and Survival of Artistic Reputation* (1990).

Howard Jones, *Union in Peril: The Crisis over British Intervention in the Civil War* (1992).

Robert L. Dorman, *Revolt of the Provinces: The Regionalist Movement in America* (1993).

Peter N. Stearns, *Meaning Over Memory: Recasting the Teaching of Culture and History* (1993).

Thomas Wolfe, *The Good Child's River*, edited with an introduction by Suzanne Stutman (1994).

Warren A. Nord, *Religion and American Education: Rethinking a National Dilemma* (1995).

David E. Whisnant, *Rascally Signs in Sacred Places: The Politics of Culture in Nicaragua* (1995).

Lamar Cecil, *Wilhelm II: Emperor and Exile, 1900–1941* (1996).

Jonathan Hartlyn, *The Struggle for Democratic Politics in the Dominican Republic* (1998).

Louis A. Pérez Jr., *On Becoming Cuban: Identity, Nationality, and Culture* (1999).

Yaakov Ariel, *Evangelizing the Chosen People: Missions to the Jews in America, 1880–2000* (2000).

Philip F. Gura, *C. F. Martin and His Guitars, 1796–1873* (2003).

Louis A. Pérez Jr., *To Die in Cuba: Suicide and Society* (2005).

Peter Filene, *The Joy of Teaching: A Practical Guide for New College Instructors* (2005).

John Charles Boger and Gary Orfield, eds., *School Resegregation: Must the South Turn Back?* (2005).

Jock Lauterer, *Community Journalism: Relentlessly Local* (2006).

Michael H. Hunt, *The American Ascendancy: How the United States Gained and Wielded Global Dominance* (2007).

Michael Lienesch, *In the Beginning: Fundamentalism, the Scopes Trial, and the Making of the Antievolution Movement* (2007).

Eric L. Muller, *American Inquisition: The Hunt for Japanese American Disloyalty in World War II* (2007).

John McGowan, *American Liberalism: An Interpretation for Our Time* (2007).

Nortin M. Hadler, M.D., *Worried Sick: A Prescription for Health in an Overtreated America* (2008).

William Ferris, *Give My Poor Heart Ease: Voices of the Mississippi Blues* (2009).

Colin A. Palmer, *Cheddi Jagan and the Politics of Power: British Guiana's Struggle for Independence* (2010).

W. Fitzhugh Brundage, *Beyond Blackface: African Americans and the Creation of American Mass Culture, 1890–1930* (2011).

Michael H. Hunt and Steven I. Levine, *Arc of Empire: America's Wars in Asia from the Philippines to Vietnam* (2012).

Nortin M. Hadler, M.D., *The Citizen Patient: Reforming Health Care for the Sake of the Patient, Not the System* (2013).

Louis A. Pérez Jr., *The Structure of Cuban History: Meanings and Purpose of the Past* (2013).

Jennifer Thigpen, *Island Queens and Mission Wives: How Gender and Empire Remade Hawai'i's Pacific World* (2014).

George W. Houston, *Inside Roman Libraries: Book Collections and Their Management in Antiquity* (2014).

Philip F. Gura, *The Life of William Apess, Pequot* (2015).

Daniel M. Cobb, ed., *Say We Are Nations: Documents of Politics and Protest in Indigenous America since 1887* (2015).

CPSIA information can be obtained
at www.ICGtesting.com
Printed in the USA
LVHW041502050123
736439LV00004B/398